NEW CARS · USED CARS · TRADE-INS · CAR LOANS · LEASING · CAR AUCTIONS · CAR-BUYING SERVICES · SELLING YOUR CAR

Bob Elliston—an insider in the automotive industry for more than twenty years—is breaking every rule in the book! He's revealing all he knows about how dealerships get maximum prices . . . and how you can turn the tables to purchase a car at or *below* the dealer's cost.

This means a saving to you of hundreds, even thousands, of dollars on a new or used car!

This great guide to a great deal puts into hard print the sales pitches that manipulate you into buying, the responses that put you in control, and the "magic" words that will get you the best deal possible. It dares expose the hidden profits the dealer counts on. It tells you the best-kept secrets that car salespeople do not want you to know. And it gives you the ultimate car-buying strategy that insures that you will beat the dealer . . . every time!

WHAT CAR DEALERS WON'T TELL YOU

BOB ELLISTON, President of Automotive Consumer Information Service, Inc., has worked inside the automotive industry for more than twenty-two years. ACIS was created to provide the kind of inside information that is not readily available to automotive consumers. It gathers information from the experience, knowledge, and resources of people actively working in and for the automotive industry, thus bringing a truly unique perspective to the car-buying experience. ACIS believes that to be forearmed with the facts is to be forewarned of the shopping experience.

WHAT CAR DEALERS WON'T TELL YOU

The Insider's Guide to Buying or Leasing a New or Used Car

BOB ELLISTON

A PLUME BOOK

AUTHOR'S NOTE

This publication is designed to provide accurate and authoritative information about the new, used, and leased car market. While it was designed to help readers save money and make a better and more informed car purchase, lease, or sale decision, Automotive Consumer Information Service, Inc., cannot make any guarantees about the outcome of using the information contained in this book. This book is sold with the understanding that neither Automotive Consumer Information Service, Inc., nor any of its employees or representatives is engaged in rendering legal, accounting, or mechanical services. If any legal or accounting advice or other expert advice and assistance is required, the services of a competent professional should be engaged.

PLUME
Published by the Penguin Group
Penguin Books USA Inc., 375 Hudson Street, New York, New York 10014, U.S.A.
Penguin Books Ltd, 27 Wrights Lane, London W8 5TZ, England
Penguin Books Australia Ltd, Ringwood, Victoria, Australia
Penguin Books Canada Ltd, 10 Alcorn Avenue, Toronto, Ontario, Canada M4V 3B2
Penguin Books (N.Z.) Ltd, 182–190 Wairau Road, Auckland 10, New Zealand

Penguin Books Ltd, Registered Offices:
Harmondsworth, Middlesex, England

First published by Plume, an imprint of Dutton Signet,
a division of Penguin Books USA Inc.

First Printing, October, 1996
10 9 8 7

LIBRARY OF CONGRESS CATALOGING-IN-PUBLICATION DATA:
Elliston, Bob.
What car dealers won't tell you : the insider's guide to buying or leasing a new or used car / Bob Elliston.
p. cm.
Includes index.
ISBN 0-452-27688-8
1. Automobile—Purchasing. I.Title.
TL162.E43 1996
629.222'029'6—dc20 96-16018
CIP

Printed in the United States of America
Set in Century Light
Designed by Jesse Cohen

Dedicated to everyone who has ever felt at a disadvantage when buying or leasing a new or used car, van, or pickup.

Contents

PART II: ABOUT BUYING USED CARS

PART III: ABOUT LEASING

Part IV: About Buying at Auction

Part V: About Car-Buying Services

PART VI: ABOUT SELLING YOUR CAR

PART VII: THE CHECKLISTS

I

About Buying New Cars

If You Know Their Rules . . .
You Can Play Their Games

1. Introduction

To be a smart car, van, or pickup buyer you need three things:

1. An *understanding* of the automotive selling business:
   - How a dealership operates
   - Their selling strategies
   - Their ploys and games
2. A *basic strategy* designed to help you buy the right vehicle at the lowest price possible
3. The *determination* <u>not</u> to be intimidated by the process

We can help you with the first two, but the third *you're* going to have to supply. Hopefully, once you've read this book, your knowledge of the car business will give you the confidence to take charge of and remain in control of virtually any car, van, or pickup truck buying situation.

Buying Is Negotiating

Unless you plan to walk into a dealership and pay the asking price for a vehicle, every buying situation is a negotiation. And, as with most negotiations, there are different phases or steps.

Step 1. Assumptions

Every negotiation begins with assumptions, even before the two parties meet. In car sales it is not uncommon to find many customers entering a dealership assuming that the salesperson and the dealership are going to do their best to "take" them in one way or another. On the other hand, many salespeople in the dealership assume that customers are going to try to "beat them up" on price and lie about anything from the number of places they've shopped to the condition of their trade-in. The trouble with assumptions is that they are just that: assumptions. Left untested by facts, they can make a negotiation very difficult for both parties.

Step 2. Fact-Finding and Information Gathering

Good negotiators always make an effort to get all their facts before the negotiation. In the car business this means that you should research the vehicle you want to buy, determine the real cost of that vehicle, know the actual wholesale value of your trade-in, and shop for the best financing.

This process begins before you walk into a showroom and continues throughout the sales encounter.

On the dealership side, good salespeople begin by knowing their product thoroughly—obviously before the customer walks in. Once in front of the customer, good salespeople conduct their fact-finding and research by asking questions, listening, and observing. Their objective is to learn as much about the customer's needs, wants, and purchase ability as possible.

Step 3. Confrontation

Once the sales process begins to focus on price, the lines are drawn and the issue becomes: *your money and how much of it you're willing to pay in exchange for the desired car*. There are two possible outcomes to the confrontation phase:

1. You do not come to an agreement on price and leave.
2. You come to an agreement and buy the car, van, or truck.

Step 4. Agreement

There are three kinds of negotiated agreements:

Win/Win: This is an agreement in which both sides feel that they've gotten a good deal.

Win/Lose: An agreement in which, from your point of view, you've won by getting a great price and the dealership has lost. *Be warned:* Sometimes salespeople will act as though they have lost when, in reality, they have won. However, to make you feel good, they pretend to have taken a "beating" on the price. (They almost never do.)

Lose/Lose: This is an agreement, of sorts, in that you have "agreed" not to buy the car and the salesperson has "agreed" not to sell it to you because you simply could not agree on the price. In this case the salesperson has invested time but earned no commission (very much a loss). You have invested time but not managed to purchase a car. (Sometimes this might be construed as a loss since it means you're going to have to continue shopping. Other times, it may well be a "win" in disguise because your refusal to give in may lead to a better deal later on.)

Of all these steps there is none more important than number two: fact-finding and information gathering. In "About Buying New Cars" we're going to focus on the kind of information you should have before you enter the dealership. It is our belief that the more you know about how dealerships and salespeople think and work, the stronger and more secure you'll feel when it comes time to negotiating the price. To put it another way, the better you understand their rules, the better equipped you'll be to play their games.

2. Profile: The Ideal Salesperson

"Yes, Virginia, There Are Good Car Salespeople."

There may be an inclination—a strong one, in fact—to assume after reading this book that all car, van, and pickup truck dealers are something less than ethical and that salespeople are simply not to be trusted. Unfortunately, in more than a few cases that may well be true. However, we want to make it clear that there are very good, very ethical dealerships that work very hard to deliver good value, stand behind their products, and will do whatever is necessary to assure that their customers remain satisfied throughout the ownership experience. Their rewards, not so incidentally, are the benefits that come with running a very successful business.

There are also a good number of salespeople who proudly regard themselves as "professionals." They work very hard to develop and hold their customers. They go out of their way to make themselves "valuable" to their customers long after the sale has been completed. These are the people who send thank-you notes for your business. These are the people who make it a point to be on hand when you bring your car in for its first service. These are the people who will always be your voice in the dealership should you have problems or special needs.

And They Want to Make a Living

Make no mistake, these salespeople are in business to earn good commissions. They are not going to "give the store away." But then, would you expect any less of a good salesperson? They know that they will make more money in the long run if they develop a list of very satisfied customers. These "professional salespeople" realize that every sales transaction must be a win/win. They know that their customers must leave feeling that they have received, and will continue to receive, good value for their money.

At the same time, professional salespeople conclude the sales transaction knowing that they have made a fair profit for the dealership, that they've earned a good commission for themselves, and that, most important, they have laid the groundwork for developing the kind of ongoing relationship with their customers that will generate new customer referrals and repeat sales.

If you're fortunate enough to deal with one of these "professionals," here is what is likely to happen:

The Greeting

You walk into the dealership and within moments a professionally dressed salesperson—meaning that both the men and the women look as if they work for IBM or Xerox—greets you with a smile and an extended hand:

"Welcome to Good Motors. My name is ______."

As you answer they might present you with their business card. From this point they will probably adjust their personalities and demeanor to match your personality. If you're a no-nonsense, let's get down to business type, they will be all business. If you're what car people classify as a "pipe smoker," i.e., someone who says little but wants to know all of the facts and generally gives the impression of a college professor—they will become your information resource. If you're outgoing, gregarious, and open and regard car shopping/buying as fun, they will be your alter ego.

Qualifying—Understanding Your Needs

After making you feel welcome in the dealership—expect to be offered a cup of coffee or a soft drink—they will direct the conversation toward what you're looking for in a car, van, or pickup and try to determine your price range. While there are certain pieces of information that you, as a buyer, will choose not to reveal at this time (more on this later), you do want to tell them which model and features you're interested in.

An astute professional salesperson is not going to mention prices, deals, discounts, or trade-in allowances at this time. Even if you bring up the subject of price, professionals will make every effort to have you focus on the car and its ability to satisfy your needs before they discuss price. Their first objective is—or at least should be—to understand your needs and to show you a car that addresses those needs.

"Hot Buttons"

During what salespeople call the "qualifying" stage, the salesperson may ask you to identify what is really important to you:

"What's your number one priority in any car you decide to buy?"

Often, this will be the first time you've ever given the question much thought. Is it safety, performance, reliability, durability, resale value, or maybe even prestige? These are what salespeople regard as the "hot buttons." The value and importance you place on these "hot buttons" will eventually be one of the primary reasons you'll decide to buy one make or model over another.

Once good salespeople discover your "hot button"—that is, what's really important to you—they will build their presentation to make sure that you fully appreciate why this car or that pickup addresses your needs. Smart salespeople always sell the value *before* they talk about price.

The Presentation

For a professional salesperson to be able to show how their product addresses your needs, they have to know everything there is to know about each model they sell. If you want to know engine displacement, they'll be able to give you the figures. If you want axle ratios, they'll know. If you want to know about crumple zones and air bags, they will provide you with a complete explanation.

If you're a female buyer, they will treat you with respect but never with condescension. Good salespeople are "gender blind," and they gear their presentations to your level of need and interest, not to your sex. To put it another way, they will treat you as *you* want to be treated.

The Demonstration Drive

Once the car has been presented and you've had a chance to sit behind the wheel and ask questions, the professional salesperson will always invite you to take a demo drive. If you're serious about buying the car, take the demo drive. You owe yourself time behind the wheel to see if the vehicle meets your expectations.

On a demo drive the good salesperson will drive first. After a few minutes he or she will pull over, stop the car, and invite you to change places. At that time the salesperson will explain how to adjust the seat, headrest, steering wheel, temperature controls, and be sure that you're in a comfortable driving position.

During the demo drive you'll be taken on a route designed to show off the car's suspension, steering, and acceleration. In addition to talking about the attributes of the car, the professional will continue to "information gather" with questions like:

"How soon will you be needing a car?"

"Is there anyone else who will be involved in the decision?"

If you answer "soon" and "your spouse," don't be surprised if the salesperson suggests that you take the opportunity now to show the vehicle to the other person.

They will also ask if you're planning to trade in your current car, if you plan to finance, or are considering a lease. As we'll discuss in the strategy section, it may not be in your best interest to provide direct and definitive answers at this time. But don't hold it against a salesperson for asking. This is part of the qualifying process, and your answers provide them with the information they need to prepare themselves for the negotiation.

Trial Closes

Trial closes are questions designed to help the salesperson determine how close you are to making a purchase decision. While "trial closes" might take place anytime during the selling process, they are most often heard near the end of the demo drive. Trial closes are questions like:

"Do you feel this car meets your needs?"

"How do you like this color?"

"When were you thinking about taking delivery?"

"How do you plan to register this vehicle?"

The Close

Once back at the dealership, the salesperson will invite you to sit down at his or her desk. You will be asked if you have any questions. If you do, they'll be answered and then the salesperson will use any of several "closes" to ask for the order. Good sales training programs teach various types of closing techniques. The most popular is to simply take out a buyer's order and begin to write up the specifics of the deal. Once everything is on paper, the salesperson will ask for "your approval"—in writing—so that he or she can take your offer to management.

At this point, of course, price comes into the picture and the negotiation begins. While it's true that your salesperson would like to close the deal on your first visit (a "spot delivery," it's called), professionals understand that this is not always going to be the case, especially if they're dealing with an educated auto buyer.

Let's assume you announce that you "want to think about it" or that you "want your spouse or friend to see the car." Most salespeople will assume that your real intent is to shop another dealer to compare prices. Once they know you're determined not to buy that day, they will give you a packet of literature, make sure you have their business card, and suggest that when you return the two of you can settle on the final price. No professional is going to "put you out on the street" with the final price offer that you can use as leverage with another dealer.

Pre-Sale Follow-up

After you've left, the professional car salesperson will sit down and write you a letter thanking you for coming in, suggesting that he or she knows that you can get together on price, and that if you'd like, the salesperson will be happy to bring the car out to your office or house for another demo drive. The letter arrives the next day and you're impressed. Who wouldn't be? Here's someone who is really interested in earning your business. Expect a phone call as well.

Making the Deal

Eventually you return to the dealership and negotiate a deal. The good professional will always be just that—professional. He or she does not want to give away the store, but at the same time doesn't want to lose your business. When you finally come to an agreement, the salesperson will put all the "give and take" of the negotiation behind and extend a hand congratulating you on your purchase.

You'll give the dealer a deposit—but not the whole amount—to secure the deal, and the salesperson will arrange for a convenient time for you to come in and take delivery of the vehicle. The professional will ask that you allow forty-five minutes to an hour so that you can complete the paperwork, go over the owner's manual, service books, and guarantees, and review the operation of all the features on the car.

The Delivery

The professional will make the delivery of your vehicle a special event. When you arrive, your car, van, or pickup will be sitting in a special place out front for everyone to see. The interior and exterior will be spotless. When you enter the dealership, your salesperson will be waiting, and immediately you'll sense that he or she is just as excited about this moment as you are. You'll go to the desk to complete the paperwork. Really savvy professionals will even go so far as to clear the top of their desks of everything but those papers and booklets relating to your purchase. They want you to know that nothing is going to distract them from giving you their total attention.

Once the paperwork is done and you've handed over the check, the salesperson will take you back to the service department and introduce you to the service manager and, very possibly, to the service writer who will be assigned to you. In good dealerships these people will be genuinely happy to make your acquaintance and welcome you to their family of customers. Parenthetically, the author has been in dealerships where the service department is so much attuned to customer needs that customers will continue to buy their cars from the dealership even if some other dealer beats their price. There's an old saying in the car business: "The first car is sold by the salespeople and the second by the service people." Very true.

Anyway, after you've met the service people, the professional will take you out to your new vehicle. Don't be surprised to find a small gift waiting for you. Some of the best professionals we've known always have a bouquet of flowers for their female customers. Key holders, document pouches, and the like are all very common for men.

During the delivery you'll be given a complete "walk-around" of the car. You'll be shown how to open the hood and check the oil and transmission dipsticks, windshield wiper reservoir, and where to find the fuse box.

Inside the car, the salesperson will review the seat adjustments, air conditioning, heater, radio, and all the other features. Depending on the car and the situation, the salesperson might offer to take you for another demo drive to be sure that you fully understand the vehicle's operation. One other nice touch that some dealerships and salespeople add to the delivery experience is to drive with you to the nearest gas station—or use the dealership pump, if they have one—and buy you a full tank of fuel. The act of having someone buy your first fill-up is one of the more powerful ways to cement a good customer-salesperson relationship and lay the groundwork for referrals and future sales. In a good dealership the dealer or general manager will come out and thank you for your business and tell you that their door is always open if you have questions or concerns.

If the professional has done his or her job, you will feel very good about the entire experience. But there's more to come.

Post-Sale Follow-up

Sometime within the next two days your salesperson will give you a call to ask if everything is okay and to inquire if you have questions.

The smart professional will use this opportunity to set up an appointment for your first service.

Sometime during the first week a letter will arrive from the salesperson formally thanking you for your business and suggesting that if you were happy with the purchase experience and know of anyone in the market for a car, an introduction would be greatly appreciated. This is where the professional's approach begins to pay off. If he or she has really managed to lay the groundwork for a long-term relationship, your endorsement of that performance to friends will, on average, generate three additional customers for that salesperson.

When you arrive for your first service, your salesperson will be there to greet you and reintroduce you to your service writer. The professional will make it clear that he or she is always a phone call away if ever you have questions. On the anniversary of the purchase, you'll get an anniversary card from your salesperson.

In Conclusion . . .

The bottom line here is this: If you are fortunate enough to encounter the kind of professional salesperson described here, latch on. This person can become a valuable resource. You may even find that it's worth paying a little more just to assure that your salesperson and the dealership really are prepared to go the extra mile to guarantee your satisfaction.

3. Understanding How a Dealership Operates

In business, in life, and in the car business, good negotiators like to "get into the heads" of their opponents and learn as much as they can about how they operate, how they do business, and how they plot their negotiation strategies. In this segment we're going to show you the world from the dealership's perspective in the belief that the more you know about the car business, the more prepared you'll be to deal with their tactics.

Identifying the Enemy

"They have identified the enemy and he or she is you." (Or at least one of the enemies.) From a car dealer's perspective (and fortunately this is not universally true) there are two kinds of enemies:

Enemy #1. Those customers who have taken the time to do their homework, who refuse to accept less than the true wholesale value for their trade-in, and have established a budget beyond which they will not go. These people are also the type who maintain a pleasant, even attitude—no sign of anger or malice in these folks—and they make it clear they are prepared to walk out and shop another dealer if they don't get what they want. Salespeople will, in private, also reveal their feelings about customers with the expression: "Buyers are liars." In truth, sometimes they are. As you learn, there are times when a white lie—or at least an avoidance of the truth—works very much to your advantage. (More on this later.)

Enemy #2. *Any* and *every* competitive dealership. Most salespeople are firmly convinced that a competitive dealership will all but "give away their vehicles" if that's what it takes to "steal" a customer. *Make note:* This very real and often fierce competitiveness is one of your best weapons.

Floor Planning

The manufacturer sells its vehicles to dealers at set invoice prices. But since most dealers don't have the kind of money it would take to buy and hold a full inventory, they enlist the help of their bank or other financial institution. This is called "floor planning."

For the purpose of this explanation, let's assume the dealer uses his local bank. The bank lends the necessary invoice price to the dealer and then charges the dealer interest (usually prime rate plus points) for that period between when the dealer takes delivery of the vehicle and when he sells it to the customer. When the car is sold, the dealer repays the bank the invoice cost, settles the interest due, and keeps the remainder as profit. The longer a car sits on the lot, the greater amount of interest it accrues. That's why dealers want to move cars as fast as they can and why they prefer to sell you a car or truck from their stock rather than having you request one that must be ordered from the manufacturer.

Dealer Markup

You will find that there are two sets of markups on most cars. One markup is the profit on the base car. That is, the car without any of its options. The second markup, which is frequently higher, is for the options. For example, you'll find that the markup for a Chevrolet Corvette is 15½ percent for the base Corvette. The options are marked up 17 percent. You should consult a consumer guide like *Edmund's New Car Price Guide* to identify the base vehicle and option markups for the car of your choice.

Front-End Profits

The amount of profit from the sale of the vehicle is called the "front end" of the deal. From this they have to pay the salesperson's commission and contribute to the dealership's overhead. Clearly, the new vehicle sales side of the dealership's operation is successful if they can:

1. Sell cars or trucks in volume
2. Earn a good gross profit on each vehicle sold

Back-End Profits—Profits after the Sale

If a dealership had to exist on the front-end profits alone, most would probably be out of business in short order. For that reason they will work very hard at selling "add-ons" after you've agreed to buy the car or truck. These include rust protection (which they sell to you for $150 but which costs them less than $10), extended warranties, and life, accident, and health insurance. All of these are major profit sources for the dealer. They will also try to convince you to finance your car through them. That becomes another source of profit.

Sometimes, car companies offer financing rates that are better than those you will find at your bank or credit union. This low APR (annual percentage rate) is usually part of the manufacturer's effort to move an oversupply of inventory. While we recommend that in most cases you say no to dealer-offered life, accident, and health insurance, there are some situations in which these add-ons can be of value: specifically, if you are elderly and in poor health and find it difficult to get insurance.

KEY TIP

> When it comes to after-sale add-ons, you will want to be sure that you aren't spending a lot of money on items you don't need or that you could find cheaper elsewhere.

Dealer Hold-Backs

Currently, most manufacturers are "holding back" from the dealer anywhere from 2.5 to 3 percent of the markup in their cars. In other words, if a car has a list price of $17,100 and an invoice of $15,000, that is a 15 percent markup. What the manufacturers do is hold back 3 percent of the profit—in this case $450—so that the dealer can, if he so chooses, show an invoice of $15,450 to a customer to prove how "close we are to tissue." Once the car is sold, the manufacturer sends the dealer a check for the "hold-back."

One of the interesting side notes on this "hold-back" process is that it has negatively impacted many sales commission checks. Usually the salesperson earns a commission based on the total profit in the deal. Even though the "hold-back" is, in fact, profit, many dealers are not figuring that into the salesperson's commission. Needless to say, this does not sit well with the salespeople.

Your Trade-in as a Dealer's Profit Source

If the dealership has a used-car operation, your trade-in can also represent a source of additional profit. Let's say that a new car has a sticker price of $18,000 and that the dealer's price, or invoice, is $16,000. Further, let's assume that the buyer trades in a car with a wholesale value of $8,000 and that the dealership agrees to put that $8,000 of used car equity against the new car. The buyer turns over the used car and a check for $10,000. The dealership now has to pay off a floor plan on the new car. The floor plan would be the invoice plus whatever interest has accrued.

For simplicity, let's say that the dealer's payment to the bank or financial institution amounts to $16,200—the invoice plus the floor plan interest, which will round off to $200. Because $8,000 of the deal is in the equity of the trade and $10,000 is in cash, the dealer has to make up the $6,200 difference. That "difference" will come from the used car.

If he has given the customer $8,000 as a trade-in allowance, it's probably because he knows that the car will bring at least that and probably more at auction. However, if it's a nice car, he may sell it himself in order to improve his profit on the transaction. It would not be unusual for him to put the car on his used-car lot with a price of $10,995, which is about a 37 percent markup. If he sells it for $9,995, that means he has received $10,000 in cash and a trade-in, which as a result of the resale grossed him $9,995 for a total of $19,995. Subtract what he paid the bank for his floor plan—$16,200—and his total profit on the new car transaction is $3,795.

Now, factor in the back end of the deal, hold-backs, and possibly even a factory-to-dealer incentive payment, and the total gross profit to the dealership could be several thousand higher. You see? There is a reason why car dealers live in big houses.

And What If the Trade-in Is a Dog?

While dealers prefer to make money on trade-ins, they don't want to lose the new car sale (and all the profitable add-ons) just because they know they will have trouble selling a "dog" on their used-car lot. When the condition of the car raises doubts about its retail marketability, the dealer will often arrange with a wholesaler to buy your trade even before you have closed your deal. As you can understand from the above example, a dealer must be sure that his costs and profit margin will be covered by the value of the trade-in.

Let's say that you have a car that has a true wholesale value of $2,200. Furthermore, let's assume that after the dealer calls around to several wholesalers, the best offer he gets is for $2,000. Often the salesperson will greet you with a long face and say that the best they can do on your trade is $1,800. If you agree, they'll pocket the difference. Sometimes—and we'll go into this in more detail later—the salesperson may come back and say that the dealership can "allow" you $2,400, or maybe more, on your trade. What the dealership is doing is simply taking the additional $200 out of the profit side of the deal (money that otherwise might have taken the form of a "discount") and putting it on your trade. This is usually a tactic reserved for those people who are more concerned with what they receive for their trade-in than they are with the price of the new vehicle. By taking money off one end and putting it on the other, car sellers can make the buyer feel good about the trade-in price without really impacting the dealership's profit.

Dealer Financial Pressures

The dealer is under constant pressure to move his inventory in order to minimize floor-plan interest and generate the funds necessary to offset the overhead. Unless a dealership has a line of cars that is "really hot," they will be inclined to take a definite profit *now*—even if it's below what they had planned to get. They know that the next buyer may be days away, so it's really a case of "take the money and run." Currently the competition for your business is fierce, and sales managers are putting a great deal of pressure on salespeople to close deals. As we'll explain later on, you can use this pressure to your great advantage.

How "Supply and Demand" Impacts the Deal

If you've got your eye on a car that is in great demand and in limited supply, you probably are not going to be able to buy that car below the asking price. In fact, occasionally the dealers will actually jack up the price over the manufacturer's suggested retail price (MSRP) and charge a premium for a hot car. On the other hand, if the dealer has a lot full of slow-selling vehicles that have been generating a ton of interest for the bank, you'll probably be able to make a deal very near the invoice price.

Why Dealers Deal

Most dealers would rather take a small profit than lose the sale to a competitor. Furthermore, they know that for every "short" deal there will be customers who will end up paying them close to full sticker.

Dealers know that they have several opportunities to profit from a sale in which there is only marginal front-end profit. They can sell the back end—financing, rust-proofing, insurance, etc.—and potentially make a very attractive profit. They can make money on your trade-in. Finally, they know that if you service your car with them, you'll become an ongoing source of profit.

Dealers are often paid on a "turn and earn" basis. The factory wants them to move cars. For that reason, the number of cars sold each month is often more important than the profit. Factories reward dealers who "move a lot of iron" by giving them special bonuses and providing them with larger allocations.

A sales manager once summarized the main "moan" of most salespeople when he asked: "How would you like to be in a sales business in which the customers come in and tell you how much profit they're going to let you make on your product?" That's essentially what consumers have the power to do in most car-buying situations. But the key is up-front information. In order to tell a salesperson how much profit you're willing to give the dealership, you have to know all of their numbers and, you have to be fully aware of the ways in which they can recoup losses on the front end of the deal by selling you unnecessary and expensive items on the back end.

How They Sell Below Invoice

This is a wonderful sleight of hand in which the salesperson shows you his or her invoice and then offers the car at a price just above cost. The question is, how do they make money on that kind of deal? As it turns out, they have several sources of profit. First, there is the factory holdback, which can amount to up to 3 percent of the sticker price. Second, the factory probably has offered the dealer an incentive to help sell the car. Some dealers will pass the incentive on to the consumer; others put it in their pocket. On some luxury cars, this incentive might total $5,000 or more. Often the factory will increase the incentive payments as the dealer sells more. Third, there's still the back end of the deal and your trade-in. Keep in mind, there's a reason why car dealers live in big houses.

"No-Haggle" Cars or the "No-Dicker Sticker"

Currently, companies such as Saturn, Oldsmobile, Ford, Chevrolet, and Buick are offering "one price" models that typically have more standard features than the base models but are priced for less. The intent of this pricing strategy is to help the dealer maintain a reasonable profit margin while giving the buyer a better value without the haggle. This concept has worked for Saturn for two reasons: First, they sell all their cars with a "no-dicker sticker." Second, Saturn's ability to offer a no-dicker sticker lies in General Motors' decision to create exclusive franchise areas for the Saturn dealers. These areas are large enough so as to discourage and reduce the consumer's ability to play one dealer off another. Furthermore, it is their policy not to offer rebates or other incentives but to maintain, as much as possible, a supply that does not exceed demand.

What Saturn has done is create a pleasant no-pressure sales environment in which consumers are treated very well. In return for this courteous treatment, the consumers get to pay Saturn more than they would for a comparable car in which the dealer is obliged to compete with other dealers. It's interesting to note that according to industry figures, the average Saturn profit is about 13 percent over dealer cost, while the average selling price of negotiated cars tends to be just below 7 percent. The message here is that you "pay" more for not having to haggle over price.

Other car lines have tried to launch the no-dicker sticker on some of their models while the rest of the line remains negotiable. To date, they have had marginal success because they don't have the exclusive sales territories Saturn has and because there is always some dealer who is willing to make a deal in order to meet monthly quotas or to reduce his inventory. And it's been shown that a good number of the no-dicker dealers will change their price to reflect factory incentives, inventory levels, and when they need the units to qualify for a larger allocation.

No-Dicker Trade-ins

We would also suggest that you take care when it comes to your trade-in. Reports suggest that at times customers get so comfortable with the no-hassle environment that they let their guard down when it comes to insisting on and getting a fair price for their trade-in.

The upside of the Saturn is that you won't be hassled. The downside is that you'll pay more than if you were to negotiate aggressively for a comparable car. Moreover, the difference in money might well buy you a more upscale car or at least a comparable one with more features and options.

The bottom line is that the car market is one of supply and demand. The car dealers are the ones who introduced the negotiated price, and now, until they find some other way of selling cars, they have to live with the reality that most people have been taught not to pay sticker.

The Nearly Impossible Dream

Most dealers dream of having a line of cars for which demand is just slightly higher than supply. And sometimes, on certain models, this is the case. Show me a dealer with a hot car in great demand, and I'll show you a stone wall when it comes to negotiating. However, this tends to be the exception. Because manufacturers must meet their financial forecasts, they press their dealers into accepting more cars than there is demand for. The idea is to get the cars on the dealers' lots and then let the dealer "blow them out," which is industry parlance for selling cars at lower prices in order to reduce the inventory. Dealers know that when sales are slow and the production line is outproducing sales, the factory representative will come around pressing them to take more cars.

Now you might assume that a dealer would just say: *"Hold it. I've got a two-month supply, and I won't buy any more cars until I've sold some."*

While factory representatives might sympathize, their job is to push cars into dealer lots. So if they have a dealer who resists taking his or her quota, the factory representatives will sometimes retaliate by shorting or denying the dealer the hot-selling cars—the ones that make the big profits. Or the representatives might unload a bunch of cars with colors that are in low demand. The standard joke is: "If you don't cooperate, you're going to find an awful lot of green cars in your next allocation."

Bottom line: If the dealer wants to get the hot-selling cars and keep the factory representative on his side, he accepts the inventory, then moves it out with special sales, sales spiffs, rebates, tent sales, and just about any ploy or gimmick he can think up.

4. "Their" Selling Strategies—How the Salesperson Works

The Steps of the Sale and Controlling the Customer

Earlier, we took you through the steps of the sale and showed you what it would be like to deal with a truly professional salesperson. One who, while trying to make a profit, is also intent on making you a truly satisfied customer. We're going to go through the steps of the sale again, but this time we're going to help you understand some of the strategies, tactics, and ploys that salespeople use to control you and the selling process. The intent is to show you what's going on behind that smiling face. As we explained earlier, there are eight basic steps to the sale.

1. Meet and greet the prospect and establish rapport
2. Qualify the prospect. Find out what they're looking for and determine what they can pay and how they intend to pay
3. Present the car
4. Take the prospect on a demo drive
5. Answer and overcome any objections
6. Close the sale
7. Deliver the car
8. Follow up and ask for referrals

1. Meet and Greet

Any salesperson worth his or her commission will want to make a good first impression and establish some degree of rapport. In the best of circumstances, they want you to think of them as someone you can trust and someone who has just become your new best friend.

As the old saying goes, "You don't get a second chance to make a first impression." With that as a given fact of life, you have to wonder why so many salespeople act as if you're imposing on their time, as if they would really rather be reading the newspaper than selling you a car.

In any event, a smart salesperson will try to establish a good relationship, and that's as it should be. While smart buyers recognize that this person is never really going to be their friend, they also know that it is better to deal with someone who is basically pleasant and tries to lower the stress level for all concerned.

Going for the Close from the Open

Sometimes a customer will come in and ask, "What's your best price on this car?" The more inexperienced, desperate, or lazy salesperson will immediately start dealing, and the negotiation begins—and sometimes ends—within minutes. The only time you want to start dealing from the get-go is when you've decided that it's in your best interest. We'll talk more about this type of situation later and offer some strategies for you to consider.

Roles They Play—The Salesperson as an Actor

Often in automotive sales training the point will be made that the salesperson is like an impromptu actor. The customer comes in, sets the stage, and it's up to the salesperson to play whatever part the customer's needs, personality, attitudes, experience, or demands dictate. This probably could be said of just about any salesperson who is interested in being responsive to his or her customers.

A salesperson will also try to determine if you have anything in common: Do you know the same people? Do you live in the same area? Do you like sports? Are there hobbies you share? The more a salesperson can make you believe that he or she is a lot like you, the greater the chances of building rapport.

In sum: Salespeople try to sell themselves to you and to establish the basis for a working relationship by finding a common ground. There's nothing wrong with this so long as you understand that, in the end, their goal is to sell you a car. If they're smart, they will also try to establish the basis for an ongoing relationship. Unfortunately, most car salespeople's vision ends with their commission check.

2. Qualifying

One of the first steps in virtually any sales situation is for the seller to qualify the buyer. In car sales, the salesperson is looking for two types of information:

1. Vehicle-related: Vehicle-related information has to do with the kind of car you're looking for, the features you want, and how you plan to use it.

2. Financial-related: Financial-related information has to do with finding the answers to questions like:

1. How much are you planning to spend?
2. How much do you owe on your current car?
3. How much do you think your trade-in is worth?
4. Are you a "payment" buyer?
5. Are you a "difference" buyer?
6. Are you a "cash" buyer?
7. Are you planning to finance?
8. Are you planning to lease?

A good salesperson understands that his or her first task after learning your price range is to sell you a car that is both within your price range and satisfies your *needs*. Then, having convinced you that a particular vehicle satisfies your driving needs, they begin to deal with the financial side of the deal. Unfortunately, most salespeople are so anxious to sell you a car, they cut the car presentation short and attempt to go right for the close.

Depending on what you tell the salesperson about any or all of the eight questions listed above, the salesperson will use that information to decide his or her sales strategy.

What Your Answers Tell the Salesperson

1. How much are you planning to spend?

If you tell salespeople that you're planning to spend $15,000, they'll show you a car with an MSRP (manufacturer's suggested retail price) of $15,000. They know that you will probably want to negotiate the price. It's their hope that they will sell you the car for around $14,000 and then make up the additional thousand by selling you an extended warranty, rust proofing, life insurance, and anything else they offer as add-ons.

If you have allocated $15,000 for a vehicle and want to get the maximum car, van, or truck for that amount, you should enter the dealership knowing the true "invoice" or "dealer cost" of the car. In this example, if you've got $15,000 to spend, then the car ought to have an invoice price of something less than $15,000. Therefore, you should ask to see a car that is 15 to 20 percent above your budget. In this case you'd tell the salesperson that you're thinking about something in the $17,000 to $18,000 range.

2. How much do you owe on your present vehicle?

Assuming you plan to trade in your current car, your answer to this question tells the salesperson:

1. How much equity you have in your current car, and
2. If your payoff is so large as to make it difficult to structure a deal

For example, let's assume you bought a car last year for $15,000 and financed 75 percent of the car, or $11,250. Further, let's assume that you've paid that down by $3,000, leaving you with $8,250 still owed. Now here's the shocking news: With few exceptions—those being certain luxury cars and high-demand sports vehicles—your one-year-old car, van, or truck has dropped in value anywhere from 40 to 60 percent. That means that on the wholesale market your car is now worth, at best, about $9,000, leaving you only about $750 equity in your trade.

Should you decide to try to sell the car on your own, you might be able to get a couple of thousand over the wholesale price and use that as a down payment on the new car. On the other hand, if the salesperson knows that your car is fully paid for, that tells him or her that:

1. You've got $9,000 in equity to put against a new car, and
2. Your additional out-of-pocket payment is only $6,000

This information could then lead the salesperson to try to sell you on a more expensive car. What's another two to three thousand dollars?

3. How much do you think your trade-in is worth?
Once you have made it known that you intend to trade in your current car, the salesperson will try to establish if you have a price in mind. If you suggest a number that is higher than the car is worth on the wholesale market, that will suggest that either:

1. You need to be educated, or
2. You are one of those buyers who is more concerned with getting a "good price for their trade" than they are about the total cost of the transaction

If your estimate is lower than the car is worth you've told them that:

1. Their used-car department can "steal" your trade.
2. They can quote you a low trade-in figure at the outset and then use the difference between your estimate and its real wholesale worth as a means of reducing the difference between the trade and the price without hurting their profit margin.

The lesson here, and one that we will discuss frequently in this book, is to know the true wholesale value of your trade-in before you start to shop. We'll provide instructions on how to do that later.

4. Are you a "payment" buyer?
While they won't ask this question in so many words, they will try to determine if you're one of those people who is really only concerned with the amount of the monthly payment. If you are, you've given them a license to steal.

5. Are you a "difference" buyer?
If you're not a payment buyer, you may be a "difference buyer." This is someone who is primarily concerned with the difference between the

allowance on the trade-in and the price of the car. Again, this kind of buyer is considered fair game.

6. Are you a "cash" buyer?
Many buyers assume that because they are prepared to pay cash, they have some degree of negotiation advantage. They don't. Actually, cash buyers usually find themselves listening to a dozen reasons why it makes more sense to finance through the dealership than to lay out the cash. And why are dealerships so interested in advising you on the best use of your cash? Because if you finance through them, they make more money on your deal.

7. Are you planning to finance?
If they think you are looking to finance, they immediately recognize an additional profit opportunity. As noted above, dealerships make money by financing or taking a commission for arranging the financing.

8. Are you planning to lease?
If you're a lease customer, this information immediately tells the salesperson to talk in terms of monthly lease payments. And guess what? Those payments are almost always based on the full sticker price, except when the manufacturer is providing a subsidy.

A Key Tactic for You to Keep in Mind

While you can't blame salespeople for wanting to qualify you financially, it's in your best interest to reveal only your price range (which, as we pointed out, you should inflate by 15 to 20 percent to provide room for negotiation). When they ask if you plan to trade your current car, or if you plan to lease, whatever, put them off with a response like: *"Right now I'm only interested in finding out if the car meets my needs and if your price is competitive with the other dealers' in town."*

This sends two unmistakable signals:

1. The salesperson is going to have to *sell you* on why you should buy the car
2. That you plan to shop for the best price

At this point an aggressive salesperson might counter with what we call the *"If I could, wudja?"* question which goes something like: *"If we find a car you like and I could get you that car at $3,000 less than the sticker price, would you be prepared to buy that car today?"*

Naturally your inclination might be to say: *"Sure, who wouldn't buy a car with that kind of discount?"* But understand this: The salesman has no intention of selling you a car at $3,000 off. His sole objective is to see if there is some price at which you would buy a car "right now . . . today." If your answer tells him that for the right price you're ready to buy *now*, he instantly labels you as a "hot prospect" and will turn up the pressure. We suggest that you answer that question this way:

"I have no idea. I think maybe we ought to see if I like the car first."

If the salesperson persists with this line of questioning, suggest that since he or she seems interested in only the price, it might be better for you to visit another dealer first in order to learn more about the car and then come back and let the salesperson bid for your business. Rest assured, no dealership (at least none that we can imagine) is going to let you walk off their lot if they think you're a buyer. You'll find that once you let it be known you're going to leave, there will be an immediate attitude change. If there isn't? Walk. You don't need the hassle, and unless you live in East Nowhere, there are many other dealers who will be very happy to accommodate you.

KEY TIP

> The less salespeople know about your true financial intentions and the less you tell them about how you plan to pay, i.e., cash, finance, or lease, before the negotiation, the more control you have. Make no mistake, information is the key to control. The more information you hold back, the harder they have to work and the more control you retain.

3 & 4. The Presentation and Demo Drive

During the presentation of the vehicle and the demo drive, salespeople have two objectives: First, they want to convince you that the car meets your needs. Second, they want to see if they can elicit buying signals from you. That is, they are looking for comments that suggest you are getting ready to buy.

Know that good salespeople will listen for buying signals like:

"If I buy the car, how soon could I have it?"

"I've always wanted a car like this."

"Do you have this model in silver?"

"My wife would kill me if I bought this car."

When they hear statements and questions like these, salespeople sense you're ready to make a deal. If they're smart, they will hustle you to their desk as fast as possible.

5. Overcoming Objections

At some point during the negotiation, you might begin to raise objections. Usually these objections occur in relation to the price. You should understand that there are really two different categories of objections with which the salesperson must deal. The first are called "Stated Objections." With "Stated Objections" there's no question as to what's holding the buyer back from making a purchase decision:

"The price is too high."

"I've really got to get more for my trade-in."

The second category of objection is called "Implied Objections." These are usually disguised as excuses such as:

"I need to talk to my wife about this."

"I'd like to think about it."

Beneath the Implied Objections

One thing most salespeople assume about the implied objection is that underneath the excuse is an unstated objection. More often than not, the price is at the root of this implied objection. Smart salespeople will begin to ask questions to see if they can uncover the barrier to making the sale. Does the spouse have to approve it? Does the customer want to shop to see if the car can be had for a better price? Is the customer afraid to make a decision? Whatever the case, be it a stated or implied objection, the salesperson will try to remove the obstacles and sell you on the deal.

6. The Close

Trial closes are questions designed to determine your readiness to buy without coming right out and asking if you're ready to sign the purchase order. Trial close questions might take the form of simple questions such as:

"What do you think of this model?"

"Have you got a particular color in mind?"

"How soon will you be needing a car?"

"Does the car have the performance you're looking for?"

Or they might be designed to get you into a yes mode:

"This is really a smooth riding car, wouldn't you agree?"

"Isn't this the kind of car that would look great in your driveway?"

"If the price is right, do you think that you might be interested in this one?"

Your answers give the salesperson an idea of how close you are to making a buying decision.

Asking for the Order

For some salespeople, the most difficult part of the sale is asking for the order. And the reason is simple: They don't want to suffer a turndown. On the other hand, some salespeople have developed very effective closing techniques. Here are some that have proven to be most effective.

The Assumptive Close

This closing technique is designed for people who can't make up their minds or seem afraid to make a decision. This method is designed to force you to act or make a decision by default. To put it another way, salespeople simply proceed as though they assume you want to buy the car. What they're doing is giving you the task of stopping them if you don't want to go through with the purchase. Here are several examples of how they might set up the assumptive close:

1. They will begin filling in the order form.
2. If you're interested in leasing, they will offer to introduce you to the leasing manager.
3. They will call the sales manager and have him or her approve the appraisal.
4. They will ask you to fill in some financing, leasing, or credit forms. In each instance they will have created a positive action designed to lead to the close of the sale.

The Direct Close

As the name suggests, this is where the salesperson candidly asks for the order:

"Shall we write up the order?"

"All I need is your signature and the car is yours."

Normally, the direct close is used when the salesperson feels confident that you are ready to buy and there are no obstacles standing in the way of your decision.

Summary Close

Here the objective is to summarize all the reasons why the car satisfies your needs. You'll hear something like:

"Ms. Customer, you told me performance is your number one

priority. Let me remind you of all the performance features in this car."

At that point they will summarize the key performance features and say:

"Now, let's get the paperwork done so you can start enjoying your new car."

Some closes are built around time pressure:

"If you buy today, you can get a great discount."

"There is someone else interested in that same car."

Other Closes

Some salespeople like to begin their close by asking an either/or question. The answer or answers to this type of question will provide them with a signal to write up the order or to keep selling:

"Do you want me to register the car in your name or in both your name and your spouse's?"

Still others are designed to create sympathy for the poor salesperson:

"We're having this contest, and if I can just get one more sale, I'll be able to take my poor invalid mother to Hawaii."

Finally, if all else fails, if the salesperson just can't get you to commit, don't be surprised to hear the salesperson say something like:

"You told me you liked the car. You said our price was competitive. Where did I go wrong? Was it me? Was it the dealership? Help me understand."

The intent here is to get you to talk and keep you in the dealership long enough to find some way to convince you to buy . . . now!

KEY TIP

> If you're intent on leaving, leave. Politely but firmly bring the conversation to an end. Make it clear that you have all the information you need and that more conversation would just be a waste of their time and yours. Tell them you'll be making a decision within a couple of days, if such be the case. Then shake hands and leave.

Working the Deal

There will probably come a time during the negotiation when the salesperson says something to the effect:

"Understand, I'm here to work for you, and I want to see you get the best deal possible." Right!

Unless you're offering full sticker, the moment you announce how much you're willing to pay for the car, salespeople will generally respond by suggesting they can't sell it to you for that price—they probably can, but they're not about to admit it. Then they will proceed to try to resell you on the inherent value of the car and prove it is worth more than you're willing to pay. If you should decide to up your offer slightly, you'll probably witness any variety of pained expressions accompanied by references to the boss—who will never accept the deal—followed by *sincere* comments like:

"Please understand, I'm on your side. If I don't sell you a car, I don't earn a commission. So I'm working for you. But my boss is a mean s.o.b. and I've got to convince him that he should take your deal. That's why I have to go in there with some numbers that I can defend. So if you could just come up a little . . ."

Sometimes, a salesperson will know what the house will take for a given car. More often, the sales manager doesn't want the salespeople to know what the bottom figure is because it will change according to how badly the dealership needs sales, the time of the month, the inventory, and any of a number of other different factors. The sales manager generally wants the salesperson to bring him your offer so that he alone can decide to "take it" or "bump it."

Getting You to Agree to Something . . . Anything!

In many dealerships, salespeople are told not to bother to negotiate. Their job is simply to get you to make a commitment at *some* price—*any* price—and write up a buyer's order for you to sign. Finally, they are to ask for a deposit check to prove that you are sincere. The manager will usually look at the offer and then send the salesperson back to announce that the dealership appreciates your offer, but that it's not enough. The car is going to cost you more. How much more really depends on how much higher they can push you. Given the fact that car buying is a process of negotiation, there is nothing ethically wrong with this approach. After all, they are in the business of making money. If they sold all their cars at the first price offered by each of their customers, they probably wouldn't be in business for very long. However, your attitude should be to let the other customers pay for the dealer's overhead. Your number one concern is *your* pocketbook, not theirs. Also, as you'll learn in this book, even when the dealer ends up with a "short deal," they still make money via hold-backs, incentives, or by having added another "sold unit" to their bottom-line tally. Keep in mind that the more units they sell, the more cars they are allocated from the factory.

"We Gotta Get More!"

Let's step back to the point when the salesperson said that your offer will not be enough. This is where the "grind" begins. If you hold firm to your figure and make it clear that you are ready to make a commitment today, the salesperson will eventually suggest that he write up the order at "your" price so that he can take it to the boss. As we said, the salesperson will probably also ask for a modest deposit so that the house knows that *you're serious*. Make it very clear to the salesperson that:

1. You *are* serious
2. There will be *no deposit* until the deal is approved
3. You will give them *a check for one percent* of the agreed price upon signing and that the rest will be paid when you take delivery

The salesperson won't like this and will probably say that it's dealership policy to require serious buyers to make a deposit. At which point you should stand up and say,

"Well, then I guess that's that. I want to thank you for your time. I guess I'd better look elsewhere because this is the only way I will do business."

Be pleasant, but make it clear that you are very, very firm.

More on the Deposit

There are any number of sales managers who believe that until prospects are ready to write a deposit check, they are not ready to buy. For that reason the deposit check is a signal to the manager that you're ready to be "tipped over." At the same time, the deposit also serves another very important function: It helps keep you from "walking" and gives them more time to "work you." Few people want to leave a signed check on the sales manager's desk. Car people know that there is a psychological commitment that goes with writing a check and that it works in their favor. It's their belief that if they can get you to write one check, you're primed to write another. They're right. So don't do it. Tell the salesperson to get the offer approved without a deposit and that you'll be happy to give them a small deposit once the deal has been signed by the sales manager. If he or she resists, make it clear that you will shop elsewhere.

Sometimes, when car salespeople realize that no matter what they say or do you are not going to buy that day, they will suggest that you leave a deposit to "hold the car." They might even suggest that there is another buyer interested in that same vehicle. Make it clear that you don't really care if the car is sold tomorrow because you know there are more where that one came from.

KEY TIP

Remember, until you sign the check—any check, including a deposit—you are in control.

Leaving a Deposit on an Approved Deal

Let's say the dealership has approved your deal and the manager has signed the buyer's order indicating approval. It is now appropriate to leave a deposit, but only a very small one—probably no more than $100 to $200. However, do not sign the deposit check until you know exactly the total amount you'll be paying. The details should all be on the buyer's order. If the order looks as though a chicken walked over it, ask to have it rewritten and to show all the figures with a proper explanation of each. Be pleasant about this, but be firm.

Further, never pay for the car in full until you take delivery. Do not hand over the final check until you've given the vehicle a personal inspection. If the dealership knows you're going to insist on making a pre-delivery inspection, the salesperson is going to make very sure that the car, van, or truck is spotless and ready to go. After you've fully checked out the car to be sure that it's clean, that it's got all the options you've agreed upon, and that it's got gas in the tank—only *then* do you sign the check.

KEY TIP

Let's say you've signed the buyer's order, the deal has been approved, you've left a check for $200, and suddenly you have an attack of what is known as *"buyer's remorse."* Maybe when you got home you decided that you'd agreed to spend too much, or that it's not really the car you want or that, for some other reason, you simply want out. Once you sign a buyer's order you *may or may not* be legally bound by the contract. Read it carefully before you sign. Especially all that fine print. In some cases, if you want out, the dealership will simply refund your money—although not without some cajoling and pleading. Other dealerships may let you out but will find a reason to keep your deposit. (See your lawyer if that is the case.) Still others may make all kinds of threatening legal sounds, especially if you signed a buyer's order for a car that the dealership had to special-order from the factory. If you get an attack of buyer's remorse,

you might be well advised to consult with a lawyer as to the extent of your obligations under the contract.

Once you get beyond the buyer's order and sign a finance agreement, lease, or cash contract, you are, in most states, committed fully to the terms of the contract. Again, if you have questions in this area, see a lawyer.

The Lowball Offer

You've been looking at a car and you think it's the one for you, but you want to think about it because you're still above the figure you want to pay. The salesperson knows that he or she can't close you today and that chances are you're going to shop another dealer. To assure that you'll come back, he will "put you out on a lowball." The salesperson will say something like:

"You know, I bet if I sit down and talk with the boss I can get him to knock off another $500 or $600 for you when you come in tomorrow."

Guess what? When you return to the dealership, the salesperson will have a long story about how he tried to "beat up the boss" but just couldn't get him to budge.

"But don't worry, because I really like you folks and I really want you to have this car. Here's what I'm going to do . . ."

The "Bump"

You make an offer and the salesperson goes into the manager's office to "fight for you." (It'll be a real struggle.) He or she then returns saying that if you could just *"up your offer a little the boss would have to agree."* Car sales managers don't like to leave any money on the table, and they will pressure their salespeople to squeeze out every last drop of profit.

Another variation is to have you sign the buyer's order and be told by the salesperson that you have a deal that the manager conveniently doesn't sign. Then, when you come in to take delivery of the car, the salesperson says, with tears welling in his eyes, that he made a mistake and that the boss just won't let the car go for such a low price.

"All we need is another $200. . . ."

This is one good reason to be sure that the manager signs the buyer's order to secure the deal. If someone does try to "bump" you as you prepare to take delivery of the car, ask for your deposit check and leave. If they don't get you now, they surely will find a way to get you later. This kind of practice should never be condoned.

The Turn Over (T.O.)

You've been negotiating for some time, and you've refused to budge beyond a certain figure. The salesperson has gone back and forth to the manager, but always returns saying management can't accept the deal.

"Could you just bend a little? Help me out. We're so close."

You don't budge and are about ready to leave, when the salesperson asks you to please sit down while he or she makes one last try.

The salesperson will probably disappear for anywhere from five to fifteen minutes depending on how long he feels he can leave you alone. To maintain control, tell the salesperson that you're on a tight schedule and that if it's going to take longer than three minutes to get a response, he or she can call you at home. Look at your watch. If five minutes pass, get up and find the salesperson or, failing that, have someone else find him. Announce you're leaving, but that you'll be looking forward to hearing from him at home.

Enter the Sales Manager

At this point you've established yourself as:

1. A buyer and
2. A determined negotiator

Depending on the establishment, the sales manager or possibly another salesperson will come back with your salesman and you'll be TO'd (turned over) to this new face. His objective is to point out all the many, many reasons the dealership can't sell the car to you at your price. The sales manager's attitude may range anywhere from the "friendly uncle" to "Attila the Hun." He may plead or try to intimidate. And make no mistake, at this point the salesperson and sales manager both hate you because *they* realize that you understand how to play the game. A good sales manager may try to appeal to your sense of fairness and relate his need for a fair profit to yours in whatever business you are in. You may find that he begins all his questions with *"Wouldn't you agree that . . . ?"* This phraseology is designed to elicit yes answers. The manager's purpose is to try to get you to agree that the dealership deserves more profit than you're willing to give them.

Don't get into a debate. Just smile and stay firm. Remember, their worst fear is that you'll walk out the door . . . *with your checkbook.*

Your Trade-in

As we mentioned earlier, one of the first questions you'll hear from a salesperson when it comes to your trade-in is: *"What are you looking to get for your car?"*

Their objective is to find out if you:

1. Have any idea of what it's worth
2. If you have underestimated its value, thus opening the opportunity for a "steal"
3. If you have an inflated idea of its worth and are going to have to be "educated"

Car salespeople know that most customers will ask more for their trade than they expect to get. What the salesperson wants to know is what you "really" think you'll get for your car. One ploy is to quote a purposely low bid. So low that your reaction is to defend your car with:

"My bank told me the car was worth—." Or,

"A guy at a used-car lot offered me—."

Once you've revealed what you really expect to get for the car, the salesperson has an important bit of information to work into the deal.

How they determine your trade-in's value

The fair wholesale price of a car is really what a wholesale buyer will pay to own your car so he can resell it at a profit. The industry publishes guides like the *Kelley Blue Book, NADA Official Used Car Guide,* and *The Black Book*. These books (which can be found at any library, bank, or credit union) collect reports on what the dealers are paying for trade-ins and what these cars are selling for at auction. While their figures can provide a guide, the actual value of your car can be determined only after you've had it appraised by at least three different used-car dealers. Their price will reflect what they believe they can sell it for to another wholesaler or what it will bring at auction.

Here's how a used-car transaction works. If you're selling your car to a dealer—that is, you do not plan to use it as a trade-in—the dealer will try to classify the car as extra clean, clean, good, or rough. He will then give you a price no higher than what he feels he can get from a wholesaler or at auction. If he decides to put your car on his lot, he may elect to perform any needed repairs and have it detailed (professionally cleaned inside and out). He will then mark up the car and advertise it for sale. Markups vary widely. It is not unusual to find that a car costing the dealer $1,000 will go on the lot with a $3,999 price tag. That's a 400 percent markup. Cars in the $10,000 range will show markups of anywhere from 30 to 60 percent. Above $20,000 the markups generally hover around 20 percent.

The only way to find out how much markup really is in a particular car is to learn what the dealer has invested in the car, i.e., his costs including purchase, repairs, and any applicable overhead. (We'll give you a tactic for making this determination in "About Buying Used Cars.")

When they talk about allowance

While we're on the subject of trade-ins, here's some other facts that you should keep in mind.

If your salesperson senses that what the dealership gives you for your trade will be a major factor in the deal, he will often say, "We can allow you X number of dollars on your trade." The key word to listen for is "allow." You should know that the "allowance" will usually be higher than the wholesale value because they are going to take some of the profit out of the new vehicle and put it on the trade. This is another form of giving you a discount on the new car. Be aware that if you get a healthy allowance, you probably won't be getting much, if any, discount off the new car. In most cases the car dealership is not going to give you money on both ends of the deal.

KEY TIP

Don't let the salesperson quote you an allowance. Ask for the actual trade-in value of the car. This is the only way you will know if they are in line with the three appraisals you've gotten.

Or maybe they focus on a difference figure

There are some buyers who seem to be primarily concerned with the *difference* between their trade-in and the price of the new car. So transfixed are they on getting a good price for their trade that the difference figure becomes the basis for the negotiation. The only time you should be concerned with the difference is after the negotiation when you are determining the amount of money you'll have to pay or finance upon taking delivery. By focusing on difference many buyers lose sight of the actual cost of the car. And that's something you never want to lose sight of.

7. Delivering the Car

In today's market, a good deal of emphasis is being placed on the delivery, thanks to Customer Satisfaction Index surveys. In order to score well, a dealership is supposed to do things like review the owner's manual, introduce you to the service department, provide you with a full tank of gas, and any number of other things that a good dealership will do with or without the threat of a survey.

Having said that, there are also some dealerships that will simply take your check, have you sign some papers, toss you the key, and wave good-bye.

We're going to provide you with some guidelines and suggestions as to what to do in order to be sure that when you take delivery of your new car, you maximize the potential for a satisfactory experience.

8. Follow-up and Asking for Referrals

Sometime after the sale, a good salesperson will call and ask how you're enjoying your car and if there are any questions they might answer. Again, this follow-up activity is part of the CSI survey.

Don't be surprised if salespeople use this opportunity to ask if you know of anyone else who might be in the market for a car. If you've had a good experience and if you're satisfied with the way you've been treated, you might be very happy to recommend your friends to the salesperson and the dealership.

On the other hand, if you've had a less than satisfactory experience, you might want to make that fact known both to the dealership and to your friends.

5. The Informed Auto Buyer

The Six Kinds of Buyers

Salespeople identify essentially five different types of buyers. We are adding a sixth buyer type to the list.

1. **Cash buyers.** These are people who pay cash for the vehicle. (Dealers would prefer that you *not* pay cash. They make more money if you finance.)
2. **Difference buyers.** These are people who are primarily interested in the difference between the amount the dealer will give them for their trade-in and the price of the new car.
3. **Allowance Buyers.** These people are mostly concerned with what the dealership will allow on their trade. Because the allowance often appears to be a "good price for the trade," buyers never know what their car is really worth or how much, if any, discount they're getting.
4. **Payment buyers.** These people look at the price of a car only in terms of what it will cost them per month. Far too often they will jump at a 48- or 60-month deal because the payments are low. This

may be the only way they'll be able to afford a new car. That notwithstanding, when all is said and done they will have paid hundreds, even thousands, of dollars more for the car.

5. **Lease buyers.** This is a different category of buyer and one that we will discuss in more detail in "About Leasing."

With possibly the exception of cash buyers, each of these buying methods gives the salesperson an opportunity to confuse the customer and maximize the dealership's profits.

6. The sixth type of buyer—the one you can be—is the **Informed Auto Buyer**. These are buyers who do their homework before they buy. They understand that each element of the deal must be kept separate. The educated auto buyer always knows the answers to these questions:
    1. What is the true price of the car, van, or truck to the dealer?
    2. How much profit am I prepared to give them?
    3. What is the fair wholesale value of my trade-in?
    4. What is the total cash I can afford to put down?
    5. Where can I find the best finance rates?
    6. Which monthly finance plan fits best into my budget?

If you deal with each of these issues separately, you will go a long way toward avoiding the confusion that some car sellers try to create. You will also set yourself apart from the not so car-smart buyers.

Control Is the Key

Were you to read the training manuals created for automobile salespeople, you'd find that a good deal of emphasis is placed on *controlling the customer*. Traditionally, salespeople are taught to follow a multistep sales plan—or a variation thereof—that we outlined in Chapter 2 (page 5ff). These steps, plus carefully focused questions, various ploys, confusion tactics, and even facial reactions, grimaces, and expressions are all part of the effort to maintain control. Far too many customers forget that until they sign the check, they have the ultimate control. And that's just fine from the dealership's perspective.

Your objective is to take control of the process. The way to do this is to:

1. Have your research done ahead of time. Your research should include:
    a. Deciding upon the make, model, and options

   b. Determining the dealer's costs
   c. Investigating and deciding on your financing options
   d. Setting a limit on what you'll spend
   e. Being able to recognize dealership ploys and tactics
   f. Knowing how to use counter tactics
   g. Recognizing that you have the option of shopping many dealers
   h. Deciding at what point and under what circumstances you will "walk out."
2. Plan your buying strategy in advance. Since salespeople have a *selling plan*, there is no reason you shouldn't have a *buying plan*.
3. Be prepared to slow down the selling process with questions, with requests to review figures a second and third time, and with the determination not to buy until you are totally satisfied that you understand and are ready to agree to all the elements of the deal.

Your Attitude—A Key to Success

"Be someone that they can neither hate nor take advantage of." As strange as that might seem, this is a sound piece of advice. Car salespeople expect to deal with all kinds of people. At the one end of the spectrum are the bullies, the aggressive personalities, and people who enter a dealership determined to give the salesperson a hard time. They are convinced that the dealership is going to try to cheat them on their trade and overcharge them on the new car and "by golly" they are going to "beat up the salesperson" before he or she gets a chance to beat them up.

At the other end of the spectrum are people who dread the prospect of buying a new car. They don't want to endure the hassle. They come in hoping to find someone who will treat them fairly and not take advantage of the situation. These people often agree to almost anything just to get it over with. In fairness, some car salespeople will be "gentle." They are smart enough to know that the prospect can also be the source of future referrals. But remember, no matter how altruistic or kind-hearted salespeople might appear, they did not come to work that morning to do social work. They are there to earn a commission. Money—not you—is the ultimate bottom line.

As an informed auto buyer you're totally different. While you will enter a dealership with a strategy, an objective, and, most important, with all the facts, you will also enter with the resolve to remain calm, pleasant, somewhat reserved, but clearly very determined and focused. Salespeople work very hard to out-bully bullies and to dream up schemes to make them pay more. Salespeople don't take kindly to know-it-alls with egos who claim they know cars and the car-selling business. Generally, the ego trip ends as a very expensive ticket. At the same time, many salespeople try to take advantage of the timid and the insecure by confusing them with figures and showering them with assurances that they will see to it that the customer's best interest is always served. Sure they will!

Salespeople will tell you that the unemotional, well-prepared, in-control customer is one of their more formidable challenges. Your objective should be to convey the impression that you are pleasant but very businesslike. That you are someone who asks good questions but offers few answers. That you are someone who has clearly done your homework and knows exactly the deal you are prepared to make. And finally, that you are someone who will not be pressured or swayed. Someone who will buy only when you are ready. Someone who is prepared to shake hands and walk out to shop elsewhere if your deal requirements are not met. *Believe you this*: Most salespeople are simply not equipped to deal with someone who comes into the dealership *prepared*.

6. Pre-Shopping Preparation

Assessing Needs Versus Wants

If you want to see a truly sad situation, picture the buyers who fall in love with a car and agree to hefty monthly payments. A year later, they come back to the dealership having realized that the monthly payment is killing them financially and try to sell the car back. What they discover is that their V-8 beauty has depreciated anywhere from 30 to upward of 50 percent and that they owe more on their loan than the car is worth at wholesale. So they end up giving back the car *plus* a substantial amount of cash just to get out of the payments.

Being a smart buyer also means being financially prudent. Never buy more car than you can reasonably afford. If you want a hot car, there are any number of new and used cars that can give you the thrill of ownership without the pain of payment poverty. By the way, this is where the used-car and pickup truck market becomes a very real and attractive alternative.

Evaluating the Vehicle

Visit a dealership and ask for a test drive. Make it clear that you are not interested in buying a car, van, or pickup that day, but that you will be shortly. The fact that you're a future prospect should get you some cooperation. Of course, you may also find that the salesperson will make an effort to convert you from "looker" to "buyer" before you leave.

Your objective is to spend some time behind the wheel and really get a feel for the car. Below you'll find an evaluation sheet to help you assess how a particular make and model satisfies your needs.

NEW-VEHICLE EVALUATION CHECKLIST

1 Poor, 2 Fair, 3 Okay, 4 Good, 5 Excellent

	1	2	3	4	5
General Quality Impression					
Exterior (fit, finish, paint)	❑	❑	❑	❑	❑
Interior (workmanship)	❑	❑	❑	❑	❑
Comfort					
Ease of entry front and back	❑	❑	❑	❑	❑
Headroom front	❑	❑	❑	❑	❑
Headroom back	❑	❑	❑	❑	❑
Legroom front	❑	❑	❑	❑	❑
Legroom back	❑	❑	❑	❑	❑
Seat support/comfort	❑	❑	❑	❑	❑
Ease of access to controls	❑	❑	❑	❑	❑
Visibility	❑	❑	❑	❑	❑
Trunk space	❑	❑	❑	❑	❑
Riding and Handling					
Acceleration	❑	❑	❑	❑	❑
Passing acceleration	❑	❑	❑	❑	❑
Hill climb power	❑	❑	❑	❑	❑
Cornering	❑	❑	❑	❑	❑
Steering response	❑	❑	❑	❑	❑
Road feel—bumps	❑	❑	❑	❑	❑
Braking	❑	❑	❑	❑	❑
General Impression					
Interior noise	❑	❑	❑	❑	❑
Rattles/Squeaks	❑	❑	❑	❑	❑
Sound system	❑	❑	❑	❑	❑
Convenience features	❑	❑	❑	❑	❑
Safety Equipment	**Yes**	**No**			
Air bags—driver	❑	❑			
passenger	❑	❑			
side	❑	❑			
ABS brakes	❑	❑			
Traction control	❑	❑			

How do the experts rate it?

Take time to do some third-party research on the make and model you'd like to buy. What do the car magazines say about it? What kind of rating does it get from *Consumer Reports*? What do current owners have to say? If you're concerned about the safety performance of a particular model, you can contact the Insurance Institute for Highway Safety, 1005 N. Glebe Road, Arlington, VA 22201 (703-247-1500). They can provide crash-test reports and cost-of-repair information. Keep in mind that those vehicles with better safety records usually have better insurance rates.

Twins

As you begin to consider various makes and models, keep in mind that most American manufacturers offer what the industry calls twins. What this means is that manufacturers will produce two cars, give each a slightly different look, give each a different name, but build them with essentially the same components. For example, Mercury Sable is essentially the same as a Ford Taurus. However, the Sable will generally run anywhere from $500 to $1,000 more for essentially the same car.

General Motors also produces twins. If you look closely at the Oldsmobiles and Buicks and compare them to Pontiacs and Chevrolets, you'll see that their primary difference can be found in some front and back styling variations and levels of interior trim. A number of years ago somebody at General Motors decided to display the full line of the cars at the General Motors building in New York. And because it was the Christmas season they thought it would be nice to have all the cars in white. What no one realized, until it was too late, is that the basic similarity of the cars made even more similar with the common color pointed out an unassailable fact: The primary difference between a Buick, Oldsmobile, Pontiac, and Chevrolet lies not in the styling, but in the price tags.

When it comes to imports, twins are not as common. Usually Hondas, BMWs, Audis, Jaguars, and Mercedes are one of a kind. However, there are a few foreign cars that are marketed under domestic nameplates. You'll find, for example, that a Chevy Nova is basically a Toyota Corolla assembled in California. Plymouth Conquest is the same as a Mitsubishi.

From the manufacturers' perspectives building similar cars and marketing them as separate models helps them offer more selection without having to go to the expense of building two different models. Obviously, this concept is not unique to the car industry. The point we want to make is that in some cases it is possible to save money and get the benefits of a more expensive car or truck by buying its less expensive twin.

KEY TIP

If Twins Are Good, Maybe Quads Are Better!

Years ago the author was doing some work for the Oldsmobile division of G.M. during the time that they were announcing their first compact, the Omega. In looking for an advertising theme that would help the public identify the Omega with the presumed aura of an Oldsmobile, it was suggested that they use a very simple and straightforward tag line: "Omega is an Oldsmobile." Everyone liked it but the lawyers. As it turned out, Omega was not an Oldsmobile at all, but a Chevy Nova built for Oldsmobile on the Chevy line. Somewhat irreverently we suggested that maybe the tag line should read: "*Omega is an Oldsmobile built by Chevrolet*."

It was then that we discovered that the last three letters in the Chevy Nova were the first letters of the three siblings: *O*mega (Oldsmobile), *V*entura (Pontiac), and *A*pollo (Buick). Hey, if twins are good, why not quadruplets?

Options

Needless to say, price is a major key in car marketing. For that reason, manufacturers will build and advertise base cars which come with few features in order to provide an attractive price point for their advertising. *"New Zapmobiles starting at just $12,995"* looks a lot better in print than "The New Zapmobile, like the one you will probably end up buying with all the nice features like AM/FM with cassette player, air conditioning, power steering, etc., for $15,995."

By breaking out the options, dealers can advertise more attractive come-on prices and then "sell up" once they've got you hooked. Plus, options tend to carry a higher percentage of markup than the cars themselves. Even Mercedes-Benz, which for years offered fully equipped cars, has now elected to go the option route in order to make their advertised pricing more competitive. Obviously, there's nothing wrong with this, but it does behoove the potential buyer to realize that in most cases the advertised price is what the industry calls a "Sally Rand." Translated, that means a "stripper" model that has been stripped of all its features and, like Sally Rand, is presented without much on it.

Option Packages

In order to avoid having to build cars with hundreds of different option combinations, manufacturers offer what they hope you'll find to be attractive option packages. As you shop for your car, keep in mind that a higher—and thus more expensive—model in the line may come with more options standard and represent a better value, at less price than it would for you to buy a base model and then begin to add the options you want. At the same time, however, be sure that the option package does not include equipment or trim that you don't want or need. Our advice when it comes to options is to examine the option packages carefully and then consult one of the price guides to determine the dealer cost and the markup. (We'll go into more detail on this in a moment.)

Depreciation

Another factor to consider when you buy a car is how fast it will depreciate. This is particularly important if you think you might be trading it in two or three years from now. Cars lose their value at different rates. Some, for example, may have lost as much as 40 percent of their value after the first year; others with similar features and engines may have lost only 15 or 20 percent. If you'd like a better fix on the projected depreciation of your target car, get the Automotive Lease Guide's *Residual Percentage Guide* by calling 1-813-791-4955. It comes out every other month and sells for $12.50 plus shipping and handling.

Evaluating the Service Department

One of the reasons to buy from one dealership over another has nothing to do with price or the vehicle. A good, customer-oriented service department that makes a real effort to take care of the dealership's customers can be a legitimate reason to pay more for a vehicle at one dealer than at another. While most manufacturers insist that their dealers will service all customers—no matter where they purchased the vehicle—it is true that you are looked upon with more favor if your car, van, or pickup bears their dealership logo. Be that as it may, it makes good sense for you to ask your salesperson—prior to making your deal—to show you the service department and introduce you to the service manager.

Look at the service department. Does it look like a junk shop or does it appear to reflect someone's pride? Ask about loaners and courtesy buses for their service customers. Ask if you will be assigned a service writer and inquire about roadside service. If you get the impression that the service manager and service writers are truly proud of their operation, make that a plus in the dealership's favor. You might even consider asking some of the service customers in the waiting room how they rate the dealership's service.

Getting the Retail Numbers

Before you begin to negotiate, you need two sets of numbers or prices.

The Costs You See

The first are the prices listed on the window sticker—officially called the Monroney sticker. This sticker is required by federal law to appear on all cars sold in the U.S. It must show the following:

1. The manufacturer's suggested retail price for the car and the factory-installed options
2. A transportation or destination charge for shipping the car from the factory or the port of importation to the dealership
3. EPA city and highway fuel-economy estimates

At present the law does not require dealers to put a Monroney on vans, four-wheel-drive vehicles, and light trucks. However, most do so voluntarily. If they don't, you might be well advised to steer clear.

Supplemental or "Pack" Stickers

In some cases you'll find a second sticker listing optional accessories added by the dealer or services like rust proofing that he has performed. In far too many cases, dealers use these supplemental stickers as a means of adding more profit. For example, in one lot we visited we found a supplemental sticker reading:

Dealer Delivery and Handling	$199
Auto Protection Package (Paint Sealers)	$249
Pin Stripe	$99

Since the Monroney sticker already showed a transportation charge, "Dealer Delivery and Handling" is labeling sleight-of-hand that the dealer is using to add a few more dollars to his profit. If one of today's vehicles needs a paint sealer, you might want to find out why and what kind of sealer they are talking about. Possibly if you live under an acid rain shower and don't intend to wash your car but once a year this might be a worthwhile investment. Only the pin striping appears to be a legitimate charge. By the way, an educated guess suggests that of the $547 of pack prices, the real cost to the dealer probably amounted to something less than $50. Clearly, this is nothing more than another means to squeeze some additional money out of the buyer.

Advertising Fees

Some dealers will add a separate charge for advertising. Their excuse is that the manufacturer charges them a fee on every car to help defray the cost of reaching you with their ads and commercials. You might respond by saying:

"Since I never see any of your ads, I guess I won't have to pay the fee."

Or you might suggest that since advertising is a cost of doing business, it should be built into the profit. If they insist on adding the fee to the price, make it clear that since you are shopping, the additional cost could put them at a disadvantage against the other dealerships you plan to visit. A statement to this effect will not be lost on a salesperson. If the dealership will not budge on the advertising fee and you decide that, all other things being equal, this is the dealership where you'd like to do business, try and use your agreement to pay the advertising fee to win a concession on another point.

Destination Charges

All manufacturers charge their dealers a destination or transportation cost, and this number is shown on the Monroney. This is a standard pass-along fee and one that they will not negotiate because there is no profit for them in the charge.

The Costs You Don't See

The second set of numbers is what the manufacturer charges the dealer for the car and the options. This is referred to as the invoice or "tissue" cost. The difference between the MSRP and the invoice is the markup and targeted profit figure.

During your test drive, find an opportunity to copy down all of the price information on the window sticker. Or if you prefer, just drop into a dealership and, should you be approached by a salesperson, announce that you are just looking. Usually that's enough to send them back to their desks, figuring that since you're not a buyer "today" you're not worth talking to. The major task here is to be sure that you write down all the key information including the dealer add-ons.

You might find it convenient to make a copy of the form on the next page and use it during your visit. (You'll also find a copy in your "Checklists.") Your objective is to leave the dealership with the information in columns 1 and 2 filled in. We'll discuss how to determine the dealer costs (or invoice) in Column 3 in a moment.

PRICE INFORMATION WORK SHEET

Make ____________ Model ____________ Year ____________

VIN Number* ____________ City Mileage ____________ Highway ____________

1	2 MSRP— List Price	3 Dealer Cost	4 Difference/ Profit
Price of Vehicle	______	______	______
Options			
______	______	______	______
______	______	______	______
______	______	______	______
______	______	______	______
______	______	______	______
Totals	______	______	______
Supplemental Charges— "Dealer Packs"			
______	______		______
______	______		______
______	______		______

*VIN number is the identifying number of the vehicle, which is usually found by looking through the left front of the windshield at the bottom of the support pillar. Or you can find it on the Monroney sticker itself.

Determining the Invoice Cost (Column 3)

Buy the most current copy of a new-car price guide like *Edmund's New Car Prices* or *Consumer Guide—Auto Series* and find your car. (*Consumer Guide* also advertises a fax service called *Price Fax* that, for a fee, will supply you with pricing information.) Compare the list prices with those you've copied from the window sticker. If the figures don't match, you may have an older book. You may also find some minor variation in the options, as manufacturers will change prices rather frequently, making it difficult for a publication to stay truly current. For your purposes, the figures should be close enough to provide you with enough information to complete the chart for analysis purposes.

Using the work sheet on the preceding page, find the items in Column 1 in the price book and list the dealer prices as shown in the book in Column 3. Then subtract 2 from 3 to give you the profit each item represents. When you add up the invoice-dealer cost figures, you'll know what the manufacturer is charging the dealer for the car. The total in Column 4 will show the dealer's profit before the holdback or any factory incentives are figured in. Then add the supplemental charges or "pack." Usually, the supplemental charge can be and should be challenged and made part of the negotiation.

Below, we've filled out a work sheet using figures that we obtained from a dealer offering the Volkswagen Jetta GL.

MAKE *Volkswagen* **Model** *Jetta GL* **Year** *19—*			
	MSRP	Dealer Cost	Profit
Price of Vehicle	$13,750	$12,488	$1,262
Options:			
Air Conditioning	$850	$742	$108
Power Glass Sunroof	$575	$502	$73
AM/FM Cassette	$350	$291	$59
Transportation	$390	$390	$0
Totals	**$15,915**	**$14,413**	**$1,502**
Supplemental Charges	**Price**		
Dealer Delivery & Handling	$199		
Auto Protection-Paint Sealer	$249		
Pin Stripe	$99		
Total Supplement	**$547**	**$47**	**$500**

At this point you know two things:

1. The MSRP represents a profit to the dealer of $1,502.
2. His supplement or add-ons total $547. The actual cost will be hard for you to determine, but you can be sure that most of the supplement represents profit. For purposes of our illustration,

we are assuming that the profit is about $500, for a total of $2,002 of profit that we know about.

The Hidden Profit

Now we have to look for the hidden profit. This comes from two potential sources:

1. Factory-to-dealer incentives
2. Dealer hold-backs

Factory-to-dealer incentives

Frequently, the manufacturers—often called "the factory" in car parlance—will offer their dealers incentives on certain cars in order to help move inventory. The incentives serve to lower the cost of the car to the dealer and make it possible for the dealer to offer deals, negotiate deeper discounts, and generally provide a customer with the opportunity to buy a car for a lesser price. These incentives can range from several hundred dollars to four or five thousand in the luxury car range. This is information you'd like to have for your negotiation.

One good source for this information is the industry magazine *Automotive News*, a weekly publication from Crain Communications. You can often find copies in your library, or possibly the car loan department of your bank or credit union will have a copy. In the back of the magazine you'll usually find a section called "Incentive Watch," which shows current dealer and customer incentives. In one issue we found dealer incentives ranging from $200 up to $5,000. Obviously, the higher the retail price of the car, the higher the factory incentive. Consumer incentives ranged from $300 to $3,000. Understand that these incentives are likely to change frequently.

In the case of the Volkswagen Jetta, we found that at the time of this writing—and by the time you read this it will have changed—the factory was offering dealers an incentive of $500. This is profit and should be figured into your calculations.

Dealer hold-backs

It is common practice today for the manufacturer to hold back 2 to 3 percent of the dealer's profit and then pay that profit once the car is sold. What this does, effectively, is give the dealer an opportunity—if he so chooses—to show you an invoice that is from two to three percent higher than his actual cost. If he can talk you into giving him 3 or 4 percent over "invoice," he could well walk away with 6 to 7 percent profit and maybe a factory incentive to boot. For purposes of your number gathering, assume that the hold-back amounts to at least 2.5

percent. In other words, if the difference between the MSRP and the invoice is 15 percent, you can safely assume that the true markup is between 17 and 18 percent.

In the case of the Jetta, the hold-back is 3 percent—again at the time of this writing—and that represents approximately $477 of additional profit to the dealer. When you total up the dealer's potential profit you find that:

Profit markup in the car and options	$1,502
Supplemental Charges—estimated profit	$500
Factory-to-dealer incentive	$500
Dealer hold-back	$477

Based on your research, you know that the Jetta could potentially produce a gross profit of approximately $2,979.

As we noted earlier, from this profit the dealer must pay interest on the car (his floor plan) and pay a commission to the salesperson. The amount of the commission is usually determined as a percent of the gross profit, but it will vary from one dealership to another. Finally, the dealer must make a contribution to the cost of his overhead. The rest is profit. This is "front-end" profit. There is also "back-end" profit and *profit* from your trade-in and *profit* from the parts and services you'll buy over the period of ownership. You can almost think of the new car as the stopper in a bottle of profits that begins to flow into the dealership once you sign the buyer's order.

The Value of This Information

Consider the value of this information to your buying strategy. Most people walk into the dealership selling the VW—or any car, for that matter—look at the sticker, and assume that the bottom-line price of the car is $15,915 plus the $547 supplement, for a total of $16,462. They will probably assume that by being aggressive they can get a 10 percent discount, so they will start their negotiation by asking for a $1,600 discount off the MSRP. In most cases, after a good deal of "grinding," the dealership—pleading poverty and expressing the fear that this deal could force them out of business—will finally agree to an $800 discount, leaving the dealership with about $2,000 of profit—*before* they start to sell the back-end items—e.g., the financing, insurance, extended warranties, etc.

Knowing what you now know, you can elect to begin your negotiation not at the list price but at the actual price. Knowing that the dealer's cost is about $13,936 ($14,413 invoice less 3 percent hold-back of $477), you can start the negotiation by offering 3 percent over the true cost—about $418. You might even elect to agree to another $100.

Chances are, if it's the end of the month, if the dealer is loaded with inventory, and the car or truck you're buying is not in high demand, with persistence you'll make your deal.

Other Sources of Savings—Yours!

Besides what you can save by knowing the dealer's real cost, there are several other opportunities to lower your cash outlay.

Factory-to-Customer Rebates—Your Money, Not Theirs

Another of the major marketing devices utilized by manufacturers to help move product is the "consumer rebate." The upside of a rebate from the factory's and dealer's perspective is that it generates more interest and more sales. The downside is that consumers have become so accustomed to rebates that they tend to wait until a rebate is announced before they consider buying. That was not the way it was intended to work.

Essentially there are two kinds of rebates:

1. A cash payment direct to the customer from the manufacturer
2. A cash payment that requires dealer participation

The problem with the second rebate is that it requires individual dealers to put up part of the rebate money if they wish to participate. If they don't, there is no way for you to get a rebate from that dealer.

Often when a car is offered with a rebate, the salesperson will try to factor the rebate into the negotiation. Don't let them. *The rebate is your money*—offered by the factory—and not the dealer's unless they are participating.

Rebates or Low Financing?

Some manufacturers offer the option of a rebate or low financing. Depending on how much money you plan to put down against the car and the amount the dealership gives you for your trade-in, you may find that one option is clearly better than the other. It's important to take the time to compare both.

Example: A car has a bottom-line sticker price of $16,000. In order to help promote more sales, the factory offers potential customers a $1,000 cash rebate or 2 percent financing. Further, let's assume that your financial institution is offering 8 percent new-car financing on a 36-month loan. Which is the better deal? Take some time to figure it out or call your bank and ask for their help. They have all the tables.

Here's a comparison:

Price of car is	$16,000
You agree to pay	$15,000
You decide to finance	$10,000

Which is better? The $1,000 cash back and an 8 percent loan, or no cash back and a 2 percent loan?

The amount of your interest payment with a 2 percent loan on $10,000 over a three-year period would be $311.22.

If you were to take the $1,000 and use it to reduce the amount of money needed to finance the car, your 8 percent loan (now on $9,000) would cost you $1,153 in interest over the 36 months. Notice that if you keep the cash you end up paying it back in interest.

$1,000 Cash Back Applied to Loan		**$1,000 Cash Back Not Applied to Loan**		**2% Financing**	
8% Loan	$9,000	8% Loan	$10,000	2% Loan	$10,000
Interest	$1,153	Interest	$1,281	Interest	$311
Totals	**$10,153**		**$11,281**		**$10,311**

Another example: This time let's assume a cash-back offer of $750 and a 7 perc56ent loan, or 2 percent financing. The amount to be financed is $7,500 over 24 months.

$750 Cash Back Applied to Loan		**$750 Cash Back Not Applied to Loan**		**2% Financing**	
7% Loan	$6,750	7% Loan	$7,500	2% Loan	$7,500
Interest	$503	Interest	$559	Interest	$157
Totals	**$7,253**		**$8,059**		**$7,657**

Appraising Your Trade-in

If you have a trade-in (and let's assume that it's only two or three years old and is in reasonably good condition), take the car to three different dealers and tell them that you are interested in selling the car and that you'd like their best price. No matter what price they quote, show some pain and tell them that if they want the car, they're going to have to do better than that. When they ask, "How much better?" respond by asking for another ten or fifteen percent. You can be assured that they will probably shake their heads and say that the car isn't worth that much. If they don't make a counter offer, they've either quoted you the fair wholesale or they are interested in the car only if they can buy it below wholesale. That's why you need to visit three different dealerships. Repeat this with two other dealers and use the highest offer as the basis for what your car is worth on the wholesale market.

Now, what if your car is not in all that good condition? Maybe the interior is a little ragged, the paint is scratched, the miles are a little on the high side, and the motor needs work. In this case you're probably going to find that used-car dealers associated with new-car lots aren't going to be interested. Independent used-car dealers might, but they will only give you a price below what they know they can reasonably expect to get from a wholesaler or at auction. Keep in mind that no one is going to risk any more than they can absolutely be assured of getting back. In fact, in most cases they'll whack another ten to twenty percent off the price to be sure that they're protected.

Book Prices

The industry uses any of several books as price guides: the *NADA Official Used Car Guide*, *National Auto Research Black Book*, *Kelley Blue Book Auto Market Report,* and *Galves Auto Price List*. These books purport to reflect the average wholesale prices that various cars are bringing across the country. The only problem is that they don't agree. Compare the suggested wholesale prices for a 1991 Chevrolet four-door Lumina from the same month:

Kelley Blue Book:	$7,500 (tends to reflect West Coast prices)
NADA:	$6,750 (combination of auction and dealer reports)
Black Book:	$5,650 to $8,850 (reports from auction sales)

Your objective is to find out how your local market values your car, and the only way to do that is to have it appraised by the people who are putting up the cash. You may find that certain vehicles will be worth more at certain times of the year. A convertible will probably bring more in the spring. A station wagon will bring more as vacation time approaches and the market for family cars increases. A four-wheel-drive vehicle might do better in the North as winter approaches. The bottom line is that you won't know until you test the market.

The Appraisal

Frequently, used-car appraisers find themselves having to deal with a customer who has a totally unrealistic idea of what his or her car is worth. For many, the car has become a member of the family, and the dents, rust, and the ripped upholstery have either become invisible or are regarded as part of the character of the car.

To help "disabuse" the customer of his or her inflated impression of the car, they will frequently use a technique called the "negative walk-around." The appraiser will walk around the car inspecting it carefully as the owner looks on. The appraiser will touch all the bad spots, rub his finger over the paint scratches, and generally underscore each defect with an "Ummmm," or a "Too bad," or a "They don't make cars like they used to," every time he discovers a problem or defect. If you decide to shop for a used car and elect to use this technique, keep in mind that you'll want to point out the defects without demeaning the car or putting any blame on the owner. That could create a negative atmosphere. The sole purpose of this technique is to make sure that the owner knows that the appraiser is fully aware of all those things that impact the car's value. Don't be surprised if the appraiser uses this tactic on your car.

There are times when customers will bring in true "cream puffs" with no idea of what they're worth. There are more than a few used-car buyers who will try to steal the trade. That is, they will offer less than the car is worth, knowing that they can retail it for a significant profit. Again, take the time to get three appraisals to make sure you have determined the car's fair wholesale value.

Selling Your Car Yourself

If you've got a car that's in good condition, most used-car dealers would rather take it in on trade than let you sell it yourself. The reason is simple: Most dealerships make more money with their used-car business than they do with their new cars. And why not? Most new-car markups fall in a range between 12 and 20 percent, while used-car markups have virtually no top.

If a dealer believes your car will sell quickly for a good profit, he will try to convince you that the hassle of selling a car yourself is just not worth it. He might even point out that if you trade your car, you pay sales tax only on the "difference" between the trade-in allowance and the price of the vehicle. True, but keep in mind that it will be you, and not the dealership, who will be pocketing the profit.

Financing

Investigate your financing options. Call several banks, check with your credit union, and get quotes from the dealership you plan to shop first. Find out if they have any special rates. A difference in one or two percentage points can save you hundreds of dollars over the course of the loan. If you decide to finance through the dealership, keep in mind that their rates are usually negotiable. Remember, the dealership makes money on financing, and they would usually rather discount their rate than lose your business to another financing institution.

Dealerships usually have several loan sources, including local banks and the manufacturer's credit company. Each source sets their rates to the dealer. If the dealer can get you to pay a percent or two more above the rate, they keep the difference as profit. If you plan to finance through a dealer, always shop other sources so that you will know the going market rate in your area for vehicle loans. Also, be sure to negotiate the price before you reveal that you are thinking about dealer financing. If they know ahead of time that you plan to finance, they will frequently try to confuse the issue by giving you a lower rate on a higher price or a lower price at a higher finance rate. (Your refusal to identify how you intend to pay for your car is a strategic ploy that we'll discuss in more detail later.)

Another point to keep in mind is that wherever you finance, the more you can put down in cash and in trade-in equity, the lower your monthly payments.

Shopping for Your Loan

Here are some tips that are important for you to keep in mind while shopping for your loan.

1. ***Decide on a price range.***
2. ***Decide how much you can put down as a down payment.*** As we mentioned earlier, too many buyers accept long financing arrangements in order to minimize their down payment. If they decide to trade the car in the first year or so, they often find that they actually owe more on their car than it's worth. Not a pleasant prospect, to say the least. A good rule of thumb is never to finance more than 80 percent of the true cost—i.e., the dealer's invoice—of the car. At least 20 percent (some recommend more) should be paid in cash or in the equity of your trade.

   In other words, if the car has an MSRP of $21,495 and the dealer's cost is $18,800, your total finance package should not be more than $15,040. Remember what we said about depreciation? The moment you drive the car, van, or truck home, the actual value will have dropped about 40 percent, and the wholesale value of the vehicle will be about $13,000. If you sold it yourself you might be able to cover your payoff and maybe recoup some of your down payment.

3. ***Go to your bank or credit union and ask them to figure the monthly payments on the amount you intend to finance for both a 24-month and 36-month loan.*** Don't let yourself get trapped into a 48- or 60-month loan. Sure, the

monthly payments look attractive as compared to those of a 24- or 36-month loan, but add them up and you'll see just how much more these 48- and 60-month loans cost in actual dollars. Be aware that *interest charges vary widely* for the same amount of money. So take the time to shop and compare.

4. ***Once you've shopped for money, found the best rate, and have an estimate of the monthly payments, make a hard-nosed personal decision about whether the payments will fit into your budget.*** Remember, the thrill of taking delivery of an expensive, sporty new car will become the reality of monthly payments. Keep in mind that today there are nearly 600 different models of car, van, and light truck on the market. With all those choices there has to be at least one that will fit into your budget and still create some pride of ownership.
5. ***Determine the equity in your trade-in.*** If your car has a wholesale value of $6,500 and you owe $1,500, your equity is $5,000. On the other hand, if your car has a wholesale value of $6,500 and you still owe $7,500, you've got a $1,000 negative equity, and you might want to consider trying to sell it yourself. While selling privately can be more of a hassle, at least you'll give yourself the chance of getting enough profit over wholesale to pay off your negative equity.
6. ***Once you have a fix on your finances, start to shop.*** But stick to your budget. In fact, make it a point to try to buy your car under your budget. By using these books and doing your homework, there is no reason you can't.

Work sheet example

Here's an example of how to figure what you'll need in the way of cash, equity, and financing to buy a new car. For purposes of illustration, let's assume that your current car has a wholesale value of $6,500. In other words, this is what a used-car dealer will pay to buy your car. At the same time, let's also assume that you owe $800 on the car.

Next look at the amount of money—cash—that you plan to take from your savings account, or other sources, to put down on the car.

Let's use $1,500. With the trade-in price, less the payoff, plus the cash you can put $7,200 down on the car. Now decide on the car you want to buy. Let's say it has an MSRP sticker price of $20,200. Using a source like *Edmund's*, you find that the actual cost of the car to the dealer—the invoice or "tissue" price—is $17,750. That's a profit margin of about 14 percent. Now, let's assume that the strategies we will outline enable you to negotiate a sales price of $500 over the invoice. That would make the total cost of the car $18,250. (And by the way, you'll find that in a number of cases you can actually buy it for less. Again, this will be explained.) To the cost of the car you have to add transportation charges, taxes, and registration fees.

$ 6,500 Wholesale value	$18,250 Price you'll pay for car
− 800 Payoff on current car	+ 200 Transportation charges
$ 5,700 Equity in current car	+ 823 7% sales taxes based on price less trade-in
+ 1,500 Cash to be applied	+ 100 (Est.) Title, registration, misc.
$ 7,200 Cash and equity to apply to new car	$19,373
	− 7,200 in Cash and Used-Car Equity
	$ 12,173 needed to finance

Of course, there's also the matter of interest

At this point you should visit your bank, credit union, or lending institution and look at the monthly payments for two- and three-year car loans. Remember, interest should always be factored into the equation when you're figuring the real cost of buying a car. Even though it dribbles out over a period of two years or more, it ultimately comes out of your pocket.

One of the traps far too many people fall into is spreading the payments out over four, five, or six years—sometimes even more—because the monthly payments look *sooooo low*. And don't think that there aren't a few salespeople who have sold their customers on long finance deals in order to make it easier for them to "get into a new car." (By the way, there are more than a few experts who will tell you that—except in some special circumstance—you should probably never finance for more than 36 months. If for no other reason because you will probably tire of the car and want the option of considering a new one.)

Look at what the number of years does to the finance costs and therefore to the actual cost of the car. For purposes of simplification and illustration, we've rounded the loan to $12,000.

The Actual Out-of-Pocket Cost of a New Car over the Life of the Payments			
	24-Month Loan	**36-Month Loan**	**60-Month Loan**
Loan principal	$12,000	$12,000	$12,000
Total interest at 8.2%	$1,052	$1,577	$2,668
Total amount owed bank	$13,052	$13,577	$14,668
(includes principal and interest)			
Your Monthly Payment	$544	$377	$244
Total Paid Over Life of Loan			
Loan (principal/interest)	$13,052	$13,577	$14,668
Cash and equity (trade-in)	$7,200	$7,200	$7,200
Fees, taxes, misc.	$1,123	$1,123	$1,123
Insurance, gas, repairs, and	$0	$0	$0
misc. expenses not included			
Total Cost of Car	$21,375	$21,900	$22,991

Some salespeople like to refer to the purchase of an automobile as an investment. If you'd bought a Mercedes Gull Wing back in the fifties, that would have been true. All but a very few exotic cars today are expenses, not investments, and the next chart illustrates why.

After one year you decide you hate the car and want to sell it. Get out the bath soap!

Let's say you've taken out a 36-month loan and that for some reason you decide that after one year you want to get rid of your new car. Prepare for a financial bath.

For the average car, the wholesale value—the amount that someone is likely to pay for your car—will be based on the original MSRP less the depreciation. Typically, a vehicle will suffer between 15 and 40 percent depreciation during the first year to eighteen months. It all depends on the car, the model, and market demand. Here you can see what your decision to sell after one year would mean.

Original selling price (MSRP)	$19,200.00
30% depreciation	$6,720.00
Wholesale value (what a car buyer would pay you)	$12,480.00
Less loan principal still owed bank	$8,000.00
Cash Left to You	**$4,780.00**

Dealer financing

You also want to look at the financing packages offered by dealers. Keep in mind that financing is a profit source for dealers. If they are participating in the package or if they are just getting a fee for having delivered you to a financial institution, money goes into their pocket. At times, dealership financing can be very high, and they can use it to all but extort more money from customers.

At other times, especially when they are trying to make room for more inventory, they will offer below-market loans from the manufacturer in return for your buying from their stock. Over the life of the agreement, these loans could save you hundreds of dollars. However, there's often a catch: The low-rate financing package is available only on cars that they want to sell, i.e., the slow movers. Or you may find that while the rate is low, the price of the car is not. The message here is to consider dealer financing as an option, but to compare it to other sources before you agree to anything.

Some Not So Hidden Other Costs

Insurance

Many car companies and lending institutions will offer you insurance on your loan. On the face of it this seems very inexpensive. However, before agreeing to the extra few dollars a month, consider the following:

Loan insurance covers only the amount of money you owe the lending institution. In other words, let's say you finance $15,000 and you purchase insurance for $10 per month over a three-year life of the loan. If you die the first month, the $10 will pay off the entire $15,000. However, if you die in the last month of the loan the insurance will pay only what's owned, i.e., the last month's payment.

Consider if instead of buying loan insurance you purchased level term for the same $10 per month. At rates quoted in 1995 for a person 40 years of age, $10 will buy you $15,000 of level term. With this insurance, whether you die in the first month or after the last month of payments, you get all $15,000. Now, while we recommend that for peace of mind you cover your loan with insurance, why not put your money where it will return the most cash in the event of an untimely death?

Accident and health insurance

If you're in poor health and feel that you can't qualify for other programs because of your age or current health status, the A&H may be of some value. However, if you're in good health and have enough existing insurance, take a long look at this type of policy. Generally the only ones who benefit are the sellers.

While a lending institution can require you to cover your loan with insurance, they cannot, in most states, require that you buy the insurance from them. What you can do is assign the lending institution a current insurance policy purchased elsewhere to cover the loan. You probably should consult your insurance agent for details and for requirements as they apply in your state.

Conveyance and advertising fees

Some dealers will try to get you to pay a conveyance fee for preparing the paperwork and another for their local advertising. We suggest that you remind them that both of these are a cost of doing business and refuse to pay. If they insist, take your business elsewhere.

What's a Fair Profit for the Dealer?

Like beauty, fair profit is all in the eye of the beholder. If a dealer has a really hot car in large demand, the fair profit is going to be a whole lot higher than on a car that's been sitting on the lot for three months with 20 other cars of the same make and model.

Dealers always complain that they aren't getting enough profit on their cars. When you look at a car that has an invoice price of $15,500, a 3 percent profit or $465 would seem to be very small indeed. But remember, most dealers floor-plan their cars, which means that the cars are owned by a financing institution. It's almost as though the cars were given to the dealer on consignment with the understanding that they will pay monthly interest on the cost of the car. Usually that interest is prime plus a point or two. For purposes of illustration, assume that a particular vehicle costs the dealer $120 a month in finance charges for the opportunity to sell the car.

Now, let's say you decide that a 3 percent profit is what you're willing to pay. What you probably didn't know is that most manufacturers include a two to three percent hold-back in their invoices. Which is to say the invoice price—the price the dealer pays the manufacturer—is actually 2 to 3 percent higher than the real cost. Once the car is sold, the manufacturer sends the dealer the additional 2 to 3 percent. Using the illustration we showed you several pages back, if you were to agree to a 3 percent profit over invoice, and add that to the manufacturer's hold-back, the dealer would have over $900 in profit. In addition, if he can get you to pay for stripes and some other miscellaneous charges, it's not unlikely that his total profit on the deal will be about $1,250. Subtract one month of interest—$120—and a commission of $100 to the salesperson, and his profit before overhead and expenses will be just over $1,000. Not a bad return on a $120 investment.

Where does their profit come from?
Now in "fairness" even with this amount of return on their investment, there is no way that a dealership could survive by just selling new cars. Even if most customers were to pay list price, the dealership would need other sources of income. You'll find that most successful dealerships realize the bulk of their income and profits from their used-car operations, service departments, parts sales, and from convincing you that it makes sense to buy *their* financing, *their* life insurance, *their* health and accident insurance, *their* striping, *their* rust proofing, *their* extended warranties, and whatever else they can sell you.

We offer this bit of insight so that when the manager appears and talks about "fair," you will have a slightly different perspective of what's really fair.

Deciding on Your Offer

If you are determined to make a good deal, decide how much profit you want to offer the dealer and then stick to it. If you want to make an initial offer and then come up a bit to help the salesperson save face with his or her manager, that's your call. Remember, when your money walks out their door, so does theirs. You represent profit that will help pay for the interest, the sales commission, and contribute to overhead. When your money walks out, so do all the dollars you'll spend in the service department.

The other thing that walks out if they don't make a deal is the possibility of your recommending a friend to the dealership. Don't be swayed by sob stories, fairness pleas, and other pressure tactics. As salespeople will tell you, *the toughest customer in the world is one who comes in knowing what he or she wants, who has all the figures neatly written down, and who makes it clear that they will give the dealership one, and only one, opportunity to sell them a car at their price*. If the dealership won't deal, thank them nicely and go elsewhere. There are an awful lot of dealerships out there just waiting for a chance to get at your money.

On the next page there's a financial work sheet that we think you'll find helpful.

FINANCIAL WORK SHEET

1. If you have a trade-in: Enter the wholesale value of your trade-in as determined by having car appraised by three different dealers $ ________
2. The amount, if any, that you owe on trade-in $ ________
3. The amount of equity you have in your trade (line 1 minus line 2) $ ________
4. The amount of cash you plan to use as down payment $ ________

---

5. Total amount of cash and trade-in equity you have to put against new car (add lines 3 and 4) $ ________

---

6. MSRP (window sticker price) $ ________
7. Invoice (cost to dealer of car/options—use your *Edmund's* or similar source) $ ________
8. Dealer hold-back (Use 3% of MSRP as estimate) $ ________
9. Factory-to-dealer incentive (check second-to-last page in recent issue of *Automotive News* in library) $ ________

---

10. Actual dealer cost (lines 8 plus 9 minus line 7) $ ________
11. Total potential dealer profit were car sold for MSRP. Line 6 minus line 10 (this primarily for your reference) $ ________

---

12. Maximum amount of profit you plan to offer over dealer's cost (line 10) $ ________

---

13. Total amount you plan to pay for vehicle (line 10 plus line 12) before taxes, title, registration, and transportation charges $ ________

---

14. All other charges
    - Transportation $ ________

- State sales taxes* $ ________
- Title fees $ ________
- Registration $ ________

Total $ ________

15. Total amount of transaction (line 13 plus line 14) $ ________

16. The amount to be financed (line 15 minus line 5)** $ ________

17. Difference between the equity in your trade (line 3) and amount you plan to pay (line 13)*** $ ________

*Remember, if you have a trade-in, you pay sales tax only on the difference between what you receive for your trade-in and the final negotiated price of the car.

**It would be wise to be sure that this amount is at least 20 percent below the invoice (cost) of the car. If you plan to finance through the dealership, check their rates before you shop for the car.

***The reason for establishing this figure is so that you can compare it to the number the salesperson writes on the order as the *amount owed*. If your "difference" and their "difference" are not the same, make sure you know why and that you agree.

7. Shopping for Your Vehicle

At this point you should have collected all the relevant facts on the vehicle, the options, and the pricing. Now you're ready to plan and execute your buying strategy.

Plan your visit to the dealership for one of the times listed below at the dealership where you'd prefer to do business. Make sure you allocate enough time to permit the salesperson to take you through the entire presentation process. Have him or her present the car and take you for a demo drive. Remember, *time* is the only thing car salespeople have, and the more of it you consume, the more anxious they are to make sure that the time spent results in a commission.

The Best Times to Buy a New Car

End of the month

Car dealerships and car manufacturers work on a month-to-month basis. Virtually every car dealership is under end-of-the-month pressure to meet sales forecasts. If you've done your homework and are ready to buy, there's probably no better time than the last day of the month.

End of the year

Dealers are under pressure to move out the current year's inventory at the end of each year. Many manufacturers will offer dealers year-end or clearance incentives to motivate them to offer bigger discounts and move the cars off the lot. While you can make a good deal at this time, it's important to recognize that if you buy a leftover, you should plan to trade for your next new car at the same time of year. Many year-end leftover buyers fail to recognize that 12 months after they've purchased the car, the used-car market regards it as a two-year-old vehicle and the wholesale price will reflect that fact.

If you buy a car at the end of the model year, negotiate a deal that reflects the first year's depreciation. To determine what that depreciation is expected to be, you might want to consult a resource like Automotive Lease Guide *Residual Percentage Guide* by calling 1-800-418-8450. For a fee, they will be able to tell you the projected depreciation after one year.

Rainy days

If the weather has been bad, you can assume that business in the dealership will be a little slow. Slow periods make sales managers very nervous because their general manager and/or dealer is probably pressing them to move some cars. After all, the interest on their floor plan doesn't know it's raining.

When car sales are slow

Another time to buy a new car is when business is bad and dealers have a higher than normal inventory on their lots. Generally, dealers like to have a 50-to-70-day supply of cars. This gives them ample choices for their customers without greatly impacting the cost of financing that inventory. But when that supply begins to climb to over an 80-day supply, dealers get very nervous, and they will generally do whatever they have to do to "move the iron"—including giving large discounts. To learn which car companies are having inventory problems, go to your library and ask for the current issue of *Automotive News*, the industry's weekly newspaper. In the back you'll find inventory and sales data for each make and model.

Targeting the Best Opportunities for Deals

We've already talked about the realities of supply and demand. If a vehicle is in high demand by buyers and there is limited supply, the chances for making a good deal are reduced. However, if the dealer has a large inventory and if that inventory has been sitting on the lot for several months, you will be in a position to deal. Keep in mind that every day a car, van, or truck sits on a dealer's lot, the bank is collecting another day of interest. One of the key pieces of information you'd like to have prior to negotiation is how long the car has been sitting on the lot. One clue to the answer is to open the driver's side front door and look for the metal manufacturer's label, which will tell you the date that the car came off the assembly line. If you assume that it took about a month to get the car from the factory to the dealer, you will have an approximate idea of how long the car has been in inventory.

Information Resource "Fighting Chance"

To help simplify your research you might want to consider something called "Fighting Chance." This is a consumer information service that provides you with all the invoice data and the dealer and consumer incentives and hold-back percentages and amounts. They also supply you with the unit sales figures, which tell you if the car is in high demand or is a slug eating up lot space and interest money. All this information is important to have prior to shopping. One benefit over the published books that you find on the newsstand is that Fighting Chance provides you with current information. The price of their service is $19.95 plus $3.00 shipping and handling for complete information on the car of your choice. Reports on additional vehicles, when ordered at the same time, will cost you $8.00 each. They also offer a fax service. For more information call 1-800-288-1134.

Choosing a Pre-Shopping Attitude Strategy

One of the elements of your shopping strategy should be the adoption of an attitude designed to help keep the salesperson off balance—and therefore not in control. Here are two attitude strategies that are guaranteed to perplex any salesperson.

1. Indifference or "I Couldn't Care Less"

Salespeople want you to fall in love with their cars. They want you to salivate and confess that if you don't have this car you may develop terminal warts. Don't ever let the salesperson know that you've fallen in love. In fact, make them think that you could not care less. Your attitude should convey the following message:

"Yes, I'm in the market for a car, and I'll buy it when I find the car and the deal I like.

That could be today; that could be a month from today. Now, if

I find it here, great. If not, I'll go somewhere else and, in fact, I think I would really rather shop somewhere else anyway."

The idea that you might walk at any minute will make the salesperson work very hard to keep you there. Remember, the more salespeople think that they might lose you as a customer, the greater your opportunity for control.

2. Indecision or "I Can't Make Up My Mind"

Salespeople like customers who come in, identify a specific vehicle that they'd like to buy, know the options they want, and are prepared to get right to the deal. If there is one customer type that drives them crazy, it's the customer who can't seem to make up his or her mind. Sometimes referred to as "flakes," they jump from one car to another. One minute they say they are going to buy today and then the next they are going to think about it. Even when they sign the buyer's order, there's the fear that they will cancel the deal. Go ahead. Let them call you a "flake" behind your back, but keep them guessing.

When you're ready to buy, let them see a dramatic shift in your attitude: Make it clear that the only way you'll settle on a vehicle is if the salesperson can prove it's a great deal. And you'll know if it's a great deal because you will have done your homework and know exactly what the car has cost the dealer.

Starting the Process

When you go to the dealership, take your notes. There are two reasons for this: First, they will send a signal to the salesperson that you've done some homework. Second, you don't want to have to depend on your memory when you're working out the deal.

When you enter the dealership, wait to be greeted. Let the salesperson initiate the conversation and use this opportunity to assess the type of person with whom you're dealing. Does the salesperson seem in a hurry, interested, laid back, or what? When asked what you're looking for, make it clear that you have a good idea of which vehicle you're interested in buying, but let the salesperson "sell it to you." Don't jump to the close unless you've decided on the tactic in which you announce that you know what you want and you're giving the dealership one and only one opportunity to bid for your business. This tactic is usually more beneficial when you're "shopping the price" given you by the first dealership—the one where you'd prefer to do business.

What Information to Provide

The only thing that you want the salesperson to know at this point in time is your name, what you're looking for, a price range that is inflated by 15 to 20 percent *over* what you actually plan to spend, and the fact that you are in the market "now" and plan to buy "soon." This will establish you as a buyer and someone deserving of their attention.

Don't reveal anything about how you plan to pay, i.e., cash, finance, or lease. When asked questions relating to the method of payment, respond by saying that you really haven't decided yet. When asked if you plan to trade your car, respond by saying that you're not sure:

"I may keep it, or sell it myself . . . or maybe I'll trade it in. At this point, I'm really only interested in seeing if your car meets my needs."

The message you're delivering is: "*Sell me the car first, then we'll talk about trades and financing.*" If the salesperson persists with questions related to how you plan to finance and whether you plan to trade, make it very clear that you first have to decide on the car and then decide if you want to buy it at this dealership.

The Presentation and Demo Drive

Insist on a full presentation and then a demo drive. There are two reasons for demanding these. First, you want to be sure that this is in fact the car or pickup that you want to buy and that it does meet your needs. Second, the more time a salesperson invests in you, the more anxious they're going to be to realize a financial return on the invested time.

You should know that while the sales manager insists that the salespeople grind for every nickel of profit, salespeople will, in turn, grind the sales manager to give a little so as not to lose the deal and the commission. If you walk, you're out some time, but the salesperson is out both time and commission.

Agreeing on a Price for Your Trade-in

If you plan to trade in your car for the new one, announce to the salesperson after the presentation and demo drive that you'd like to get an idea of the value of your car should you decide to trade it in. Candidly admit that you've already shopped it around so that you have a very good idea of what it's worth. Make it clear that you don't want to talk about the price of the new car until you have the *appraisal* (not the *allowance*). You want to know what the dealership believes is its fair wholesale value. Undoubtedly, the salesperson will ask what other figures you've gotten. Don't reveal them. Rather, respond with something like: "*I'm sure your appraisal will be in the same ball park.*"

If the appraisal does not match the highest figure that you received from the three used-car operations, tell the salesperson that you have a higher offer and that if the used-car department can't do better—don't tell them how much better—you may have to look elsewhere. At this point, the salesperson may suggest that you write up the deal. Indicate that you'll be prepared to deal when the appraisal is competitive with those you've already received.

Appraisal, Not Allowance

If the salesperson comes back and talks about how much they are prepared to "allow" you on your trade, be pleasant and remind the salesperson that you did not ask for an *allowance*, but an *appraisal*. Your objective here is to eliminate—or at least minimize—dealership-injected confusion by keeping each element of the transaction as a separate issue.

KEY TIP

When a dealership offers you more for your trade-in than the wholesale price, it may be that you have a car that is so much in demand they are confident they can sell it immediately for considerably more than they're paying. Or the salesperson may perceive you as someone who is more intent on getting a good price for your trade than getting a discount off the new car (a "difference" buyer). All the dealership is doing is moving the discount off the new car onto the trade-in price of your current car.

Negotiating the Deal

Assuming that the dealership raises their offer to an acceptable amount on your trade-in, you can turn your attention to the new car. Tell the salesperson, in a nice way, that you'd like to see if you can make a deal and that you hope the two of you can come to some agreement within the next half hour because you have an appointment at another dealership. (Salespeople like to use a time-pressure ploy on their customers. This is one way to turn it back on them.)

Also, inform the salesperson that if you aren't satisfied with the deal, you will shop other dealerships, and the one with the best price on the new car and the best offer on the used car will get your business. Said with conviction, this will strike fear into the salesperson's heart. *You* will be in control.

Maintain that control by telling the salesperson that you have carefully calculated the actual price of the new car and that you are prepared to offer the dealership a price that reflects a profit of X. (If you use the financial work sheet as we suggested, you should determine that figure before you enter the dealership.) As a rule of thumb you might begin with a profit margin that amounts to about 2 percent over the invoice—dealer's cost—and be prepared to raise your offer once—and only once—to a figure that amounts to 3 percent.

The salesperson will either show great pain and suggest that management won't accept your offer or agree to write up the order and take it in to see if it can be approved. If the salesperson balks, insist that your offer be taken to management and suggest that you will leave if it is not. Keep in mind that in most dealerships, management does not want a buyer to walk before they've had a chance to counter an offer—*any* offer.

Writing the Buyer's Order

When the salesperson begins to write up the buyer's order, make sure that the difference between your trade-in and the negotiated price of your car matches with the one on your work sheet. Make sure that they show you the cash difference before they add in all the additional charges. Your objective is to prevent the salesperson from trying to add some confusion in hopes of getting a few more dollars. By isolating the trade-in appraisal, the total amount to be paid, and the total amount of additional charges, the only opportunity for them to extract a few dollars is via the back end of the deal.

Once the buyer's order has been written up, the salesperson will ask you to okay it (translated: *sign it*). The salesperson will ask for a deposit so that management knows you're serious. Tell them that you'll sign a buyer's order confirming your offer, but that you will not give them a deposit until the deal has been approved. Mention that the fact you've just spent the last hour or so in the dealership should be proof enough of your seriousness.

The "Sincerity" Deposit

Some dealerships believe that unless you give them a deposit, you're not ready to buy. They know that the psychological commitment that goes with writing a check works in their favor and that if they can get you to write one check, you're primed to write another. They may tell you that the deposit is their standard operating procedure and that it will show management your offer is *sincere*. In fact, it's just another way of keeping you in the dealership while they "work you." Never give a dealership a deposit until they have approved your deal. Also, before you sign the check, be sure you know exactly the final amount you'll be paying and that the amount is in writing.

A Message to Management

As the salesperson gets up to take your offer (*sans* deposit) to management, deliver one last message. A message which might go as follows:

"Please make it clear to your management that I am not interested in getting involved in a series of offers and counteroffers. I would like to buy here. I want you to have my business. However, if necessary, I will continue to shop until I make 'my' deal."

And then say no more. Your message will most certainly be delivered.

Rejecting Your Offer

You can almost put money on the probability that the salesperson will return with a long face saying that management has turned down your offer. If you have properly selected the timing of your visit to the dealership, if you are negotiating for a vehicle whose supply is well in excess of demand, it's a good bet that the dealership is just testing you.

How to Test Back

Shake your head sadly and begin to busy yourself by gathering up your notes and papers as though you're getting ready to leave. Say something to the effect that you're sorry you couldn't get together. Then don't say anything.

Be aware that the salesperson—who comes up empty if you walk—is going to try to get you to increase your bid. Your response might be something like:

"I haven't really shopped around enough to know if I really need *to up my bid.*

But for the sake of discussion, how much are you looking for?"

Again, say nothing. Force the salesperson to respond. Chances are he or she will come down, but not to your figure. Get out your pad and pretend to be doing some heavy figuring. (By the way, salespeople love to do this to customers to create the impression that they are really trying to find some way to further reduce the price. Usually the "heavy figuring" is all part of the show.)

Finally, up your offer by whatever amount you're willing to pay to make the deal. Tell the salesperson that this is all you're willing to go and that it is your final offer. Suggest that he or she think about it and if the dealership is willing to make a deal, fine. If not, you'll be on your way. And then say nothing.

Remember the old negotiator's motto: "*He who speaks first loses*."

The salesperson will believe he's convinced you to negotiate and that you can be talked into at least another bump or two. Surprise him. Make it clear that your offer is firm and that you're prepared to look elsewhere. Stand up, offer your hand, and thank him for his time and then leave. Chances are, if you've followed our suggestions for determining the actual list price, if you've timed your visit to fall at the end of the month or the end of the year, and if you're negotiating for a car that is not in heavy demand and one that can be purchased easily from any of several dealerships, they will stop you before you leave the dealership and you'll make your deal.

The T.O.

If you've convinced the salesperson that you are absolutely serious about your offer, he or she will probably leave and return with the sales manager, who will give you a whole list of reasons why they can't accept your offer. You can translate those reasons to read: "*We think we can squeeze you for a lot more money before we risk having you walk on us*."

After the sales manager has told you why they can't accept the deal, respond by saying that you're sorry you were unable to have come to an agreement and that you would really have liked to have had the car this weekend.

If they understand that you do not intend to negotiate further and appear to be ready to walk out, the manager, fearing the loss of even your marginal profit plus the opportunity to make a substantial profit on your used car (this assumes that your current car does have some retail value) may agree to your price. He may then suggest that you give the dealership a check for the entire amount. *Refuse!*

Tell him that if your offer is approved and he signs the order verifying the dealership's acceptance, you will give them a one percent deposit and the rest when you take delivery. Be very firm in your determination to pay the balance *only* after the car has been cleaned, fully prepped and after you have had a chance to make a final inspection.

Signing the Buyer's Order

The buyer's order is a contract that outlines the deal to which you are agreeing. If you are getting your financing through the dealership, the buyer's order will be replaced by a financial contract.

When you sign the buyer's order you are committing yourself to the deal as outlined on that order. However, the contract must be signed by the dealership management before it becomes valid.

Once the salesperson has written up the buyer's order, check all the information against that which you've developed before you began the negotiation. The key is to be sure that the amount you have agreed to pay is indicated and that, if you are trading, the amount of the dollar difference between the trade and the new car is exactly what you expect it to be.

Be sure that a manager has signed the buyer's order indicating that the dealership has agreed to your deal before you give them a deposit.

Your buyer's order should contain the following information:

BUYER'S ORDER CHECK SHEET

1. The date of the transaction
2. Make and model of the car your are buying
3. The VIN number of the car you are buying
4. The total amount that you have agreed to pay for the car
5. The amount of money they are giving you for your trade
6. The amount of the payoff on your current car
7. The VIN number of your trade-in
8. The difference in dollars between what you have agreed to accept for your trade (less any payoff due) and the amount you have agreed to pay for the car
9. The amount to be financed if you are financing through the dealership
10. The number of payments if you are financing through the dealership
11. Annual percentage rate (APR) if you are financing
12. A list of all the fees beyond the price you've agreed to pay: e.g., title, taxes, etc.
13. A clear statement of the warranty that will come with the car

F&I and the Back End of the Deal

Virtually every dealership has a finance and insurance (F&I) person who you'll meet once you've agreed on a price for the car. His job is to sell you the back end of the deal. He may appear to be your friend, but he's not. The F&I guy has but one objective: to squeeze more money out of the deal. If you intend to pay cash, he'll try to convince you to finance and save your cash. Is this because he's interested in your financial welfare? Hardly. When you finance, the dealership gets a commission from the financing institution or, if they are participating in the finance package, they get part of the interest.

The F&I person will try to sell you extended warrantees, rust protection, fabric protection, health and accident insurance, and anything else they can tack on the deal. We know of one situation where a woman came into a dealership, paid full price for a $14,000 car, and then let the F&I talk her into an additional $10,000 of options, insurance, financing, and other back-end items. While this is an extreme example, the lesson here is to understand that the F&I person is not there just to fill out the contracts but to *sell*. In more than a few cases, the dealership makes more money on the back end of the deal than they do on the car itself. This is one more reason for you to have done your homework ahead of time. Keep in mind that most of what the F&I person would like you to buy is really of marginal value. Specifically we refer to rustproofing, fabric sealer, and most extended warranties. Some items like loan insurance, etc., can be purchased outside the dealership for less money.

Taking Delivery

When you return to take delivery of your new car and to give the dealership your used car, be true to your word: inspect your new car. Make sure that it is the same car that you looked at.

Backing up for a moment: After you've agreed on a price with the dealership and before you leave the lot, copy down the VIN number of the car. That way you'll know if they've tried to switch cars. Now, why would they do that? Well, one possible reason is because they have two identical cars on the lot. One they may have acquired several months ago before the manufacturer decided to raise the dealer cost by $500. If they can push off the older car—maybe only three or four months older—they will be able to pocket the $500 as profit. Or worse, there have been dealers who try to substitute the car you've chosen for the exact same model with the same options. The only difference is the second car fell off the delivery truck and had to be repaired. Hey, it happens.

Before You Sign

Understand everything you're signing!

Mileage Statement

If you are trading in your car, you will be asked to sign a mileage statement. Before you sign, be sure that the actual mileage of your car has been entered on the appropriate line in ink. Then sign the mileage statement. Don't leave it blank with the promise by the salesperson to fill it in later. Be advised that if the future buyer of your car should discover that the mileage at the time you sold it to the dealer was wrong, you, not the dealer can be sued. So fill in all the blanks before you sign.

New-Vehicle Mileage

The seller is obliged to provide you with a mileage statement. It should be the same as on the odometer.

Used-Vehicle Mileage (Used-Car Purchase Only)

The seller is obliged to give you a copy of the mileage statement signed by the previous owner. If there is no mileage statement, don't buy the car.

Power of Attorney

The dealer will need power of attorney in order to change the title on both your new car and the one you're trading in. If you have signed the buyer's order, you can sign these forms without their being filled in. However, if you want to be totally secure, ask that the forms be filled in before you sign.

Finance Contracts

If you decide to finance your car through the dealership, your buyer's order will be replaced with a finance contract. This contract will have so much fine print that it would take a couple of hours to read it. Most of the fine print is *boiler plate* that is dictated by law. The key things you want to check against your buyer's order are:

1. Is the VIN number the same on the buyer's order and finance contract?
2. Is the figure for the amount you intend to finance the same on both?
3. Look at the finance charges and be sure that they are as agreed. This section will also contain any other charges that you may have agreed to such as insurance.
4. Is the annual percentage rate as agreed?
5. Look at the amount and number of payments. Be sure that they reflect the total number of months you have agreed to pay and that the dealer has not tried to slip in some extra payments.

Warranty Agreements

You will be given a paper detailing the warranty. Read it carefully and be sure that you understand what is and what is not covered. Have the seller write down the exceptions. The warranty should be signed by the dealership's management.

New-Car Warranties

There are basically two kinds of new car warranties:

1. The manufacturer's warranty specifically states what it covers and the length of time and/or miles that it applies.
2. The other new car warranty is provided by the selling dealer and is an "adjustment warranty." This is designed to cover smaller problems like rattles, leaks, alignment, noise, and other problems that develop within the first 60 to 90 days. You should ask about the length of the adjustment warranty and have the salesperson confirm, in writing, that these adjustments will be fixed free.

Extended Warranties

These are warranties or service contracts that purport to cover your car after the factory warranty runs out. Generally these warranties represent just another way for the dealership to make money. Some make a 50 percent or greater profit on each extended warranty sale. (As of publication of this book, dealers are not required to reveal the profit they build into these service contracts. This may change.)

If you read the fine print you'll find that most of the things that could or will go wrong after the manufacturer's warranty expires are not covered. In addition, many of these warranties have a deductible.

Take time to read all the fine print, even if it takes you a half hour. When you've read all the fine print, you might want to ask the salesperson if he or she really feels that their car is so poorly built that it needs this added coverage. You might even suggest that if the dealership has so little faith in the reliability of their vehicle, they should throw in the extended warranty free or that maybe you should reconsider the whole deal. Watch them try to squirm out of that one.

One other note: If you should decide to buy an extended warranty, make sure it's one that is backed by the factory. Avoid third-party warranties. All too often owners discover that third-party warranties end up offering no more value than the paper they're written on.

BEFORE YOU SIGN—CHECKLIST

❑ **Mileage Statement**
- Has the mileage of your trade-in been entered?
- Are all the blanks filled out?

❑ **New-Vehicle Mileage**
- Is the mileage statement on the new car the same as on the odometer?

❑ **Used-Vehicle Mileage (used vehicle purchase only)**

- ❑ **Power of Attorney**
- ❑ **Finance Contracts**
  - Is the VIN number the same on the buyer's order and finance contract?
  - Is the figure for the amount you intend to finance the same on both?
  - Are the finance charges the same as you agreed?
  - Are there other charges to which you have agreed?
  - Check the other fees normally associated with a new car purchase.
- ❑ **Is the APR (annual percentage rate) as agreed?**
- ❑ **Do the amount and number of payments reflect the total number of months you have agreed to pay?**
- ❑ **Warranty Agreements**
  - Have you read the warranty?
  - Do you understand what is and what is not covered?
  - Are the agreed exceptions in writing?
  - Has the warranty been signed by management?
- ❑ **Have you received the owner's manual and maintenance record books?**
- ❑ **Did you receive two sets of keys?**
- ❑ **Has the dealership arranged for the license and registration?**
  - Do you have all registration records?
  - Have you arranged for your insurance?
  - Is your insurance form in the glove compartment?

8. Alternate Buying Strategies

Tactic 1. "I May Have Started Too Low"

If you feel that for some reason your final offer may actually be less than they can take—for whatever reason—and you're inclined to raise your offer . . . *don't*. This tactic is designed to help you stay in control while forcing them to give you their best price. At an appropriate point stand up and say the following:

"I am prepared to buy and take delivery of a car like the one you've showed me within the next two days. And I will buy a car within that time frame. However, I am looking for the best possible deal. Maybe, as you have suggested, my offer is unrealistic. Therefore, after I leave, I would appreciate your deciding what is, in fact, the lowest price that you'll accept for this car. While you're doing that, I'm going to visit two or maybe three other dealerships and give them the same opportunity. Like you, they will have one and only one opportunity to bid for my business. There will be no negotiation. If your price is competitive with theirs, I'll probably give you the business because of the time you've invested with me.

You have my phone number, I hope to hear for you no later than this evening."

And with that, walk out. Chances are they will try to keep you there with more questions, but be resolute. Walk! If you agree to raise your bid at this time, you've opened the door for more "grinding" and sent a signal that says you can be "worked." In this case control is maintained by making them chase you . . . at home.

Tactic 2. "Using the Fax"

Let's say that for one reason or another you'd like to do business at a particular dealership. Maybe it's close to home and you feel you'd get better service if you bought your car there. However, you want to be sure that you've gotten the best possible price. Here's one approach you might try:

Visit the dealership within three to four days of the end of the month. Decide which car you'd like to buy and make it clear that you intend to buy before the end of the month. Ask the salesperson to give you the dealership's best price. Write down the number and then using the MSRP sticker on the window, write down everything—including the options—that is included in the car. Tell the salesperson that you intend to shop the price, but that you'll give him or her the last shot at making you a deal.

Go home and call four or five other dealers in the area. Ask for a salesperson and tell them that you must buy a car before the end of the month. Tell them it's for tax reasons or anything else you can think of. The key is to convince them that you're a buyer with cash that's burning a hole in your pocket. Tell the salesperson that you're going to fax him or her a description of the car you're looking for. Suggest that you could be flexible on the exterior and interior colors, but that basically the car you're describing in the fax is the car you want. Finally, tell the salesperson that you're giving them one and only one chance to bid for your business. Emphasize that because you're in a hurry to buy the car, you haven't got time for dickering. You just want their best price. Give them your fax number and tell them that you need the price no later than noon tomorrow.

Some dealerships will refuse to send you a price. But others will bid willingly. The prospect of having a live customer who's ready to buy will usually motivate most dealerships to give it a shot, especially if it's the end of the month and sales have been slow. Now, be warned that some dealers may give you a lowball bid. The lowball is designed to get you into the dealership so that a salesperson will have a chance to work you into a deal. The fact that a lowball bid will probably not be honored is of no concern in this scenario. The reason is because you're going to use the competitive bids to force down the price quoted by the first dealer.

Once you have the faxed bids—and assuming they're lower than the price you've gotten—take the lowest back to the first dealer, show it to the salesperson, and ask if he can beat the lowest price. Emphasize that you want the salesperson and the dealership to have your business and that you're ready to write the check, but that you don't want to pay more than you have to. Always, always be very, very pleasant. While the salesperson may be angry inside, it's very hard—and a rather poor bit of salesmanship—to show that anger to a person with a friendly smile on their face.

Chances are very good that unless the competitive bid is below their actual costs—including rebates and hold-back—they'll beat the competitive price rather than risk you and your checkbook walking out of the dealership.

Tactic 3. "I Can Wait"

If time is not a factor in your purchase decision, if you're looking for a car with the most common options, and if color is not a major consideration, you might consider this tactic:

Visit three or four dealerships—more if you like—and tell a salesperson that you know exactly what you're looking for, that you're flexible on options and color, and that you are willing to pay $200 above the invoice price. Explain that while you understand that they may not want to make you that kind of deal at this time, they may, at some time in the future, need one more sale to "make their month." Leave your card and on the back write:

"I will pay your true invoice plus $200 for the following model. Call me when you're ready."

Then, every month, call each of the salespeople and remind them that your offer still stands.

At this point you might be asking: Why would any car dealer accept this deal at any time? There are several reasons.

As we pointed out earlier, car manufacturers are always pressing their dealers to make their numbers. That is, to move a certain number of cars each month. The pressure to make these numbers is what makes it easier for you to negotiate a better deal at the end of each month. If a dealer knows that he's got a deal hanging out there—even at invoice—and he needs sales to make his quota, you could very well get a call.

A second reason is that if the sales of a particular model begin to slump, the manufacturer will often support it with a factory-to-dealer incentive to help the dealer move the cars. Here's how this works:

Let's say a particular car has a factory invoice of $18,000 and the MSRP reflects an 18 percent markup at $21,240. If the dealer has inventory on the lot—inventory that's costing him interest at the bank—the factory is going to press him to move product. So they find your name in the file and call you up. *"Okay,"* they say, *"we can give you the car at our invoice plus $300."* Expect them to try to "up" you a few dollars. You want the car, so you agree. The dealer claims to be losing money, but the facts show otherwise.

MSRP	$21,240
Invoice	$18,000
You pay $300 over invoice:	$ 300
Factory gives dealer $1,000 incentive	$ 1,000
Factory gives dealer 2.5% hold-back	$ 531
Total Gross Profit to Dealer	**$ 1,831**

Now, no dealer wants you to think that they are actually making money on your hard-nosed deal, so they will make you feel good by sobbing, gnashing their teeth, and bemoaning that they have just given away the store and have no money to buy shoes for their children. As we said earlier, good car salespeople are good actors.

The dealership will probably give the salesperson a $50 commission—after all, he or she only made a $300 profit. If the car has been on the lot for under 30 days, the dealer owes a month's interest that might amount to approximately $120 to $150.

When you consider that the dealer has risked only the cost of the interest—remember, the financial institution has paid the manufacturer for the car, and the salesperson only earns a commission after the sale—you realize that the dealer's made a darn good return on his investment. How many other businesses do you know that earn that kind of return on their money? But the profit stream is just beginning. There's more money on the way.

Let's say that you decide to use your current car as a trade-in to help pay for the new car. Let's further assume that the true wholesale value of your car was $7,000, but the dealer convinced you it was only worth $6,750. (In this scenario you have not taken the time to find out its real value and the lure of the new car for just $300 over invoice motivated you to make the deal.) The dealer will then turn around and put the car on his lot for $9,600 and end up selling it for $8,500, which adds another $1,750 to the total profit generated by your purchase. Now add whatever they might sell you on the back end of the deal plus the money (be it warranty work or your own cash) that you spend in the service department over the next several years. As we said earlier, the bottom line is this: There's a reason why car dealers live in very nice houses.

But Remember... You Don't Have to Be One of Those Reasons

Because you used this book, you would have been aware of the factory-to-dealer incentive (you would have checked the "Incentive Watch" in *Automotive News*), and you would have factored in the dealer hold-back. When they called you to say that they were willing to accept your offer, you would have told the salesperson that your offer was made on the *true* invoice cost, and since the factory-to-dealer incentive has reduced the cost by $1,000 your offer is on the lesser price. Hopefully, this little ploy on your part would have helped you reopen the negotiation, which, in turn, might have resulted in an additional savings.

Advantage: Women

One of the little-known facts about the car business is that, according to several research sources, 50 percent of all cars are purchased by women and that 80 percent of all car purchases are directly impacted by women. Which is to say that married men seldom, if ever, buy a car their wives don't like.

Based on these facts, one would assume that car salespeople would go out of their way to cater to women. Not so. In fact, in far too many cases salespeople—particularly males, although female salespeople are also guilty of this—make the assumption that the woman is:

1. Just looking
2. Not the decision maker
3. Will not be the check signer
4. Will have to get approval from a male—e.g., husband, boyfriend

As a result, more than a few women leave dealerships feeling insulted, poorly treated, and determined to spend their money where they are treated with the respect that every buyer is due. But this is reality, and while it's just plain stupid for salespeople to be so myopic, their insensitivity and ignorance does offer women a rather unique opportunity. We call it "jujitsu shopping." As you probably know, the art of jujitsu is based on using the attacker's force to throw him to the ground and gain control. In jujitsu shopping, women have the opportunity to use a salesman's insensitivity to gain control and throw his profit expectations to the ground.

Tactic 1. You're Talking to the Wrong Person

Having done all your research, you go to the selected dealership accompanied by your husband, boyfriend, brother—any adult male will do. When the salesperson arrives to greet you, tell him or her, very specifically, that you are in the market for a car. If the salesperson is one of those who assume that the man is in charge—even though you've told him that you are buying the car—he will probably direct most of his conversation and presentation to the man. At some point—possibly ten minutes into the presentation—the male should interrupt the salesperson and say something to the effect:

"I don't know why you're telling me all this. She's the one buying the car. I'm just along for the ride."

At that point, without smiling, you nod in concurrence and say:

"He's right. It's my money. It's going to be my car, and it will be my decision. Now, why don't we start all over again."

The salesperson will immediately recognize the error. Don't be surprised to see a little sweat break out on his or her forehead. You're now in control, and you should be prepared to use any or all of the counter tactics outlined in the next chapter.

Tactic 2. Make an Appointment

If you just want to reduce the hassle and if you're not interested in hand-to-hand combat with the salesperson—figuratively speaking, of course—you might consider calling a dealership and making a specific appointment with a salesperson to show you the car. Be very specific in terms of what you're looking for. Don't ask questions; make requests.

"Hello, my name is Mary Jones, and I'm in the market for a new ______. I intend to make a decision within the next week and would like to make an appointment to learn more about the car and take a test drive. I have time tomorrow or Thursday at three p.m."

If for some reason the salesperson refuses to take you seriously or sounds as if he or she is about to brush you off, you can strike a blow for your ego by saying:

"It sounds to me as if selling me a car might be an imposition on you. Possibly you can transfer me to your sales manager. (And you might want to find out his or her name prior to the call—just

in case.) I'm sure that he can find someone in the dealership who might show a little more interest in selling cars."

Tactic 3. "Go Ahead . . . Make Their Day"

If at any time you feel you are being mistreated or abused—and it should be clearly blatant—get up and walk into the sales manager's office and, in a very firm, unemotional, but determined manner say:

"I have come here to buy a car. Clearly the salesperson I'm dealing with does not take me seriously (or . . . needs work on his interpersonal skills . . . or, has other things to do . . .) and I would appreciate your assigning someone else to me. If this is not convenient, you can call me at home. Meanwhile, I intend to shop your competitor."

Again, no manager wants to see a checkbook walk out of the dealership. Chances are they will grovel a bit in hopes of placating you. On the other hand, you may find a sales manager who is just as insensitive. In any event, a letter to the dealer expressing your displeasure and the suggestion that your story will make good conversation with your friends will most certainly make the salesperson's day . . . *miserable.*

9. Dealership Ploys and Your Countertactics

The following chapter describes a number of dealership ploys, devices, and games designed to control the sale and extract the maximum amount of profit. Here again, if you know their rules you can play their games. Or more accurately, if you can recognize their ploys, you can counter with your tactics.

Advertising Come-ons

When a dealer makes an offer in an ad that seems too good to be true, it probably is. Keep in mind that advertising is designed to do one thing: get you to come into the dealership.

Your countertactic

Read the fine print. See the "About Leasing" segment for examples of what we mean.

I'll Call You Right Back

You decide to shop by phone. You ask for a salesperson and tell him or her that you're interested in a certain model and ask what the dealership has in stock and what kind of discount they are giving. The salesperson will usually find a reason he can't talk to you at that moment.

SALESPERSON: *Mrs. . . . I'm sorry, I didn't get your name.*

CALLER: *Mrs. Jones.*

SALESPERSON: *Mrs. Jones, I'm with a customer at the moment, but I'll be wrapped up in five minutes and I'll call you right back. That will also give me a chance to get our inventory cards.*

At this point, you give them your number. One of the reasons salespeople want to call you back is to check to see if you're legitimate and not just another salesperson checking competitive prices. Also, once they have your number they can continue to follow up. Some dealerships will quote you prices and offer discounts over the phone.

Sometimes the discounts are real; other times they are designed just to get you to come in. Many stores do not permit their salespeople to quote prices over the phone because all it does is give the customer information to use in dealing with other dealerships.

Furthermore, if you should ask for a certain car, nine out of ten salespeople will tell you they have it, or that it's coming in, or that they can get it. They'll tell you anything you want to hear if that's what it takes to get you to come in. Once you're in the dealership, they hope they can sell you something that really is in stock.

Your countertactic

If for some reason you don't want to give out your telephone number, simply ask the salesperson when would be a good time for you to call.

The Tent Sale

Often dealers will put a tent up on their lot, park a bunch of cars under it, and advertise that they are having a big tent sale. The impression is that these cars are terrific deals and that a buyer can save a bundle.

Your countertactic

Don't believe it. All the balloons, clowns, and hoopla are part of an effort to break down your resistance and create the sense that there will never be another deal like this one.

We're Having a Sale

A dealer may be having a sale, but his objective is to find every way possible to extract as much of your money as possible. Easy-payment plans, no down-payment offers, and other come-ons should be viewed with skepticism.

Your countertactic

Understand that for the informed auto buyer, every day is a "sale" day.

Control the Sale

As we've discussed, salespeople and dealerships have developed any number of tactics designed to control the sale.

Your countertactic

There are any number of ways you can take control. One is to utilize a diversion created by a "helper." Specifically a second person who appears to be helping the buyer make a purchase decision. When you and the friend walk in, make it clear to the salesperson that the car, van, or truck is for you and that you will make the decision. Prior to your visit, instruct your friend to carry a pad and pencil and make notes. The person should say virtually nothing to the salesperson. However, occasionally they should lean over and whisper in your ear as though imparting some useful strategic information. In reality, it could be the time of day. The presence of the "helper" and the whispers will drive the salesperson crazy and leave you in control.

A variation on this is for you to use a pad and make notes throughout the presentation. This will bother the high-pressure salesperson because it suggests that you are not being swept away by his or her sales pitch and intend to analyze every aspect of the deal closely.

Still another is the "broken record" routine. This tactic is one in which you lay out the price you're willing to pay and then just keep repeating it until you get your way. Kids have been using this technique with their parents for years.

Are You a Buyer... Today?

One of the first questions many salespeople will ask is designed to qualify you as a buyer or a looker.

"How soon do you plan to buy a pickup?"

"Are you looking to buy a car today?"

No mystery here. The salesperson wants to know if you're a hot prospect or someone who's just kicking the tires with no real plans to buy. If you're just a "looker," most salespeople will do their best to get away from you as soon as possible. Rather than lay the groundwork for a future sale, they'd rather take their chances with the next up.

If you tell the salesperson that you "might" be ready to buy today or within a couple of days, he or she will do their best to get you locked into a car that day. "Today" buyers instantly become a salesperson's new best friend.

Your countertactic

Our advice is to be honest when asked this question. Let the salesperson know your buying plans. However, make it clear that you are not committed to buying at any one dealership and that your final decision will depend on the price. Make it very clear that you intend to shop to get the best price.

Keeping You Off Price

Most car sales training teaches the salesperson to sell the car *before* discussing the price. This means that when someone walks in and starts discussing the price, the salesperson needs to get the conversation off the price and onto the car. The theory is that if a salesperson can build your enthusiasm for the car and present it as the answer to all your driving needs, you are going to be easier to deal with when it comes to the negotiation.

So if you come in and ask for price, a good salesperson (notice we said "good") will deflect your question possibly as follows:

YOU: *I'm interested in a V-8 road monster, and I want your best price.*

SALESPERSON: *You've come to the right place. Let me ask you a question—is this car for you or for your spouse?*

YOU: *Well, for both.*

SALESPERSON: *Do you plan to use it for work or pleasure?*

YOU: *Work mainly.*

What's happening here is that the salesperson is asking questions that demand something other than a *yes* or *no* answer. He or she will keep firing them until you've either decide to postpone the price question or have forgotten it.

YOU: *But you haven't answered my question. What is your best price?*

SALESPERSON: *Let me put it this way, price for us will not be a problem. However, before we can even begin to discuss price, I think it makes sense to be sure that the road buster is really the right car for you, wouldn't you agree?*

YOU: *Well . . . yes.*

Your countertactic

There may be times when you'll want to dispense with the preliminaries and get right to the issue of price. Open your conversation with *"I just want your best price."* Most salespeople hope that they are about to make a quick sale and will start negotiating. If you have a salesperson who is good enough to try to deflect your question as illustrated above, your tactic is to simply stay focused.

"I know what I want. You don't need to sell me on the car. I'm ready to buy today if the deal is right. All I want is your best price. If you're ready to deal, we can save each other a lot of time."

Follow Me

For some reason customers become lemmings on a car lot. When skilled salespeople decide it's time for a demo drive and sense that a prospect may be reluctant to invest the time, they will simply turn their backs and start to walk away, saying, "Come with me a minute." Like dutiful dogs, the customers follow and find themselves on a demo drive. More than just getting the person into the car, the ability to motivate the customer to follow confirms to the salesperson that he or she is in "control."

Your countertactic

In order for you to gain control, you have to be somewhat unpredictable. If you find a salesman suddenly turn his back calling for you to follow, surprise him: *Don't.* When he turns around and finds you're not there, *you'll* be the one in control.

Getting an Early Commitment

One of the ploys salespeople use to confirm that you're a buyer today and to test what you're willing to pay is the "If I could, wudja?" test. If you're asked a question like:

"If I could get you this car for just $50 a month more than you're paying now and if I could get you a great deal on your trade, would you buy today?"

If you answer yes there are two things you can count on: First, the salesperson is going to try to structure a deal for $50 or more per month above your current payments, and second, his or her conception of a great deal on your trade will be entirely different from yours.

Your countertactic

Your best response to "If I could, wudja?" is something along the lines of *"I don't know. It all depends on what the final numbers look like."*

Feeding Your Ego

Salespeople love to turn your ego and pride into larger profits for themselves. When someone comes in and claims that they know cars and that they know what cars should cost, they're usually priming themselves to be taken. A classic sales response is:

"You know, it's a pleasure to deal with someone who really

understands this business. I can't tell you how many people have no idea of how to make an intelligent purchase decision."

All too often the customer relaxes, thinking he or she has the upper hand, and the salesperson goes to work earning a nice profit for the dealership.

If, during the negotiation, a salesperson tells you that you appear to be a very intelligent buyer and for that reason he or she is going to be *"completely honest with you,"* watch out! You're being set up. Chances are whatever comes next is, if not an outright lie, a stretch of the truth.

Your countertactic

It's best to keep a low profile. Keep what you know to yourself until it's time to use the information to your advantage. The less a salesperson knows about you, the harder it is for them to develop a control strategy. If you have a big ego, park it outside until you've made the deal. Then you can brag about how smart you are to your friends—later.

Playing Cupid with a Car

If a car salesperson can generate a love affair between you and a car and if he or she can get you to admit, *"This is the car I've always dreamed of owning,"* all the control has jumped to the salesperson. When you let it be known that you *"have to have this car"* you've given up all your bargaining power.

Your countertactic

Even if you are so in love with the car you could drool, don't. In fact, try to give the impression that you are not really all that sold on the car and that you really are somewhat indifferent. In fact, if you're shopping with someone else, it won't hurt to have the person suggest aloud that they *"really like the car at the other dealership better."*

The Price Feeler

If the salesperson determines that you're a payment buyer, they will talk price only in terms of monthly payments.

"If I could get you out the door for $249 a month, could we write up a deal today?"

If you answer *"yes"* or *"I think so"* you may have given up significant ground in the negotiation.

Your countertactic

While you certainly want to know your monthly exposure, don't say yes to this question even if the number sounds good. Why? Because the seller may be quoting you the payment for a five-year finance program. Or he or she may be just testing to see if you're ready to buy at any price. Your best answer is to respond with questions:

"How many months are you quoting me?"

"What does that include? Taxes, transportation, title, registration?"

Understand that when a customer tells a salesperson, *"I'm looking for a payment in the $200 range,"* the smart salesperson will simply find the terms—48 months, 60 months, or even 72 months that will put you at that figure. Or they will quote you a number slightly above your range in hopes of splitting the difference and adding more profit to the deal.

The Boss Is the Enemy

One of the classic ploys is for the salesperson to tell you that he or she is on your side working against "the boss." The boss is presented as the bad guy who is out to squeeze customers for every last drop of profit. At the same time, he is depicted as someone who can be dealt with (if only you'll just "meet us halfway"). And lo and behold, it turns out that your sales rep is your new best friend and protector who is ready to fight the good fight on your behalf.

Yeah, right!

The only "bad guy"—or maybe a softer and kinder word is "adversary"—is you. You have the money and your unwillingness to okay the deal stands in the way of a nice commission. So why wouldn't you be the bad guy?

Your countertactic

If you find that your salesperson has to make more than two trips back and forth to the "bad guy" to win approval for your deal, take control and short-circuit this charade. Tell the salesperson that if your deal is not approved on his or her next trip, you are going to leave.

Chances are this message will bring the manager out of his or her office to meet you. Remember, behind the handshake, the welcome, and the smile is someone who—more often than not—sees you as a checkbook. He or she will probably thank you for coming in and then go to some lengths to suggest that you look like a fair-minded person. That will lead to a sob story about overhead and how unreasonable you are to ask the dealership to part with one of their cars at your price. The manager may even suggest that the real, *real* bad guy in this situation is "the dealer," who lives in a cave counting his money. Whatever the sales manager's ploy, listen for a while, and then say very calmly.

"I appreciate that you want to make every dollar of profit that you can on your car. I expect that. But at the same time, we both know that this is a buyer's market. You have my offer and it is my last offer. If you'd like to sell me a car at that price, I am ready to sign a buyer's order right now. If you'd like to review my offer, you have my phone number. If you find it totally unacceptable, then I thank you for your time."

At that point, stand up as though you're ready to leave. Chances are the manager will ask you to sit down so that he can continue to make his case. Don't let him. Interrupt with:

"I hope that I've made my position clear. Now, unless we have a deal at my price, I don't want to waste any more of your time, and I'm sure you don't want to waste mine."

If he continues to plead, shake hands with the salesperson and do the same with the manager and reiterate that they have your phone number should they change their mind. Then, just to add a little insult to injury, say: *"What is the best way to 2334 Main Street?"* which they will know is the address of their nearest competitor. Unless you've totally miscalculated, they will agree to your deal before you get out the door.

How might you miscalculate?

1. If you haven't done your homework and your price is below their costs, they probably won't accept your offer.
2. If the vehicle you're trying to buy is in such demand that the dealership can barely keep one in stock, they probably won't accept your offer because they feel confident that there's a buyer right behind you ready to pay full list.

Testing the Pain Threshold

Another ploy some car salespeople use—especially with buyers who are focused on the monthly payment and not the actual cost of the car—is to quote a monthly payment that the seller knows is out of the prospect's budget range. The salesperson will let the buyer suffer briefly and then offer to rework the deal, usually at great personal sacrifice to the dealership, to their commission, and all the orphans and widows he supports. The new figure will be just a little higher than the prospect had originally intended to pay. However, the second figure feels so much better than the first that the buyer jumps at the deal.

Your countertactic

If you've done your research and know your numbers ahead of time, you will never let them get into a payment discussion.

Confuse the Price Issue

If the salesperson perceives you as a *payment buyer*, then he or she is going to try to come up with a payment plan that meets your budget. To maintain the profit margin on the car they will adjust the payments by quoting you rates based on 48-, 60-, or even 72-month terms. You'd be surprised at how many people think they getting a great monthly payment only to find out that it's based on a four- or five-year payment plan.

If the salesperson senses that you're a *difference buyer*, he or she will talk about "allowing" you a certain amount for your trade and never mention the actual appraisal or retail price of the car. You'd be surprised at how many people make purchase decisions because the "difference" sounds reasonable.

Your countertactic

If you've done your homework, the salesperson will quickly understand that "allowance" and "difference" are not going to impress you. You will know the facts because you will have:

1. Established the fair value of your trade
2. Determined the true cost of the new car
3. Made a decision about how much profit you'll offer
4. Settled on your monthly payments based on the difference you've calculated between what your trade is worth and the price you're prepared to offer for the new car

It's hard to confuse someone who has all the facts.

I Have a Buyer for Your Car

Sometimes to get a phone shopper into the store, the salesperson will tell the caller:

"Wonder of wonders, this is your lucky day. I have a customer who's looking for a car just like yours. I'll bet that I can help you get a terrific price for it. Why don't you come in so that we can have a look at it?"

Or they'll use the bogus buyer as bait for a customer who has "walked" because they were not offered enough for their trade.

If the customer bites and comes in, the salesperson will all too frequently announce that the "someone" changed his or her mind or found another car.

But since you're here, why not let me take you for a demo drive in our . . ." Or if the customer is back for a second visit:

"Let's see if I can't get my guys to give you more for your trade," or "The boss is in a good mood today. Maybe we can get him to bend a little more."

Your countertactic

Be aware that most car salespeople are not in business to make this or any other day "your lucky day." Unless you have a truly unusual car, the chances of a salesperson having a legitimate buyer are akin to the odds of winning the lottery.

Time Pressure

When it gets down to the wire, you'd be amazed at how many contests, sales bargains, and "one time only prices" come out of the woodwork as an enticement to make you commit to buying a car. Sometimes salespeople will suggest that the prices are going up next week—often they are. Or that a major sales contest ends that night and they are only one deal away from winning.

Your countertactic

Don't be taken in by any time-pressure ploy. Even if what the salesperson says is legitimate, you should never make a purchase decision in order to beat the clock.

Create Sense of Obligation

Salespeople often try to make you feel obligated to them for the time they've spent selling you a car. It's almost as if you're an ingrate for not understanding that by having given freely of their time, you are somehow beholden to them.

Your countertactic

Have you ever been in sales and made a pitch for some business that you got because the prospect felt responsible for having taken up your time? Not likely. Remember, the only person you're obligated to is *you.*

I'll Show You the Invoice

A dealership offers to sell a certain model at just two or three hundred dollars over invoice. They give you the idea that they are giving the cars away. What they don't tell you is that there is a factory-to-dealer incentive on those cars of possibly $1,500 which gives them a $1,700 profit on the front end. Add in the dealer hold-back plus a couple hundred on the back end of the deal, and it adds up to a very profitable couple hours of work.

Your countertactic

Check *Automotive News*—you should find copies in your library. If their incentive watch confirms that there is factory money behind the car, use that fact in your negotiation. Also, figure an average of 2.5 percent dealer hold-back.

The Bump

One of the ploys used by a dealership to squeeze a few more dollars out of your pocket is for the salesperson or even the sales manager to come back and announce:

"We're so close" or

"We've come this far" . . . followed by:

"If you could just come up a little."

"If you could help me out, I know I can get the deal for you."

"All I need is a buck a day."

While they try to make it sound like just a few cents—*"Do you mean to say that you would deny yourself the pleasure of driving this car for just pennies a day?"*—keep in mind that those "pennies" will add up fast. A "bump" of 75 cents a day over a four-year finance period will amount to $1,095.

Your countertactic

Say once, and only once, that they have your last offer and then start to leave. Salespeople don't deal well with people who refuse to negotiate. If they want to sell the car, they won't let you leave.

The Misplaced Car Keys

In years past, some dealerships have held customers by claiming to have lost the keys to their trade-ins. While they frantically search for the keys, the potential buyer is subjected to more pressure to sign on the dotted line. You should know that under the law, if a dealership purposely denies you your keys—whatever the pretense—that is grounds for a false imprisonment charge.

Your countertactic

If you ever encounter this lost-key routine—and let's hope that most dealerships are beyond that kind of nonsense—simply point out that if anyone is found to have purposely hidden the keys, that is grounds for a possible felony and that you'd like to use the phone to call your lawyer.

Someone Else Is Interested in This Car

"B-Backs" are the bane of the car salesperson's life. These are people who come in, spend time looking at a car, and then tell the salesperson that they have to "think about it." As they exit their last words are, *"I'll be back."* Car people know that most "B-Backs" never return. Usually they go to another dealer, and the salesperson undercuts the first dealership's bid and gets the business. That's why car salespeople will do just about anything not to let you off the lot until you've bought a car.

One of the older and more tired ploys is to create a sense of urgency. Once you've decided on a car and shown a real interest, the pressure mounts for you to make a commitment. If you decide you want some time to think about it—and by the way, this is always a good idea—the salesperson will announce that someone else is interested in the car and will be coming in later that day. They will then suggest that you give them a small deposit to hold the car. Car people know that once you've written a check, even a small one for a deposit, you're going to have to return and that will give them the opportunity to close the deal.

Your countertactic

Never, ever give anyone a deposit to hold a vehicle. There are always more of the same model out there. And this applies to both new and used. Once you've signed a check, even for a deposit, you lose some of your control.

Unhorsing the Buyer

Another ploy designed to control the buyer is called "unhorsing." Let's say you are in the process of trying to work out a deal. You're close, but you're insisting on getting more for your trade. The used-car buyer in the dealership plans to "blow it out" to a wholesaler, but the wholesaler won't commit until he sees your car. *"By the way,"* the buyer will say, *"the wholesaler won't be here until tomorrow."* If the dealership lets you out with your current car, they're afraid you might take a detour on the way home past one of their competitors. So they "unhorse you" and prevent you from shopping your car by loaning you one of their demo cars for the night. With your car sitting on their lot and you driving their demo, there's no way you can conveniently shop another dealer.

Your countertactic

Stay on your "horse," unless you feel that they will meet your deal.

Good Guy/Bad Guy

During the negotiation the salesman might bring in another person—it could be the store "closer" or the sales manager who will become the bad guy and accuse you of trying to steal a car or of not being realistic about your offer. Generally, their tactic is to position them as the bad guy and imply that there is no way you can buy the car at your price. At some appropriate moment, known only to them, they both leave. Almost immediately your good guy salesman steps back in, apologizes for the brutish behavior of the "bad guy," and tells you that he has come to the rescue. He will get you the deal . . . *if only* you can help him out a little and raise your offer. You agree and, lo and behold, he goes into the sales manager's office and comes out with a signed buyer's order.

Your countertactic

Don't put up with this routine. When you sense the bad guy has arrived, listen patiently for a minute or so to be sure you understand that the good guy/bad guy ploy is being used. Then stand up, tell the good guy salesman that he has your offer . . . and your only offer . . . and that if he'd like to do business, to give you a call. In the meantime, make it clear that you plan to shop other dealerships. Keep in mind that the last thing in the world they want is to see a checkbook walk off their lot and into a competitive dealership. Chances are, unless your deal is below their true costs, or unless you're trying to buy a car that is in great demand but in low supply, you'll make your deal.

The Lowball Offer

If the salesman knows you are determined to shop, his last resort is to "put you out on a lowball." This is the term for an unrealistically low offer which is the equivalent of saying: "You go out and shop and if you can't beat (he names a low figure) then come back and we'll do business."

What you'll find is that the lowball figure is so low no other dealer will match it. Finally, after you've dragged this unrealistic figure around to several dealers, you come back to the original dealership where your salesman will say, "Gee, I'm sorry, the boss changed his mind. I just can't sell you the car for that price. But I'm sure we can make a deal that will make you happy." At that point, the salesperson hopes you're so tired of shopping that you'll agree to make a deal more favorable to the dealership.

Your countertactic

Keep in mind that if a price sounds too good to be true, it probably is.

First We Need Your Life History

In some dealerships, even before you've agreed on a car or a price, the salesperson will want to fill out a credit application. This is a ploy designed to establish your ability to buy, i.e., are you a real buyer or a deadbeat? In addition, the more information they can get from you up front, the greater their advantage.

Your countertactic

Don't give them any information other than your name until the deal is made. If they insist that they have to have a credit application before they can negotiate a price, make it clear that until you do have a price, you do not plan to provide them with any additional information. If they balk, you can walk.

The Car Switch

Some dealers have been known to agree on a deal for a specific car and then switch it with another car—exact same year and model—which has been damaged during transport and then repaired and repainted. If the repair job is marginal, they might even arrange to deliver it to you at dusk or at night, when it will be harder for you to notice any telltale signs.

Your countertactic

Always write down the VIN number of any new or used car you decide to buy and then check it against both the title and the car itself when you take delivery. Chances are you'll never run into this ploy, but it doesn't hurt to take precautions, especially if the negotiation has been difficult and you sense that the dealership would somehow like to get even.

Rustproofing

Once you've agreed to buy a car, many salespeople will try to add some profit through back-end sales. It's common for them to offer you rustproofing or upholstery protection at a price usually in excess of $100. The rustproofing spray material and the labor usually cost the dealership about $10 or less. This is usually a waste of money and, in some cases, the rustproofing can seal drain holes in the body that were inserted to give moisture a place to run out. When these holes are sealed you can actually induce rust and, worse, invalidate the factory-guaranteed protection against rust-through.

Your countertactic

You should keep in mind that today most vehicles use galvanized steel in areas subject to potential corrosion. Virtually all vehicle bodies are completely submerged in an electrostatic dip during assembly that coats and seals all the metal surfaces inside and out. In addition, most cars receive a factory undercoating to add further protection. If a salesperson tells you that rustproofing is really a good idea to protect your investment, you might want to question the quality and durability of the car. Tell the salesperson that since the car needs more protection than the factory has given it, you might be better off shopping for a different make. Watch the seller try to squirm out of that one.

10. System Selling—Beware of

System selling or "track selling" is a concept that some larger dealerships use to control the customer and squeeze as much profit as possible out of every deal.

Some systems are designed to generate "spot" deliveries. This means getting you to shop, buy, and take delivery of a car during your first visit.

System selling is designed to control you through confusion. In some dealerships you are met by a greeter who turns you over to a salesperson whose job it is to qualify you. The salesman's job is to see if you've got the money and/or a reasonable credit history to enable you to buy *today.* They then turn you over to another salesperson who will help you find the car you want and take you for a demo drive. This person turns you over to a "closer," who insists that you fill out a credit application before you negotiate a deal. Their job is to sell, sell, sell. Then once you've started negotiating, the salesperson will write up your order and ask for a deposit before he or she takes it in to the manager. *"Company policy, you know."*

The offer goes in and, not infrequently, even if it is for the full sticker price the salesperson will come back with instructions to try to sell you more options, move you up to a higher-priced model—anything to add more profit. Assuming that your initial offer is much lower than the list, the system store process is designed to work this offer-counteroffer process until the first "closer" has gotten all he's going to get. At that point you're turned over (TO'd) to another salesperson or manager who will try to bump you until "there's no money left on the table."

There are dealerships that will resort to intimidation and browbeating and treat you as if somehow you've never left grade school. Once you've come to a figure and signed a deposit check, they turn you over to the finance person. His job is to convince you to finance the vehicle through the dealership (so they can add to their profit) and to buy loan, accident, and health insurance (so that they can add even more). The finance person will toss figures all over the place and keep you as confused as possible.

Wheeling and Dealing in a "Track Store"

The best way to beat the system is to never give it a chance. If the store is putting you on a selling track, surprise them, jump off, and go to a smaller dealer. If you insist on dealing with a system store, *go in with the facts.* Do all your research before you shop. Know exactly what the car you intend to buy costs the dealer. When the "closer" begins his pitch, let him go on for a while and then suggest that it's time to cut to the chase and get on with the deal. Interrupt him in midsentence with a time-out signal. The more you can control the conversation, the stronger your position.

If he wants you to fill out a credit application, tell him it won't be necessary because you've got the money in your checkbook. Tell him to write up the deal. As he gets out the order form, hand him a list of all the options that you want on the car. Let him write all these on the order form. When he's done, hand him a second piece of paper that shows the *dealer's actual invoice cost* for the car and the actual dealer cost of the options plus a 3 percent profit. (All this information can be found in your local magazine store in the new-car price guides.) Don't be surprised if his whole demeanor changes. Salespeople don't expect this kind of non-compliant behavior from the customers.

Furthermore, tell him that there *will be no deposit* until the deal is approved, and even then you'll give them only $200 and the remainder when you pick up the car. Finally, make it very clear that *this is your one and only offer.* You might say something like:

"If you can't make the deal, then I don't want to waste your time or mine." And then, most important, say nothing. Remember, he/she who speaks first loses.

At this point the salesperson is going to come at you with every ploy, tactic, and retort that he has ever used. Listen for a moment and then calmly point to the paper.

"Maybe you misunderstood what I said. That's my deal. There is no other. If you find it unacceptable, let's not waste each other's time."

If you really want to add some dramatics, take out your checkbook and write a check for $200, but don't sign it. In the memo space write a deposit on—and write in the VIN number of the car—for a total price of $ ______ . Then say:

"If you need to check with management, fine. But in five minutes I'm either going to sign this check to seal this deal, or I'm going to say thank you very much and be on my way. I do have another appointment that I should either cancel or keep."

You don't have to say who the appointment is with. It could be with your aerobics instructor. The salesperson will interpret this as an appointment with another dealer. Again, stop and say nothing. If the salesperson continues to sell, pick up your check, look him in the eye, and say:

"I take it we do not have a deal."

Pause long enough for him to answer. If he balks or shows signs of wanting to continue the "grind," then tear your check in half and leave. Chances are the salesperson will not let you get that far and will take the deal to the manager. Be aware that, in most stores, salespeople are required to take every deal to the manager, or at least not to let you walk out until you've been TO'd to someone else. If the salesperson returns with the manager, understand that he's not there to be dazzled by such an aggressive negotiator, but rather to tell you that your offer is out of the question.

"Then we have no deal. Thank you for your time."

The key, of course, is to remain pleasant. Don't get hostile or angry—always be very businesslike. Start to leave. That's the last thing they want to have happen. Let them talk, but don't budge. Well, maybe toss in $50 or one percent more on the deal if that's what it will take to let them save face and write up the order. However, don't let yourself get into a "bump and raise" situation. One raise is all that you should ever make.

Now, let's say that they finally relent. And they probably will because they would rather take your deal than see your money go down the street to a competitor. Don't relax! You aren't through. There are still pitfalls ahead in a system store.

Protecting Yourself in a Track Store

Because they would still like to "squeeze you" if they can, keep the following in mind:

1. After you've signed the buyer's order, be sure that the car you looked at is the car on the order. Insist on checking the VIN number. Mistakes will happen.
2. Agree on a specific time for the delivery. Ask for a specific list of fees for title, tags, and taxes. If they try to add prep fees, advertising, etc., make it clear that these are not part of your deal. *"And by the way, my car will come with free mats."*
3. They will probably want a certified check, so arrange for that before you return.
4. When you come in to take delivery (assuming you don't take it right then), ask to take the car for a test drive before you close. Make it clear that you want to be sure nothing has changed.
5. Check the VIN number again. Yes, cars do look the same and some dealers aren't above slipping in a car that's fallen off the truck and been repaired.
6. Check to be sure that everything you asked for in the way of options is on the car.
7. Park the car near the door and take the keys with you.
8. Go in, sign the papers, and refuse to accept any of the add-ons.
9. Drive out knowing that you've done well and knowing too that the dealer probably made at least six percent on the deal.

Clearly this system-store strategy requires that you possess a fairly aggressive personality and that you cannot be easily intimidated. But if you're the kind of person who likes to deal with confrontation, have at it. Remember, do all your homework first.

11. Glossary of Terms

Allowance Buyers Customers who are primarily interested in the amount the dealer gives them for their current car.

Book Value The wholesale value of the car as quoted in any of several used-car guidebooks. The figures in these books will frequently vary from book to book. This is because some books collect their data from dealer-reported transactions and some collect their data from the prices paid at dealer auctions. Because salespeople know which books quote high and which quote low, they will often use a particular book when trying to convince a customer that the amount the dealership is willing to pay is fair. Case in point: Because *Kelley Blue Book* figures tend to reflect West Coast averages, East Coast dealers use the figures to help support an inflated used-car price. Beware of signs that read:

"Prices Below Blue Book Value." They may be below Blue Book, but they could be well above the Black.

Bump The effort by a salesperson to raise a customer's offer.

The Close The process of finalizing the deal and signing the order.

Closer A person in a dealership—whose primary job is to get you to sign the buyer's order.

Demos or Demonstrators Cars used by the dealership to provide customers with test drives. Frequently these demo cars are driven home at night by salespeople and other dealership employees. If you buy a demo, treat it as a used car. Most dealerships will try to convince you it's somewhere between a used car and a new car, in a class all its own.

Dealer Hold-Backs This is money that the manufacturer "holds back" from the dealer until after the car is sold. This usually amounts to two or three percent and was begun so that dealers could, if necessary, show their invoices to customers to prove "how little we're making on your deal" without revealing the additional money that will be collected after the sale.

Difference Buyers People who are primarily concerned with the amount of money required to span the gap between what the dealership "allows" on the trade-in and the price of the new car.

Equity The amount of money that the owner can expect to take out of his or her trade-in once all outstanding payoffs are made.

Floor Planning The practice of having a financial institution buy the cars from the manufacturer and then charging the dealer interest between the time of dealer purchase to customer sale. The bank then remains somewhat diligent in checking to be sure that the dealer hasn't "forgotten" to report the sale of a car. Sometimes dealers like to postpone reporting a sale so that they can use the cash received on a deal to cover other expenses. Obviously the financial institution frowns on this type of "forgetfulness."

Gross *Front-end Gross:* The profit a dealership makes from the sale of a vehicle.

Back-end Gross: The profit the dealership makes from the sale of add-ons like insurance and rustproofing.

Loan Value The amount of money that a lending institution will lend a buyer against the purchase of a used car. Usually the loan value is figured at 80 to 85 percent of the book value, but it can vary according to the vehicle and the applicant's loan history.

The Monroney Sticker The price sticker on the car is called the Monroney, after the senator who introduced legislation in the late fifties to require that each car have a label detailing the price and identifying the car by make, model, and identification number. Know that it is against the law for this label to be removed prior to the sale and delivery to the customer. What this does is prevent the dealer from changing the price on a given car to reflect an increase in factory pricing.

MSRP or List Price The manufacturer's suggested retail price. This is the price that appears on the paper form displayed on the rear side window. It is also referred to in the industry as the Monroney sticker.

"Packs" Extra profit added to the invoice by dealers. This is particularly prevalent when the dealer knows that a certain car is hot and in demand.

Payment Buyers People who are mainly concerned with the amount of their monthly payments.

Retail Price This is another way of expressing the MSRP.

System Selling or Track Selling A system designed by the dealership to control the customer and to hand him or her off from one person to another to assure maximum dealership productivity. Avoid these stores.

Tissue Another term for the dealer's invoice, i.e., the actual price of the vehicle charged by the manufacturer to the dealer.

T.O. The process of turning over a customer to another salesperson, usually to help make a better deal for the dealership.

"Up" System A salesperson-rotation system that assures that each salesperson gets to take his or her turn with customers as they walk into the dealership.

Wholesale Value This is the value of a car to a person who plans to resell it for a profit.

II

About Buying Used Cars

How to Buy a Used Car and Not Get Taken

A Word about This Segment

This segment was developed by people who know the used-vehicle market. Their objective was to provide a reference that would help you make a more informed used-car, van, or pickup buying decision. Their efforts have produced a guide that offers ideas, tips, and suggestions that you can put to use when evaluating a used vehicle, even if you have little or no automotive expertise.

A.C.I.S. makes no representations that this information will assure you of buying a trouble-free vehicle. *Make no mistake*, there are risks when buying a used car, van, or pickup. While it is possible to detect problems that could lead to costly repairs, no publication and probably few automotive experts can predict with 100 percent accuracy how a used car* will perform one month, six months, or a year into the future.

You will, we believe, improve the odds of getting a good used buy by preparing yourself before you start to shop. We offer this manual as a means of providing you with basic information that, when used with common sense, can help you decide what questions to ask of the seller, what to look for during your inspection and test drive, and when to enlist the help and advice of a professional mechanic.

It is our hope you will find this segment interesting, useful, and that it will make your used-car shopping experience a more rewarding one.

**When we talk about a used car, we are, in general, talking about issues that also relate to the purchase of a used van or pickup. To avoid the redundant use of "car, van, or pickup" we are, in the main, limiting ourselves to the term "used car" and hope that you will understand that, unless otherwise stated, it generally applies to vans and pickups as well.*

1. Pre-Shopping Preparation

The Upside of a Used-Car Purchase

If you have the right information and you know where and how to shop, many experts will tell you that purchasing a used car can be a sound investment.

A used car can provide a good return on your transportation dollar, especially if the car is no more than two to three years old. When you consider that a new-car price generally includes the dealer's markup, the salesperson's commission, the manufacturer's transportation charges, and the cost of both their advertising campaigns, you realize that a good deal of a new car's price has nothing to do with the car itself. Add to this the fact that the moment you take delivery of a new car and drive it off the dealer's lot, you have reduced the market value by as much as 40 percent or more. In addition, by the end of three years the average car will have lost, through depreciation, approximately two-thirds of its value.

In many instances, used cars have lower insurance rates, lower titling fees, and sales taxes. Plus, if you're buying a luxury car, you will not have to pay the luxury tax (10 percent of the amount over $32,500) or the gas-guzzler tax.

The Downside of a Used-Car Purchase

Having made the case for a used car, van, or truck, we come to a fundamental used buyer's question: *"Don't I run the risk of buying someone else's headache?"* The answer of course is yes. The used-car business is full of bad buys and lemons, and we do not want to suggest that bargains are always there for the picking. Buying a used car does involve some degree of risk. You should also be aware that finance rates will usually be higher on a used vehicle than on a new one. Plus, you do run the risk of more maintenance costs and repairs with a used car.

However, it is our contention that if you are prepared to do some homework and are willing to invest some time—and maybe even $40 to $90 (depending on your area) for a professional inspection—you can reduce the risk, save money, and end up with a very satisfactory automobile.

What Do I Need to Know Before I Shop?

Before you get serious about any one car, it's important to get the facts concerning:

1. The car's reliability and repair record
2. Whether the car has been subject to a manufacturer's recall
3. Current owner satisfaction or dissatisfaction with the car
4. The "real" price of the car
5. The approximate amount of markup on the car if you're buying from a dealer

Reliability and repair record

Consumer Reports, a publication of Consumer's Union, offers a section in their Buying Guide entitled "Frequency of Repair Records." This section is a reflection of over 600,000 reports supplied by the subscribers to the magazine. In it you'll get an excellent picture of the repair records of what appears to be the vast majority of recent model used cars. They provide a highly useful list of "Reliable Used Cars" and "Used Cars to Avoid."

Has the car been subjected to a recall?

Consumer Guide—Auto Series publishes a "Used Car Rating Guide" in which they offer a general assessment of individual used cars, technical data, price ranges, and a rather detailed description of the recall history. Another source for determining if a model has been subjected to a manufacturer's recall is the National Highway Traffic and Safety Administration. You can call their hotline at 1-800-424-9393 (free of charge) and ask for recall information on a specific car—year and model.

Owner satisfaction with the car

In addition to speaking directly with friends who have owned the car you're considering, you might also want to turn again to *Consumer Reports*. They offer charts showing how their subscribers rated their satisfaction with recent model cars.

2. Deciding Where to Buy a Used Car

What follows is a brief assessment of the potential for getting a car, van, or pickup at a very good price, i.e., "cheap" vs. the risks involved in dealing with each of the buying options.

Private Owners

1. Friends and Acquaintances

There are many who will suggest that the best place to buy a used car is from a friend. The upside of buying from someone you know is that he or she will be less likely to sell you what has become their repair shop nightmare—at least not without warning you. They may even be willing to take a little less for the car than they could get from another buyer. However, there are also several downsides to consider.

- First, your friend may have an inflated idea of the value of the car and will resent your trying to negotiate a lower price.
- Second, if something does go wrong with the car, an unexpected repair charge could put your friendship in jeopardy.
- Third, unless there is still some factory guarantee left on the car, a friend won't be in a position to offer you any kind of warranty.

Even with these possible negatives, a friend or business associate may still be the safest source for a used-car purchase.

Price: It will vary according to:

- Seller's concept of car's value
- How big a favor they're willing to do for a friend
- How badly they want to sell the car

Risk: Moderately low. After all, *you do know where the seller lives*. However, to assure that the risk remains low, you must follow the inspection instructions outlined in this segment, and you should be sure to have the car checked by a professional mechanic before you buy.

2. Persons Previously Unknown to You

Most people generally feel more comfortable wheeling and dealing with someone they have never met before. You can "grind" the seller on the price and then, if not satisfied with the deal, walk away without endangering a friendship or damaging your relationship with an acquaintance. As we'll explain in our strategy section, one of the keys to buying at a good price lies in:

- Finding sellers who need to sell their cars
- Finding sellers who are in a hurry to sell their cars
- Finding sellers who have not had much success in attracting potential buyers

Price: It will vary according to:

- Seller's concept of car's value
- How badly they want to sell the car

Risk: You can keep the risk moderately low if you meticulously follow the inspection instructions in this segment.

Buying from Classified Ads

The reason most people elect to sell their own cars is because they want more than the wholesale price that a dealer or wholesaler would be willing to pay. Their rationale, and it's a legitimate one, is that by selling the car themselves, they stand to make more money, even it means enduring more aggravation.

However, this does not mean that their prices should be higher than, or even the same as, the retail price charged by a dealer. The reasons are as follows: First, unless the car has some manufacturer's guarantee left, the private owner has no practical way of providing a warranty. Second, private owners do not have the same expenses or overhead as a dealer. For both these reasons, the private owner's car should be priced below its equivalent on a dealer's lot. Having said that, remember that unlike a new car there are no two used cars exactly alike. The point to keep in mind about all this is that if you find a private party asking substantially more than a dealer for essentially the same car, you either have a situation in which you're looking at an extremely well-kept, low-mileage, much in demand car, or you have a seller with an inflated concept of the car's value.

Curbing

This is the name for the practice of salespeople at a dealership selling some of their used cars from home as if they were private sellers. It's a way for them to make a few extra bucks. The only problem is that all too often the cars they offer are the ones that the dealer can't move. That's why one of the questions we suggest you ask when calling on a classified ad is whether the seller is a dealer or works for one. If he says it's his car and you find that when you check the title it's not in his name, you would be well advised to walk.

Advantage—Buying from the Original Owner

One advantage of dealing with the original owner, especially one who has taken pride in the car, is that he or she will give you a more accurate picture of the car's maintenance and repair history. Conversely, a private owner may be trying to unload his or her automotive headache. If you decide to buy from a private source we strongly urge you to have the car checked out by a certified mechanic.

Finding Eager Sellers

Clearly people who have been trying to sell their cars for several weeks or even months are going to be motivated to accept something below their asking price. The question, of course, is how do you find these eager sellers. One method is to find a four- to six-week-old newspaper and go through the classified ads. Circle those cars that interest you. Then call and without revealing that you have gotten their number from a six-week-old paper, ask about their car. If it's sold, they will say so and you can hang up. If it's still for sale, the seller need not know that you know how long he or she has been trying to sell it.

WHAT TO ASK WHEN CALLING ABOUT A CLASSIFIED AD

Use the following chart to develop a fact list of the car you're calling on. Review it with the seller to be sure that the ad reflects reality.

Vehicle Description

Make ____________________ Model designation ____________________

Year __________ Number of miles showing on odometer ________________

Color exterior __________ Color interior __________

Seat covering: Fabric ❑ Leather ❑

Engine size (number of cylinders) ________

Gas ❑ Diesel ❑

Doors: Two-door coupe ❑ Four-door ❑ Hatchback ❑ Sun roof ❑

Power equipment: Electric windows ❑ Electric seats ❑

Radio: AM/FM ❑ Cassette ❑ CD player ❑

Full spare ❑ or space saver ❑

Other items ____

After you've confirmed the description and content of the vehicle, we suggest that you ask the following questions.

1. **Tell me about the condition of the car.**

   (Phrasing the question this way should motivate the seller to provide more information. Don't waste your time with a seller who tells you that it "runs good." This usually means that the car has problems and that even he or she can't think of anything good to say about it.)

Notes:

____

____

____

____

2. What features does it have?

Notes:

____

____

____

____

3. How many miles does the car have on it?

(Write this down and check it against the odometer when you inspect the car.)

Owner's declared mileage: __________

4. Are you a used-car dealer?

(Sometimes used-car dealers put ads in the classifieds, and you'll want to know this before going any further. They could be selling a lemon or a car without a title or a car that won't pass inspection or one that they would prefer not to have associated with the car lot. This is called "curbing." Avoid these people.)

❑ YES ❑ NO

5. Are you the original owner of the car?

(If the answer is no, ask how long they have owned the car. Obviously, it's best to buy a used car from the original owner if only because you'll have a better chance of determining its maintenance and repair history. Recently we ran into a situation in which a wholesaler sells cars by masquerading as a private owner. What he does is buy cars at auction that legitimate dealers won't touch, cars that have been in a wreck and then fully repaired. The wholesaler buys them for a very low price, brings them home, and sells them out of his front yard for a price equal to those that one could charge for the car had it not been wrecked. Obviously, he never informs the buyer of the car's history, and most buyers never take the time to have the car fully inspected. Here again is another reason to take any used vehicle to a professional for evaluation.)

❑ YES ❑ NO How long owned? __________

6. Do you have the maintenance and repair records?

(Any owner that has kept the maintenance and repair records probably has taken good care of the car.)

❑ YES ❑ NO

7. What would you estimate it's going to cost to put the car in A-1 condition?

(This question forces the seller into making an on-the-spot evaluation. Most will try to give you a reasonable estimate, even though it will probably be a conservative one. If the seller tells you that it's in mint condition and you arrive to find a bucket of bolts, you'd be advised to say good-bye.)

Owner's estimated amount of repairs: $ __________

Notes:

____

____

____

____

8. Why are you selling the car?

(This question may help you learn how anxious he or she is to sell the car, and it may supply some information you can use in your negotiation.)

____

____

____

____

9. What is your asking price?

(By using the term "asking price" you are letting the seller know that you're assuming that the "asking price" is higher than what you will actually accept. Here's another question designed to test the seller's pricing resolve. This question should be asked once you feel that you've established a good rapport with the seller. Asked in a conversational, matter-of-fact manner, it can reveal much about the seller's eagerness to make a deal. *What do you expect to get for your car?*

Asking price: $ __________

It's a good idea to have a car inspected by a professional auto mechanic no matter *where* or from *whom* you buy the car.

Franchise Automobile Dealers

The major advantage of shopping the used-car lots of new-car dealers is that they frequently have the widest selection of low-mileage, late-model used cars. If you decide to buy from a new-car dealer, we recommend that you buy a used car from the dealer who sells that same car new. In other words, you're probably better off buying a used Ford from a Ford dealer than from a dealer who sells an entirely different line of cars.

Chances are that a new-car dealer's used cars will be more expensive than other sources because the dealer is selling only the "cream of the crop" of cars taken as trade-ins. Lesser cars, cars with high mileage, body damage, or in need of repair, are frequently sold at auction. Most new-car dealers offer the added advantage of a stronger used-car warranty, and they usually have people who know how to service your car. Plus, the better new-car dealers are very conscious of building a base of satisfied customers. The smart ones know that if you're satisfied with their used car and the service they offer, you may one day be looking at one of their new cars.

Price:

- The asking prices of franchise dealer used cars are generally the highest of any source. They are also usually in the best condition and have the best warranties.
- Asking price is based on a variety of market factors.
- Dealers will almost never sell below the wholesale value of the car.

Risk:

- Moderate to low

Independent Used-Car Dealers

You may find that there are independent dealers in your area who have a reliable record of selling good used cars. Generally, your best guide is the recommendations of friends who have had firsthand experience with the dealer.

However, in many cases used-car dealers who are not affiliated with a major new-car franchise are the sellers of last resort. Often their cars are the ones no one else wanted to peddle. Their selection is often heavily peppered with fleet cars, taxis, and cars bought at auctions. Many of these dealers are interested in only one thing: *today's sale*. While there are exceptions, most don't expect repeat business. Many don't have on-premises repair facilities, and they are much less inclined than a new dealer to think about long-term customer satisfaction.

One potential advantage of dealing with an independent is that often it's easier to get them down closer to the wholesale price. First, they don't usually have the backup capital of a franchise dealer, so they are more likely to accept a low deal than to let your money walk off their lot. Second, because they won't have as much overhead to account for, they can afford to accept smaller margins. If you have the financial ability to write a check right now, right here—you have serious negotiation power.

They'll love you today, but will they fix it tomorrow?

There are few people who like you more than a guy on a used-car lot before you buy his car. However, if you have a problem the day after your check has cleared, you may find that yesterday's friendship was just that. Does this mean that independents are out to take the public?

Some are.

Most aren't.

Like franchise dealers, licensed independent used-car dealers must conform to the various lemon laws and state or federally dictated disclosure laws. Unlike franchise dealers, most independents have no facilities either to fix a car before it's put on their lot or to provide you with after-sale service.

But he said it had a warranty!

And maybe it does. Many used-car lots offer warranties through independent companies. Commonly, these warranties require you to pay for the repairs and then submit a claim. Unfortunately, far too many of these non-dealer warranties cover very little and are hardly worth their paper they're printed on. Curiously, the negatives of an independent dealer can also be turned to your advantage in a negotiation. Every time you point out a risk, you can lower what you're willing to pay.

However, as we've said before and will keep on saying: Before you write the check, we strongly urge that you perform the complete inspection outlined in this segment and then, if it passes your inspection, take it to a professional mechanic.

Price:

- Moderate
- Very sensitive to going market prices

Risk:

- Moderate to very high
- Quality of car is almost always a key concern
- Car's history is frequently unknown
- Warranties can be next to worthless

"Nearly New" Used Cars

Domestic manufacturers sell large numbers of cars to rental agencies with the understanding that after a set period of time or a given number of miles, they will buy the cars back. The industry calls these "program cars." They are reconditioned and then sold through dealerships. Many of these cars are also being offered in used-car lease deals. (See "About Leases" for more information on used-car leases.) If you want to suggest to a dealer that you have some insight into the industry, ask him if he handles "program cars."

Price:

- They are low mileage and have been regularly serviced by the rental agency and then reconditioned by the dealer or the factory.
- They may still have some factory guarantee left.

Risk:

- They have been driven by many drivers, most of whom probably were indifferent to how they treated the car.
- You cannot call the previous owner to inquire about problems or strange quirks that might have developed in the car.

The key thing to keep in mind about "program cars" is that they should be subjected to the inspection process outlined in this segment.

Factory Executive Cars

Factory "demonstrators" or executive cars can also be options worth exploring. Often the factory offers attractive purchase deals to their employees who, in turn, seek to sell their cars at the end of each model year before purchasing a new one. Usually, these cars are low mileage, in good condition, and still under factory warranty.

To check out this source of used cars you might want to select a make and then call the home office for the location and phone number of the zone or district office in your area. Ask for information about purchasing "executive" or "company" cars.

Rental Agency Sales

Finally, some of the rental car agencies sell a portion of their used inventory through their rental lots and special sales locations. These cars offer many of the same advantages and disadvantages as program cars. Further, you may find that the rental agencies are averse to negotiation. Rather, they try to give you the impression that their "take it or leave it" price represents a good deal. It probably does. But for whom?

As with every other source of used cars, it is always a very good idea to have the car inspected by a professional mechanic before you agree to buy.

Used-Car Pricing

A franchise dealer with a used-car operation usually prices his cars at some percentage over what the car is deemed to be worth on the wholesale market. The wholesale value of a car is usually determined by such things as the demand for the car coupled with the age, make, model, options, mileage, and general condition.

The dealer's markup on a used car, van, or pickup is frequently determined by any or all of several factors:

- First, there's the price he paid to acquire the car. He might have taken it in trade against a new car—which means that he accepted the car in lieu of cash or he might have purchased it from a private seller, a wholesaler, or bought it at auction.
- Second, he will add what it has cost him to repair and recondition the car.
- Finally, he'll add a markup to cover his profit objectives and to pay for his overhead.

The markup will also reflect such things as the condition of the car, the mileage, the make, model, options and, most important, the market demand. The point, simply, is that used-car markups vary greatly for any number of factors. As an educated used-car buyer, your objective is to discover the fair wholesale price and what the dealer "has in the car." In other words, what has it cost him to buy and recondition the car and put it on his lot. That will give you the basis for planning your negotiation. More on this later.

Asking More Than They Plan to Get

Many dealers also include a "negotiation pad" in their markups. They recognize that most people won't buy a car—new or used—unless they feel they're buying it for less than the advertised price. So a dealer will build in a large enough cushion to give the buyer a discount and still end up with whatever he considers to be a reasonable, or maybe even a more than reasonable, profit.

Here's Some Insider Information on Pricing

The key to a dealer's survival and profitability in the used-car business is to buy used cars at or below what the industry calls the wholesale price and then to sell them at a retail price that, in the final analysis, is whatever a buyer will pay. Here are some actual examples:

A dealer told us that if he pays a customer $1,000 for the trade-in on a new car, he'll clean up the car and put it on his lot for $3,999. That's a 400 percent markup! He can then let the potential buyer "beat up the salesman" and believe he or she has driven away with a great deal for $3,000. The dealer and salesman laugh all the way to the bank.

Recently we saw a GM car that we discovered had been purchased by the dealer for $9,500. After spending $400 for repairs and reconditioning he put it on the lot at $13,800. That's a markup over his purchase cost of just over 45 percent. The used-car sales manager confided that he had built in room for negotiation. A buyer finally appeared and, after a negotiated agreement, bought the car for $12,450. The customer felt he'd gotten a deal, and the seller said nothing to disabuse him of that notion.

The Dealer as a "Predatory Buyer"

In a rare moment of candor a used-car manager told us that if a car is worth $25,000 on the wholesale market, he'll try to convince the seller to part with it for three to four thousand less. He called this "predatory buying," which is another way of saying that he'll say anything or do anything to screw the seller. If he's successful, he'll turn around and put it on the market for $29,995. This could represent a markup of anywhere from 30 to 40 percent. He admitted, however, that if he senses the seller is smart enough to offer the car to more than one dealer, he will be forced to offer a figure closer to the true wholesale price. He also admitted that if the car is a "cream puff," if he knows there's a lot of profit in the car and that he's bidding against another dealer, he will often go above the wholesale price.

Most successful used-car operations hold a car on their lot for somewhere between 60 and 90 days. If it hasn't sold during that time the dealer will offer it to a wholesaler or take it to auction to recover some or all of his costs. The point to keep in mind is this: Dealers seldom spend more on a car, including purchase and reconditioning, than they feel they can get were it to become necessary to sell the car to a wholesaler or to put it on the auction block. For that reason a dealer is unlikely to accept an offer that is below what he knows he can get on the wholesale market. However, any offer above the wholesale value will usually be considered, especially if the car is not in high demand, has been sitting on his lot for a number of weeks, and if the offer is made at the end of the month.

Used-Car Warranties

If the franchise dealer offers a warranty and it actually covers a substantial number of items, your risk is usually moderate to low. (Please note, however, that you will want to examine the warranty carefully and be sure that you understand exactly what's covered and for how long.)

With few exceptions (and the current used-car warranty offered by Mercedes-Benz might be one of those exceptions) you don't want to trust the current condition of the car to the future protection of the warranty. We urge you to protect yourself further by performing the inspections outlined later in this segment. Keep this in mind: A used car that at the time of purchase checks out to be in excellent condition can develop problems down the road. That's even true with a new car. The mistake most people make is that they fail to fully inspect a used car before the purchase.

You will find that most used cars come as is or with a 30- to 90-day warranty.

As Is

As is means that you're taking the car *as is* and that if it should fall apart the moment you get home, that's your problem, not the dealer's.

Full Factory Warranty

In recent years Mercedes-Benz has been offering a two-year factory-backed warranty with unlimited mileage that is almost as complete in its coverage as their new-car warranty. Once you get beyond Mercedes and one or two other luxury manufacturers, the warranties become a lot less attractive.

30-, 60-, 90-Day 100-Percent Mechanical Warranty

This is probably the best you can hope for with most used cars. It covers the mechanical parts in your car.

30-, 60-, 90-Day Drive Train Warranty

This warranty covers the engine, transmission, rear axle, and nothing more. Some of these warranties come on a fifty-fifty basis, and you should refuse to accept these.

Fifty-fifty Warranties

Often dealers offer to split any repairs for a period of 30, 60, or 90 days. Trouble is, they are the ones who set the prices, and you have no idea whether the repair invoice is the true cost of the repair or if you are actually paying the total bill.

Another variation calls for them to pay for parts and you pay for labor. Surprise! The labor is usually higher when it comes to this type of warranty.

Repairs at Cost

Oh, please! Whose cost? And how do you know the time, labor, and parts were actually performed? You don't. Forget this type of warranty.

Implied Warranties

More and more states are passing laws that say a buyer can reasonably expect the car—or for that matter, any item you purchase—to perform as designed for a reasonable amount of time without undue problems or expense. You may want to check with your local motor-vehicle authorities to get the specifics of the implied warranty in your state.

3. More on Price

How to Determine the Wholesale Price

Whether you buy from a private owner or a dealer, one of the most important pieces of information you can have is the current wholesale price of the car in your area of the country. One source of auto-price information is the car loan department of your bank. They usually have all the latest price books and possibly even auction reports that show what various makes are bringing on the auction market.

Book Prices

The industry uses any of several books as price guides: *NADA Official Used Car Guide*, *National Auto Research Black Book*, *Kelley Blue*

Book Auto Market Report, and *Galves Auto Price List.* These books purport to reflect the average wholesale prices that various cars are bringing across the country. The only problem is that they don't agree. Compare the suggested wholesale prices for a Chevrolet four-door Lumina from the same month:

Kelley Blue Book: $7,500 (tends to reflect West Coast prices)
NADA: $6,750 (combination of auction and dealer reports)
Black Book: $5,650 to $8,850 (reports from dealer auction sales)

Consumer Price Books

Frequently you will find used-car price books on your newsstand. The figures in these books provide a general range, but because they cannot account for the myriad factors that impact the costs that a dealer has in a car, they may not present a true picture of any given car's "real" price.

Getting the Price That Matters

If you're buying a used car from a dealer, the key to a good deal lies in discovering how much money he has invested in the car. In other words:

- What did he pay the previous owner?
- How much has he spent on repairs and reconditioning?
- Does he have interest and miscellaneous charges that have to be paid?

Obviously, no dealer is going to tell you what he's got in the car. Yes, in some circumstances he might claim to be giving you the number, but rest assured it will be inflated. Here's a ploy that will often help you uncover this important information. Walk onto a lot and tell the salesperson that you'd just like to look around. Most salespeople will leave you alone because you've automatically disqualified yourself as a "buyer today." When you spot a car you like, copy down all of the information you can about that car:

Make ________________ Model designation ________________
Year ________ Number of miles showing on odometer ________________
Color exterior ________ Color interior ________ Seat covering: Fabric ❑ Leather ❑
Engine size (number of cylinders) ________ Gas ❑ Diesel ❑
Doors: Two-door coupe ❑ Four-door ❑ Hatchback ❑ Sun roof ❑
Power equipment: Electric windows ❑ Electric seats ❑
Radio: AM/FM ❑ Cassette ❑ CD player ❑ Full spare ❑ or space saver ❑
Other items ________________________________

"Offer to Sell Them Their Car!"

You read that correctly. The ploy is to call the dealer and pretend to be someone who wants to sell a car exactly like the one that they have on the lot. To throw them off, you should change the color and take off 100 miles. Otherwise, the "car" you're offering to sell should be the same. Here's an example of how your conversation might go:

YOU: Hello, my name is *(make up one)* and I'm looking to sell my *(fill in the year, make, and model of the car)*. I had planned to try to sell it through the paper, but I haven't got time. I've got to sell it quick. We're moving to ______ and I won't be able to take it with me. *(Or I need the money to pay for the move. Or I need the money for ______.)*

BUYER: What are you looking to get? *(They will always ask you this to find out if you are over- or underestimating its value.)*

YOU: I don't know. I don't even know what it's worth. But I've got to sell. I know you'll want to look at it before you commit, but it would sure help if you could give me a ballpark figure. *(To encourage them to quote you a figure you might want to add):* For all I know it may not even be worth selling.

BUYER: What's it got on it?

YOU: *(In a conversational way you read off all the features that you've noted on your fact sheet.)*

BUYER: *(At this point he'll consult his books or quote you a figure based on what he assumes is a price below the true wholesale value. Sometimes it can be 15 to 20 percent below . . . or more.)*

YOU: *(No matter what figure he quotes you respond by saying):* "That seems low to me. When I bring this car in, you'll see that it's really clean. I mean, this is the kind of car that a lot of people are looking for. You won't have it on your lot for more than two days." *(The more naive you sound, the better.)*

BUYER: *(Because you are now in the role of a "seller" and not a "buyer," the used-car person is going to try to "down sell" the value of your car. He may concede that he would come up a little bit on the price, but might also point out):* Listen, I've got a car almost like yours sitting on my lot that I paid $ ______ for, and it's been sitting there for two months. *(Bingo! Now you know where to start your bidding.)*

By the way, if you don't get a price from the used-car dealership offering the target car, there is nothing preventing you from calling one or two others. Most astute used-car buyers have a very good sense of the market, and their quote on your make-believe car will help provide a reasonable estimate of the true wholesale value of the car in your area.

Using the Price Information

If this tactic works—and it has for the author—you now have a pretty good idea of what he paid for the car on the lot. Now you're ready to go back to the dealer.

"I'm looking for a ______ year-old (make and model)."

When the salesperson leads you to the target car, make him go through the entire presentation. You should drive it and then subject it to all the inspections and tests outlined in this segment—including the professional mechanic inspection. Once you're satisfied that this is the car you want to buy, offer the salesperson a couple hundred dollars less than the number the dealership's used-car buyer offered you.

Be prepared for a good deal of groaning and "can't sell it for that" reactions. Assuming you want the car and knowing, as you do, that the dealer can probably get your price from a wholesaler or at auction, up your offer to a couple hundred over the price you were quoted and don't budge. (If you're the type of person who really enjoys a negotiation, start below the price they quoted. When you budge, do so very slowly. Keep in mind that, eventually, you will probably have to offer an amount above the wholesale price. Also, keep in mind that if you've got your heart set on a one-of-a-kind car that is really hot, this tactic won't work. Remember, demand drives the price.) Assuming that there are any number of similar cars available at other lots in the area, this tactic should eventually bear results. As they try to "up" your bid, just keep pointing out that:

1. You are ready to buy today.
2. You have your checkbook with you.
3. You would like to buy from this dealer, but you know there are a lot more cars out there and you will shop other lots if necessary.

Determining the True Wholesale Value of a Private Seller's Car

If you're buying from a private owner, you'll want to know the true wholesale value of the car. Here's a tactic that has worked for us. After you've performed the inspection outlined in this segment, and before you go to a mechanic, ask the seller if you can take the car for a drive—*alone*. Leave your car as ransom.

Take the car to the nearest used-car dealer and tell them you'd like to sell the car. Use the same tactic as we outlined for the phone inquiry. If you're nervous about seeming not to know as much as a real owner would about the car, tell the used-car dealer that you're selling the car for your niece and that you agreed to get some idea of what it was worth. If you have time, make at least two stops—one at a dealership that sells the same make.

The other stop should be at a non-franchise used-car dealer. His quote will help you establish the local market value. Frequently a used-car dealer will be able to spot frame damage or other problems that you might not have seen or have overlooked.

Recently, a friend of the author's was instructed to do the above and discovered that the wholesale price was actually $4,800 below the asking price because the car had been in an accident and suffered frame damage.

Once you know the wholesale value of a private seller's car, you can adjust your negotiation strategy accordingly. More on this later.

PRICE ESTIMATE WORK SHEET

Make ________________ Model designation ________________
Year ________ Number of miles showing on odometer ________________
Color exterior ________ Color interior ________ Seat covering: Fabric ❑ Leather ❑
Engine size (number of cylinders) ________ Gas ❑ Diesel ❑
Doors: Two-door coupe ❑ Four-door ❑ Hatchback ❑ Sun roof ❑
Equipment: Power windows ❑ Power seats ❑ Power rearview mirrors ❑
Cruise control ❑ AM/FM ❑ Cassette ❑ CD player ❑ Full spare ❑ space saver ❑
Other items ________________________________

Private seller's asking price ________
Dealer price quoted to buy car ________
Used car dealer price quote ________

Two Major Mistakes to Avoid

What are the two most common mistakes people make when buying a used car?

Mistake Number One

Most used-car buyers don't take the time or make the effort to thoroughly check out the car. Neglecting this step often results in costly repair bills or, worse, owning a car that is not worth fixing.

In the following pages we will give you a list of items to check during your personal inspection and test drive. We have also included a checklist for a mechanic. Having your potential used-car purchase inspected by a mechanic will probably cost you the equivalent of one hour of labor at a dealership or repair shop. It's worth it. A good, reliable mechanic can potentially save you from making a major purchase mistake. At the same time, the mechanic can also confirm that you're looking at a very good deal.

Mistake Number Two

Far too many consumers fall in love with a particular car and let their desire to own that car cloud their better judgment. Once a car seller—especially a professional—knows a person is hooked on a car, the buyer has all but abandoned the opportunity to negotiate a good deal. Buying cars is like playing poker: Never let your opponent—in this case, the seller—know what you really think. See the section on negotiation strategies.

4. The Exterior Inspection

Important note: At the end of this chapter you will find an Exterior Checklist. This contains all the items discussed in this section. We suggest that you use the checklist during your evaluation of the exterior of the car.

A Word about Performing These Tests

If you are uncomfortable performing some of these tests—especially those involving the engine and the fluids—or if you don't trust yourself to make an accurate assessment, don't worry, *you're not alone*. Take the easy way out and simply make note to have those items you skipped checked when you have the car inspected by a mechanic. As we'll explain later, paying a professional mechanic to go over the car is a good investment.

KEY TIP

> Never inspect a car in the rain or at dusk. The car always looks better when its flaws are hidden by the rain or hard to see in the fading light. In addition, evidence of leaks or fluid puddles is not as easy to spot.

Body Condition

Outside the car, look for signs of rust inside and around the wheel wells, window trim, and at the base of the doors. Look for discolorations or blisters in the paint and check the paint inside the trunk lid and hood. Is the paint all the same color? Are there any cracks or pits in the windshield? (In some states windshield "stars" will not pass inspection.)

Look at the finish on the car. If it appears dull, that could mean that the owner has not washed it regularly. (In many parts of the country acid rain and salt will, if not washed off frequently, eat into the paint and ruin its luster.)

Open and close doors. If they squeak or groan loudly, if they bind or lift when closing and opening, that might be the sign that the car has had major frame damage. Check to be sure that the door closes easily and fits flush.

Tires

When you look at the tires, check to see if they are all the same size and type. A mismatched set of tires can be dangerous and potentially cause problems in the rear axle. For example, you don't want to have radial tires mixed with bias-ply tires. (You'll find that tires are marked on the side to indicate if they are bias-ply or radial.)

Look for uneven or irregular tire wear on the outside or inside of the tread. This tells you that the tires were not balanced properly or that there is a front-end alignment problem. If you happen to own a tire-pressure gauge, you might want to check the pressure in the tires. If you find that they are all different, this too is a sign of owner indifference.

If the car sports a brand-new set of tires, that could mean you got lucky and the owner decided to sell the car after purchasing the tires. On the other hand, the seller may have put them on to cover an underlying problem. For example, if a car has had frame damage and is out of alignment, a new set of tires can help hide that fact from the unsuspecting buyer.

Generally, a set of tires should last for about 40,000 miles. If the seller does not know how many miles are on the tires, you can determine if there is a safe amount of tread left on the tire by taking a penny and inserting it so that Lincoln's head goes into the tread. If the tread is deep enough to cover his eyes, there are still some miles left on the tires.

Suspension

Press down hard several times in rapid succession on the corners of the car. Really get it rocking, then let go. The car should dip once and then settle back. If it continues to bounce, it probably needs new shocks, and that could cost you from $100 to $400 depending on the make and model. Faulty shocks are a serious defect and can cause poor handling and premature tire wear.

Pull on the top of each front tire. If you notice any play in the wheel or if there are any chunks, it could mean that you have bad bearings or that the suspension joints are in need of replacement.

Engine Condition

Ask a friend or the seller to start the car. The smoke from the tailpipe should be barely visible. If it comes out black, that probably means too much fuel is being supplied to the cylinders and an adjustment should be made by a mechanic. However, if it comes out blue, that means that the engine is burning oil. If you notice a puff of white smoke on a cold day, that's okay; however, if there continues to be white smoke after the car has warmed up, that could mean that engine coolant is leaking into the cylinder head. Bottom line is that blue and white smoke are frequently indications of major engine problems, and it might be well to cross that car off your list.

Listen for a backfire sound when you start the car. It is usually like a muffled popping under the hood. A backfire tells you that the engine or fuel system has a problem.

Engine RPMs

Once the car is started and has reached operating temperature (this should take only a few minutes even while standing still and assuming the weather is above freezing), the car should idle at a fairly steady rate of RPM (revolutions per minute). If the car seems to run very fast at idle, or if it seems to surge, there is something wrong.

For the mechanically minded: Keep in mind that smaller four-cylinder engines should idle somewhere at about 750 to 800 RPM. If the car has a tachometer (this is a gauge instrument that is usually marked RPM × 1000) you can read the RPM here. On an eight-cylinder engine the tachometer should read around 500 to 600 RPM. The main thing you want to determine is whether or not the car idles at a smooth, consistent rate.

Listening to the Engine

Open the hood and listen to the engine. If you hear a pinging or a loud clicking, thumping, or knocking sound, that could mean trouble.

Temperature Gauge

If the car has a temperature gauge, be sure that after a long period of running at idle the gauge does not rise into the red or danger zone. This would suggest that the car is running hot and that there is a problem ranging from a leak to the need for major repairs.

Ammeter or Voltage Gauge

Some cars have an indicator that lights up to alert you to a charging-system problem. This light will come on when you turn the key in the ignition and then, if the system is working properly, go out after the car has been started.

Many cars have either an ammeter or a voltage gauge on the instrument panel. These gauges monitor the operation of the charging system. The ammeter has a range from D, for discharge, to C, for charge. The voltage meter shows the state of charge of the battery. For example, in a 12-volt system a fully charged battery will show about 13 on the voltage meter.

Changes in the voltage-meter numbers indicate how much voltage is required by the battery to keep it fully charged. The alternator must then channel current to the battery for charging. This gauge serves as a constant monitor of the charging systems and should work properly.

The Exhaust System

Get down on your hands and knees and look under the car. The exhaust system, i.e., the engine pipe, catalytic convertor, muffler, and tailpipe should be well anchored to the under carriage. The system should be secured with proper hangers and attachment devices. If you find that it all seems to be hanging six inches below the car and has been secured with wire or makeshift hanging devices, you'll want to think twice about buying the car.

The Pressure Test

If the exhaust system looks okay, you may want to perform a pressure test, although this is something that you could have a mechanic do for you.

To perform the test yourself, hold a piece of wood or cardboard tightly against the end of the tailpipe—while the car is running—to stop the exhaust from leaving the tailpipe. The engine should begin to labor and sound like it's about to stall. That's good.

However, if the engine continues to run at the same rate, does not appear to labor, and you hear noises popping out from different mysterious places, the car probably has one or more leaks in the exhaust system—usually from rust-through. This will have to be repaired to prevent exhaust fumes from filtering into the passenger compartment. While on many cars this is not all that expensive, on others it could be a major bill. This is an item that should be checked by a trained mechanic.

Checking under the Hood

If the car has 10,000 miles or more on it, don't expect to see a clean engine compartment. On the other hand, if it looks *too* clean for its age, be a little suspicious. The owner might be trying to hide something. If you see signs of oil on the engine, that may mean some gaskets need to be replaced. Depending on which gaskets are causing the problem, this could be an expensive job. After you've taken the car out for a test drive—and a test drive is a must—recheck the engine for any signs of fresh oil leaks under the car.

Fluid Checks

The car should be warmed up before checking fluid levels.

1. Check the coolant

Note: Never remove the radiator cap if the engine is hot. Most cars today have white plastic reservoir for the coolant with an easy-to-remove snap-on top. The coolant should be of a uniform color. If you find that it appears to be streaked by a secondary color—like red—it could represent rust and indicate that the coolant hasn't been changed recently. Also, if you see a greenish-white, powderlike residue on the radiator, that could signal a leak.

2. Check the oil dipstick

If the oil seems to have a lot of sludge in it, that means the oil needs changing and it could also be an indication of the previous owner's poor attitude toward car maintenance. It could also indicate a potential expensive repair is not far down the road. If the oil is clear and translucent, it is probably brand-new.

If it is grayish or milky in color, it may mean coolant is getting into the engine, and this could signal a blown head gasket or possibly bad rings. In any event, it could mean a very costly repair. A further test is to check the color of the exhaust smoke when you start the engine. As explained above, white smoke—more than you'd expect to see on a cold day—means that coolant is getting into the cylinders.

3. Check the transmission fluid—automatic transmissions

If the car has an automatic transmission, check the fluid after you come back from your test drive and the car is thoroughly warmed up. (If you don't know where to find the automatic transmission dipstick, consult the owner's manual.) The fluid should be pink or reddish in color. If it's orange, that could signal transmission problems. Sniff the fluid on the dipstick. If it smells burned, that's a sign that the car may need a transmission overhaul. Note that front-wheel-drive transmission repairs can be expensive.

4. Look for fluid leaks under the engine compartment

Look under the engine compartment for any signs of fluid or liquid that has leaked from the car. If the fluid is slippery and oily, it's probably coolant, transmission fluid, motor oil, or brake fluid. Keep in mind that the presence of any of these fluids indicates a problem, and a repair shop visit will probably be necessary.

Battery

A battery should last from three to five years. The condition of the battery and the terminals might best be evaluated by a mechanic. You'll find "Check Battery" on your professional mechanic checklist.

EXTERIOR CHECK SHEET

(The items with "$" indicate potentially expensive repair costs.)

Exterior Body Condition	**Good**	**Fair**	**Poor**
Body condition(i.e., signs of rust)	❑	❑	❑
Finish and paint condition	❑	❑	❑
Door fit/open & close	❑	❑	❑

Tires	**Yes**	**No**	
Good condition	❑	❑	$
Pass "penny" test	❑	❑	
Even wear	❑	❑	
Matched set of tires	❑	❑	

Shock Absorbers	**Yes**	**No**	
Good condition	❑	❑	$

Exhaust System	**Yes**	**No**	
System appears well secured to car	❑	❑	$
Pressure test is good	❑	❑	$

Engine	**Pass**	**Fail**	
Smoke from tailpipe	❑	❑	$
Engine idle	❑	❑	
Knocking sounds	❑	❑	$
Engine runs hot at idle	❑	❑	$
Signs of oil on engine	❑	❑	$
Coolant low	❑	❑	
Oil is low	❑	❑	
Transmission fluid is orange	❑	❑	$
Transmission fluid smells burnt	❑	❑	$
Signs of leaking fluids under car	❑	❑	

5. Looking for Accident Damage

Has the Car Been in an Accident?

The majority of used cars have not been in a major accident. However, according to figures quoted by *60 Minutes*, of the millions of used cars that enter the market each year, somewhere around one million are, in fact, cars that have been in a major accident—and adjudged to have been "totaled" by the insurance company.

At the same time, don't discount a car because it has been in a minor accident. If a car has been in a "fender bender" and has been repaired properly, it may still represent a good value. In most cases, it's only when there's been *structural damage* or when the repairs have not been done correctly that you need to be concerned. If you find the car that you're considering has been in an accident severe enough to damage the frame, walk away!

How Can You Tell?

As we suggested earlier, it's not always easy—even for a professional. A good body shop can make even a beat-up car look very good. However, even they will have a hard time hiding their work from a professional mechanic. In the final analysis, it's always best to have your suspicions confirmed or alleviated by a professional. But before you take the car to a professional for evaluation, here are some things you can do which might help you decide for yourself if the car has been in a major accident.

1. Ask the seller point-blank

One of the easiest—and often most effective—ways is to look the seller directly in the eye and ask. You'd be surprised how honest people are when they're caught off guard.

2. Paint and paint-over spray

Take the time to look for the telltale signs of body repair. Check for paint-over spray. Often when a car is repainted you'll find paint-over spray on the door moldings, rubber gaskets, and on the edge of the windows. Open the rear doors and run your fingers over the rear of the door jamb. If you feel a thin line on the paint, that could be a masking tape line. Look at the color. Does the exterior match the color in the luggage compartment, rocker panels, and spare tire well? Look at the paint itself. Does it appear even?

3. Gaps and fit

Look at the gaps between the hood and the body and between the trunk lid and rear body panels. If you find that the gaps in the lines are wider on one side than the other, the car may have been in an accident. Check the fit and alignment of the trunk, hood, and doors to see if they are really mated. Here too, if the gaps are not the same, you can suspect body damage.

4. Open the doors

Do they creak, moan, or make other abnormal sounds? Do they seem somewhat difficult to open? These may be signs of severe body damage.

5. Crab test

If you have an opportunity to drive behind the car, notice whether or not it appears to be moving slightly sideways like a crab. If it does, this is frequently a sign of frame damage. A major concern related to frame damage is that it can affect the alignment, and that ultimately could be a major safety problem.

Ask to Have the Car Checked by "Car Fax"

There is a national service available to dealers in a majority of states called "Car Fax." This is a service that car dealers can use to determine if a car has been designated by an insurance company as a "totaled" (totally wrecked, beyond repair) vehicle. All they have to do is call in the Vehicle Identification Number, and Car Fax can make the check within minutes. In many states when an insurance company decides that a wrecked car is beyond repair or "totaled," the automobile's title is marked "salvage," meaning that it may have some parts and components that can be salvaged and used as spare parts.

As a buyer in a state that demands wrecked cars be marked "salvage," you should insist that the dealer check any car you might seriously consider buying with Car Fax and show you the report. If it's been marked "salvage," look for another car.

Note: Car dealers are not permitted to hold you hostage as a means of persuading you to buy their car. But some have been known to do exactly that!

According to a weekly tabloid report, a couple was actually held hostage in a dealership. As the offending dealer said, "We don't have guns. We don't put people up against the wall." Maybe not, but they did refuse to return the couple's car keys, which they had given to the salesman so that their car's trade-in value could be assessed. When the couple discovered that the $179 lease deal offered in the paper had *just been sold*, and that they would have to pay $100 a month more for a similar car, they asked for their keys back. The manager locked the office door and said he would not let them out until they signed the paperwork for the more expensive lease. The husband picked up the phone, dialed 911, and reported that he and his wife were being held hostage. The manager unlocked the door, threw them the keys, and told them to "Get out!"

6. The Interior Inspection

Important Note: At the end of this chapter you will find an *Interior Checklist*. This contains all the items discussed in this section. We suggest that you use the checklist during your evaluation of the interior of the car.

Odometer Mileage

According to the National Highway Traffic Safety Administration, as many as one of every four of the used cars that arrive on the market each year have had their odometers rolled back. While federal law prohibits this roll-back and while you can receive up to three times the actual value of any car that you buy if you can prove that a car has had its odometer tampered with, this illegal practice continues.

While even experts will tell you that it's not always possible to spot an odometer that has been "rolled back," there are signs that suggest the mileage may not be as low as shown.

- Look at the overall condition of the car both inside and out. Does it look its age? Check for wear on the seat, driver's-side door armrest, windowsill, and on the steering wheel.
- Look at the brake pedal pad. Does it seem overly worn? Generally, a pedal pad will last up to 50,000 miles before it shows wear.
- Look at the condition of the carpet under the pedals. If it seems excessively worn or if it has holes, chances are the car has in excess of 50,000 miles. Be aware that new carpeting may have been installed to help conceal signs of the true mileage.
- Look for lubrication or oil change stickers on the front door jamb and under the hood in the engine compartment. It's possible that whoever turned the mileage back might have forgotten to remove a sticker showing the mileage when oil was changed.
- Check the tires. Normally a set of tires should last up to 40,000 miles. If the car shows 20,000 miles and the tires are nearly bald or, if they appear brand-new, find out why.

Previous Maintenance and Care

Ideally, you want to buy a car that shows signs of the previous owner's pride of ownership. Ask to see the maintenance books. If they aren't available, or if they haven't been filled out, find out why and then be doubly diligent in your inspection.

Checking the Interior

Next, inspect the interior of the car. Check out everything that turns on and everything—like the seats—that was designed to move. At the same time, ask yourself, does the car look like the owner kept it in good condition?

Make a note of your first impression. Is the car clean—inside and out? How does it smell inside? If you smell mildew there could be a leak, or worse, the car could have been in a flood. Do you smell gas? Does it seem as if someone has just emptied a bottle of air freshener in the car? Unusual smells might suggest the seller's effort to hide a problem.

Sit in each seat and bounce. Is the seat firm? Check the operation of all the seat belts. Do they extend properly, fasten correctly, and remain snug against your body? Open the glove box and check for both the owner's manual and the maintenance record book.

Electrical System

Electrical problems can be one of the biggest headaches. Check to make sure that all the electrical accessories work—all the time. Turn them on one at a time and then all at the same time and in different series. Do they work? Do the lights dim when you turn everything on? Check all the exterior lights, including high and low beams, parking lights, turn signals, brake lights, back-up lights, and trunk light. Test the wipers and the washer system if the car has one.

Instrument Panel Lights and Gauges

Check all the lights and gauges on the instrument panel. The most important are the oil-pressure and temperature gauges. If the car has dash lights for these functions, the lights should come on when you turn the ignition key to the first position. If they do not light up, they may have burned out or there may be a problem. In either case, they should be fixed before you buy.

Trunk

The last "interior" inspection is in the trunk. Be sure that the tire tools—lug wrench, jack—are in the trunk. Be sure that the jack fits the jack points as described in the owner's manual and that the lug wrench fits the tire lugs. Lift the rug or mat and check for water and any signs of rust.

On the next three pages, you'll find a checklist that you may find helpful when performing your walk-around inspection.

INTERIOR CHECKLIST

(The items with "$" indicate potentially expensive repair costs.)

Books and Records	**Yes**	**No**
Owner's manual	❑	❑
Maintenance records	❑	❑

General Appearance	**Excel.**	**Good**	**Fair**	**Poor**
Upholstery wear/stains	❑	❑	❑	❑
Rug wear/stains	❑	❑	❑	❑
Overall impression of interior	❑	❑	❑	❑
Front seats—check how they move/adjust	❑	❑	❑	❑
Window cranks (manual)	❑	❑	❑	❑
Smell (mildew, oil, gas, etc.)	❑	❑	❑	❑

Mechanical	**OK**	**Problem**	
Glove box door	❑	❑	
Ashtrays	❑	❑	
Center armrests	❑	❑	
Exterior rearview mirrors	❑	❑	
Inside rearview mirror	❑	❑	
Inside door handles	❑	❑	
Seat adjustments	❑	❑	

Electrical	**OK**	**Problem**	
Headlights—high/low beam	❑	❑	
Parking lights	❑	❑	
Taillights	❑	❑	
Brake lights	❑	❑	
Turn signals	❑	❑	
Emergency flashers	❑	❑	
Wipers (washers)	❑	❑	
Heater/Blowers	❑	❑	$
Windshield defroster	❑	❑	
Air conditioner	❑	❑	$
Radio/Stereo	❑	❑	$
Lighter	❑	❑	
Glove box light	❑	❑	
Interior dome light	❑	❑	
Rearview mirror adjustment	❑	❑	
Rear defroster	❑	❑	
Horn	❑	❑	
Power windows	❑	❑	
Power seats	❑	❑	

Instrument Panel Indicator Lights/Gauges	**OK**	**Problem**	
Oil pressure	❑	❑	$
Temperature gauge/light	❑	❑	
High beam/Low beam indicator	❑	❑	
Turn signal indicators	❑	❑	
Battery charging system (Light/gauge)	❑	❑	
Speedometer	❑	❑	
Tachometer (RPM indicator)	❑	❑	

Trunk	**Yes**	**No**
Spare tire (full spare or space saver)	❑	❑
Jack	❑	❑
Lug wrench	❑	❑
Other tools	❑	❑

Important Note: Don't let the seller hurry you in this inspection or suggest that it isn't necessary. Remember whose money you're spending.

Unfortunately, some car salespeople still don't get it. According to industry sources, 50 percent of all cars are purchased by women—on their own. Eighty percent of all car purchases are directly influenced by women. Still, far too many car salesmen do not take women buyers seriously. Clearly, that's their loss. If, as a woman shopper, you find that you're confronted with a myopic, boorish, and chauvinistic salesman, take your checkbook someplace else. Truly, that is the best revenge.

7. The Test Drive

Important Note: On pages 138–139 you will find a Test Drive Checklist. This contains all the items discussed in this section. We suggest that you use the checklist during your evaluation of the car on your test drive.

Now it's time to take the car for a test drive. Our advice is to *never buy a car unless the seller lets you drive it.* Make sure he or she understands that you want plenty of time behind the wheel. Once around the block won't tell you anything other than the fact that the car moves. If they won't let you fully test-drive the car, say good-bye.

Leave the radio off until you want to hear it and only it. Otherwise, it may mask noises, vibrations, or other signals of trouble.

Drive the Car

During your test drive, notice if the car seems to drift to one side or the other. This could be a wheel-alignment problem or it could be a frame problem. Check to see if the wheel vibrates or shimmies at highway speeds either when going straight or when turning slightly left or right as when changing lanes.

The Brakes—Straight-Line Stopping

Find an empty road or even a large vacant parking lot. Check to be sure that no one is behind you, then accelerate to 40 miles per hour and apply firm pressure on the brakes. The car should come to a smooth, straight-line stop with no pull to either the left or right. Also, note the feel of the brake. If the car does not have anti-lock brakes, the pedal should feel firm under your foot. If it does have anti-lock brakes it should still feel firm, but if you happen to be in a situation where the ABS engages—i.e., during wheel lockup—expect to feel a rapid but steady vibration, under your foot. This is the ABS system at work.

Parking Brake

Be sure to check the holding power of the parking brake. Ideally, you should find a hill and, with your foot on the brake, put the car into neutral. Then apply the parking brake and lift your foot off the brake pedal. The car should remain stationary.

Check Acceleration

Using the same hill that you used in the above test—even if it's just a slight incline—stop at the bottom, then step on the gas gently. The car should move up the hill smoothly with no hesitation, surges, or strange sounds.

On a flat road, check for traffic to be sure you're clear and then floor the gas pedal and accelerate up to the legal speed limit. If the acceleration is uneven, very slow, and is accompanied by strange sounds, you might want to write the car off your list.

Engine Overheating

Drive the car out on the highway at the speed limit for ten minutes or more. During this time, notice if there are any strange sounds and check the temperature gauge to see if the car is running hot and overheating.

Bring the car to a stop in a safe place and let the engine idle with the air conditioner on high—if it has one—for five minutes, as it would were you stopped in traffic. Does it overheat?

Checking the Alignment and Suspension

Find a reasonably rough road and drive over it at about 25 miles an hour. Notice how the car feels. Does it seem to hold a straight line? If it drifts back and forth, it may have an alignment problem. If you notice that there are times, especially over rough road surfaces, when the car jumps or seems to swing back and forth, you may have a problem with your shocks. Be alert for any loud rattles or squeaks.

On a smooth road—again, with no traffic—accelerate to about 25 miles an hour, slightly release your grip on the steering wheel, and see if the car tends to veer or drift to the left or right.

If it does, it's reasonable to assume that the car needs to be aligned. In some cases it could also point to bad tires, worn steering linkage, or defective suspension components.

Detecting Transmission Problems

As you're driving and the car is changing gears, listen for any unusual sounds. The transmission shifting should be quiet on automatic-shifting cars. Again, find someplace without traffic and stop the car. Slowly drive the car forward a few feet, stop, shift into reverse, and back up a few feet. Repeat this several times. The shifting should be smooth without noise, clanks, or thuds. The transmission should never seem to be "slamming" into gear. Then start up again and accelerate slowly. Feel the transmission shift into second, third, and fourth. Then depress the accelerator. Does the transmission down-shift to the next lower gear smoothly and without making any unusual sounds?

Standard Transmission

If the car has a standard transmission, you should find it easy to shift gears. Assuming you are proficient at using a clutch, the process should be smooth. You should not feel the gears grab, slip, or hear them chatter as you move from one gear to the next.

Test the transmission on a hill. As you shift through the gears, notice if the clutch appears to slip. If it does, this could mean a problem with the pressure plate or a leak that is affecting the clutch disc itself.

Here's another test: While driving on an uncrowded road with a speed limit of 55, accelerate to 35 MPH and put the transmission into high gear—fourth or fifth. After checking to be sure you're clear of all traffic and have an open road ahead of you, push down hard on the accelerator. If the engine "revs" and does not accelerate immediately, the clutch is probably slipping and will need repair.

Driving Evaluation

On the test drive, find a major highway and accelerate up to the speed limit and notice how the car behaves. Certain problems will show up only at highway speeds. For example, shimmies in the car and in the steering wheel, vibrations, wind noise, etc., can often only be detected at over 50 miles per hour.

Steering

Steering wheel "play" should be within reasonable boundaries. There should not be more than an inch or two of play before the wheel clearly responds to your steering input. If the steering is what the experts call "sloppy," the car will wander or drift, and there may be any number of expensive problems to fix. Check to see how hard it is to turn the wheel when the car is stopped, as if you were getting ready to parallel-park. If the car has power steering and you're having to put extra effort into turning the wheel, there's a problem. Even if the car does not come with power steering, you don't want a steering wheel that is overly difficult to turn when the car is stopped.

Retest the Accessories

During the test drive, retest all the accessories. Turn on the air conditioner and see if the car begins to overheat. Then turn on all the lights and electrical equipment to see if the charging system can keep up with the drain.

Check the Cruise Control

If the car has cruise control, accelerate up to the speed you wish to maintain and set the control. Make sure that it holds speed up and down moderate hills. Check the acceleration and deceleration buttons. Then be sure that the system disengages when you touch the brake pedal.

Engine Restart Test

When you arrive back at the seller's lot or home, turn off the engine, wait two minutes, and then restart it. Some recent-model cars with fuel-injection systems have "hot start" problems. This test is a good way to check for that condition.

Recheck the Fluids

After the test drive, open the hood and check the engine. Is there any sign of fluid leaks in the engine compartment or on the ground under the car?

TEST-DRIVE EVALUATION CHECKLIST

(The items with "$" indicate potentially expensive repair costs.)

Brakes	**Pass**	**Fail**	
Straight-line stopping	❑	❑	
Brake pedal firm	❑	❑	$
Parking brake holds	❑	❑	
Acceleration			
Hill test	❑	❑	
Acceleration	❑	❑	
Highway speed test (sounds/overheating)	❑	❑	$
Car at idle (overheating test)	❑	❑	
Alignment and Suspension			
Rough road at 25 MPH test—holds straight line	❑	❑	$
Rattles or squeaks	❑	❑	
Steering—veer/drift test	❑	❑	$
Transmission			
No unusual sounds	❑	❑	$
Shift quality	❑	❑	$
Back and forth test—no clanks or thuds	❑	❑	$
Standard Transmission			
Shifting test—smooth, no grab, slip, or chatter	❑	❑	$
Hill test—clutch does not slip	❑	❑	$
Driving Evaluation			
Highway speed performance test	❑	❑	
Shimmy and vibration test	❑	❑	$
Steering			
Steering input—no sloppiness	❑	❑	
Wheel turn test—car stopped	❑	❑	
Turn wheel hard left/right and check for squeal	❑	❑	
Retest the Accessories			
Accessory retest—turn everything on	❑	❑	
Charging system	❑	❑	

Cruise Control

Holds speed	❑	❑
Disengages at touch of brake	❑	❑

Engine Restart test

Engine restarts without hesitation	❑	❑ $

Recheck the Fluids

Oil level	❑	❑
Coolant level	❑	❑
Transmission fluid level	❑	❑
Evidence of drips or leaks underneath	❑	❑ $

Important Note: Anytime you need to start the car, either during the walk-around or for the test drive, you should be the one to do it. However, the owner should tell you if there are any tricks to starting such as having the seat belts on, the transmission in park, a foot on the brake, etc.

8. The Professional Mechanic's Inspection

Important Note: At the end of this chapter you will find a list of test items for the Professional Mechanic Inspection. We suggest that you give a copy to the mechanic as a guide.

If the car has passed your inspection up to this point, keep in mind that it is still a good, potentially money-saving idea to have the car checked out by a qualified mechanic. What follows is a description of the items you should ask the mechanic to check.

Brake Check

The mechanic should take the wheels off and check the condition of the brake pads and rotors (or brake drums if the car has the drum system). Worn rotors sometimes have to be replaced before new brake pads are installed. The rotors alone can cost more than $200.

Engine Test

Your mechanic can perform a number of engine tests including a compression check. The purpose of this test is to tell you how well the engine is able to hold the air and gas mixture that is ignited by the spark plugs when that mixture is compressed by the engine's pistons. A simple rule of thumb is that all the cylinders should have approximately the same compression-test readings. If they vary by more than 10 percent, the cylinder may have a leak, which means that the engine is losing power and wasting fuel.

Charging System

The mechanic should perform a charging-system test to make sure that the battery is being charged properly. There are also specific battery-condition tests that will give you an idea of how long the car's battery will last. With the right equipment, the mechanic can decide if the battery will hold a charge.

Cooling System

The mechanic should examine all hoses and clamps and inspect them for leaks. Older hoses increase the possibility of rupture, and that is definitely something you'd like to avoid. By using a special pump, the mechanic can pressurize the system and check it for leaks.

Emission-Level Test

Unless the car is very old, it will have some type of emissions-control system. With the right equipment, a mechanic can tell you if the system is working properly and whether or not the car will pass your state's emission test—if it has one. Excessive emissions are also a good indication of the condition of the catalytic converter.

Other Checks

Once the car is up on the lift, all visible brake lines, fuel lines, fuel pumps, etc., should be inspected. With the wheels off the ground, the wheel bearings can be checked for wear or excessive play. Most mechanics can just pull on a tire and determine if there is a bearing problem.

Also, be sure the mechanic checks:

- Exhaust system
- Alignment
- Tires
- Underbody rust
- Accident damage
- Suspension
- Rear axle
- Shocks
- Leaks
- Odometer accuracy

The Benefit to You

The key to the cost-effective use of a mechanic is to make your own evaluations first and eliminate from consideration those cars with obvious problems and in need of expensive repairs. When you finally settle on a car you like, before you "fall in love," arrange for the professional inspection.

What Do You Do with the Mechanic's Report?

The information that you get from the report should help you in any one of four ways:

1. It can confirm that you've got your hands on a good car and a good buy.
2. It can make you aware that the car is unsafe, unfit, or in need of expensive repairs and should be rejected from your consideration.
3. The information can help you in your negotiation. Depending on what is found, you might be able to use this information to help justify a lower price or, at the very least, to get the owner to agree to make the repairs as a condition of the sale.
4. A complete professional evaluation will almost certainly tell you whether or not the car will pass state inspections. If it won't, you can reasonably require the seller to make the necessary repairs to bring it up to inspection standards or, at the very least, to adjust the asking price accordingly.

In any event, because experts have both the knowledge and equipment to make effective evaluations, it's well worth your time and money to enlist their services.

PROFESSIONAL MECHANIC'S INSPECTION

Test Items	**OK**	**Needs Repair**	**Est. Cost**
Brake check	❑	❑	$ ________
Engine test	❑	❑	$ ________
Charging system	❑	❑	$ ________
Cooling system test	❑	❑	$ ________
Spark plugs	❑	❑	$ ________
Emission-level test	❑	❑	$ ________
Drive axle	❑	❑	$ ________
Suspension	❑	❑	$ ________
Alignment	❑	❑	$ ________
Tires	❑	❑	$ ________
Shocks	❑	❑	$ ________
Exhaust system	❑	❑	$ ________
Brake lines/Fuel lines	❑	❑	$ ________
Underbody rust	❑	❑	$ ________
Accident damage	❑	❑	$ ________
Total Repair Cost Estimate			$ ________

Odometer accuracy ❑ Appears accurate ❑ Questionable

Explain:

9. Negotiating Techniques

Herb Cohen, the author of *You Can Negotiate Anything*, once told us a story about shopping for a car. He sat down with the salesman and, after a period of conversation, asked, "What's the 'real' price of this car?" The salesman responded by giving him a discounted price. Herb then asked him: "Okay, but what's the 'real, *real*' price of the car?" The salesman responded with yet another discounted figure. Herb put one more question to him: "What's the 'real, *real, REAL*' price of the car?" To that the salesman responded: "For that price you'll have to ask my manager."

We offer this story to illustrate that few if any cars are purchased for their asking price. About the only cars that "get retail" are those that are in high demand and short supply—usually imported sports cars.

All other cars, both new and used, are bought on sale, at discount, or after a period of negotiation.

The Keys to Getting a Good Deal

What follows are some fundamental rules that we suggest you follow if you want to be successful in buying cheap and reducing your risk.

Rule 1. Have the money in hand

One of the keys to buying cheap lies in having the ability to write a check on the spot. Cash in hand always gets a seller's attention. Remember, the seller never knows when—or even *if*—the next buyer will come along.

Rule 2. Be flexible

While you may have a make, model, year, and color in mind when you begin to shop, it's a good idea to remain flexible. Great deals don't always arrive exactly as you envisioned them. We suggest that the condition of the car and the price are much more important than things like the interior and exterior color.

Rule 3. Be patient

Often to get a truly great deal, you have to be patient. You may have to go through any or all of the buying strategies we've outlined a number of times before you make a deal with which you're truly satisfied. If you're buying from a private owner, you may simply have to wait the seller out. Don't be in a hurry to write that check. If you find yourself in a situation where you're more anxious to buy than the seller is to sell, your chances of buying cheap are between slim and none. The key to finding a really good deal is being in the right place at the right time, and that requires both persistence and patience.

Rule 4. Be informed

Of all the advice we can offer, the most important is to be in command of all the critical information: Specifically:

- *Know the actual wholesale value of the car you want to buy.* Get all the figures before you shop. If you don't have the numbers before you begin your negotiations, you run the risk of putting yourself at a negotiation disadvantage before you even begin.
- *Know the true condition of the car before you buy.* Follow the inspection sheets and then, if the car passes your inspection, take it to a professional. As we've mentioned more than once, the failure to inspect a used car is one of the most common mistakes that used-car buyers make. In far too many cases, the mistake ends up costing them money.

Rule 5. Plan ahead

If you are buying from a private owner or a dealership, plan your strategy. If you are buying from an auction, plan your downside escape.

Rule 6. Be prepared to walk from the deal

If it doesn't feel right, if something seems amiss, if your gut seems to be telling you that your prospective purchase is a mistake—walk away. You can always find another car.

Negotiate with a Smile . . . They Can't Deal with That

When it comes to dealership salespeople, keep in mind that one of your most effective tactics is always to be pleasant and remain calm. There is nothing more difficult than dealing with a person who cannot be intimidated, rushed, pushed, or panicked. It's very hard to negotiate with nice people who simply refuse to negotiate.

When they tell you that you're not being reasonable, that you've got to meet them halfway, that they'll lose money on your deal, just smile politely and repeat: *"You have my offer. I'd like to see you earn something for all the time you've spent with me. But this is the limit of my budget."*

Summary

In sum, the key to these rules is to *follow* them. If you permit yourself to compromise or give in on even one, you dramatically decrease the odds of getting a good car at a great price.

How Much Should You Negotiate?

That really depends on how much time you want to invest, how much you enjoy the process, and how good you are. It's our suggestion that if you're like most of us, you should realize that if you're negotiating with a car dealer, you're dealing with someone who has a lot more experience than you do when it comes to negotiating. We know of car salespeople who work very hard to create the impression that their customers have negotiated a truly once-in-a-lifetime deal. They will groan and show signs of great internal pain as they slowly reduce their price and appear to give away the store to the buyer. Seldom are they giving away anything.

Should you up your bid one more time?

That's for you to decide. Ideally, you should raise your bid only once. A second raise should be made only if it means striking a compromise price that will close the deal on terms satisfactory to you. Remember however, once a negotiator feels that he can move you off your price, even a little, he will read that as a signal to keep on hammering.

Whatever you do, don't start feeling sorry for the salespeople. They don't feel sorry for you. They know, as you should know, that this is a bargain-based business and the best bargainer wins.

Prenegotiation Tips

1. Do your homework first. Don't walk onto a lot and begin to negotiate a price without having all the facts discussed earlier in this segment. Specifically:
   - The local market value of the car
   - The results of your inspection
2. Plan your buying strategy ahead of time.
3. Remember that you have the upper hand. You are the person with the money. While you can find many more used cars to consider, the seller will have a much harder time finding more buyers.
4. Have the money (or at least a preliminary approval for a loan) and be ready to act. Having money in hand—be it in cash, check, or credit card—is a powerful tool.

5. Put a limit on what you're willing to spend ahead of time. When the negotiation reaches that point—stop. Make it clear to the seller that you've got the money, you're ready to do business at your price, or you're going to look elsewhere.

During the Negotiation—Tips

1. Make up your mind to be pleasant, friendly, and uncombative. It is very hard for a salesperson to negotiate with a nice person who simply refuses to be "bumped."
2. Never let the seller know exactly what you're thinking. The only time you want to appear to reveal your true feelings is when it comes to pointing out flaws or problems in the seller's car. Consult the ploys and countertactics in "About Buying New Cars."
3. Never divulge what you're really willing to pay. If you are on a dealer's lot, one of the first questions the salesperson will ask is: "What are you looking to spend?" If you have not as yet settled on a car and are "just looking," you might find it to your advantage to give the salesperson a price range. However, offer a price range that is twenty to thirty percent higher than your actual target price. The reason is because any car the salesperson shows you is going to be priced about twenty to thirty percent above what the dealer is willing to take.
4. Always be ready to walk away. Be nice. Be polite. In fact, if you're up to it, feign some personal pain that you were unable to make the deal. As you walk away, walk slowly. If you're in a dealership, take your time getting off the lot. Chances are the salesperson will make one last attempt to reach an agreeable price. Remember, no dealer and no private buyer wants to see someone who has the money and is ready to buy today walk away from a possible sale.

Other Negotiation Strategies

The Negative Walk-around

One effective technique to use early in the buying process is called the "negative walk-around." This is a technique in which you casually mention every flaw you find. If you see a paint chip, look at it closely, touch it, and be sure that the seller sees that you've noticed. A simple *"Hmmmmm,"* or *"Too bad!"* or *"What happened here?"* will make it clear to the buyer that you've noticed the flaw and signal that you are going to be looking for a reduction in the asking price.

They Who Speak First

During the negotiation, whether it's your first offer or a counter offer, state your price and then say nothing until the seller responds. There's a saying in the car business that "He who talks first, loses." Always make the salesperson meet your counter offer with one of his or her own. If the seller responds by saying something to the effect, *"Can you go a little higher?"* or *"That's really less than we have in the car,"* just hold your ground until you get a reduced figure.

Buying from a Private Owner

Act I

The strategy we're about to outline is designed to help you get the best deal possible from a private owner. This a fairly aggressive strategy, and many people may not feel comfortable with it. However, we urge you to read it and select those ideas and concepts which you can build into your own buying strategy.

Don't Knock the Car

Some people think that they can reduce a seller's resistance to making a deal by insulting the car and suggesting that it's not worth the asking price. Don't do that. Remember, they've been living with the car for several years, and any insult or disparaging remark directed to the car is very often perceived by the seller as a personal insult to them.

This does not mean, however, that you should not conduct a negative walk-around. By all means, you want the seller to know that you are aware of all the car problems, big and small. The key is to adopt a tone of commiseration—*"Oh, wow, who did that to you?"* Or *"It's obvious you've really kept this car in great condition. What a shame that your service mechanic didn't pick up this oil leak."* Even if you know that the seller probably is fully aware of the problem and may well be the cause, always help him or her save face by blaming some third party—real or imagined—for the problem.

When you get ready to do your inspection, tell the seller that you really got taken one time and that you promised yourself, your wife, your dog—anyone you can think of—that you would not buy another car without a complete inspection first by you and then by a professional mechanic. Might as well find out up front if there's going to be any resistance to taking the car to a shop for an evaluation.

We recommend that you tell the seller exactly what you're going to do. Show him or her the checklists. If they know there's a problem with the car that they've neglected to mention, you might well see a few beads of sweat pop out on the seller's forehead.

Make your inspection

Do your inspection as outlined in this segment and keep notes. Remember, every problem, every sign of wear, every scratch, becomes fuel for your negotiation.

Take as much time as you can afford. Wear the seller out with your attention to detail. But keep reminding him or her you're a real buyer and the cash is in the bank just waiting for you to write a check. You might want to insert comments like:

"I like cash deals, how about you?"

"I really want to get that money out of the bank before my wife (or husband or whomever) decides to spend it on the house."

The message will get through.

If the car passes your inspection, make arrangements to have it evaluated by a professional. As we suggested earlier, leave your car for ransom if that appears practical and safe. On your way to the mechanic, you might, as we explained earlier, want to stop in at a couple of used-car lots to check the going market value of the car. Let's say that their estimates average about $9,100. Chances are they believe they can get a couple of dollars more at auction. Once the inspection is complete, sit down with the seller and let him or her know what you found. Go over the mechanic's report and the estimated repair costs. Be sure you point out all the problems. But do so in a positive way. Never blame the seller. Use phrases like:

"Well, you expect some wear and tear."

"What people will do to your car in a parking lot."

Finally, pose this question:

"If we were to agree on a price, would you rather make these repairs or would you prefer just to deduct them from the price?" You might also offer to let the seller call the mechanic to verify that the repair estimate and the mechanic are legit.

Getting the seller to pay for repairs

Chances are the last thing the buyer wants is to be bothered with making repairs, and he or she is certainly not interested in investing any more money in the car. So right away you've established a discount that you can factor in later. To cement the verbal agreement, make a big note on the mechanic's checklist as the seller watches:

SELLER AGREES TO DEDUCT PRICE OF REPAIRS.

It's not necessary that the seller sign it. Just be sure he or she is fully aware that you consider it to be part of the deal.

Getting to "least"

At this point, let's say you've established that it's going to take $500 to complete the repairs. After writing down the "note" about the seller's willingness to pay for the repairs, put all your paperwork and notes away and abruptly change the subject. Talk about anything, but get off the subject of the car. Your objective is to relieve the seller of having to think about the $500. What he or she doesn't know is that you've already begun the negotiation and that the first round goes to you.

Without warning and maybe even in mid-sentence, abruptly turn to the buyer and in a pleasant, almost matter-of-fact way ask:

"What's the very least you'll take for this car?"

Say nothing until the seller responds. Stare him or her right in the eye with an expression that says after all this time you and I are not buyer and seller—we're friends. No matter how great the temptation, say *nothing*!

"Well, I'd like to get $12,000," the seller says or *"I'm asking $12,000."* Score another one for your side. But you're not done with this tactic. Before he or she gets a chance to say something about your offer, come back with:

"I know what you'd like to get. But what is it that you'll take?"

If the seller responds with a number, you can generally assume that it is not the least he or she will take. But no matter what figure the seller gives you (it might be the asking price), just shake your head sadly and say:

"You know, I was looking at a car similar to this at a dealership the other day and while it had a few more miles—not many more—the price was about the same as yours. I figured that since a private seller doesn't have the same kind of expense a dealer has, I might be able to get a better price. Plus, they offer a warranty."

At this point the seller is probably going to want to know what you plan to spend. What this confirms is that his "very least" is not his very least.

At this point you act a little embarrassed and say, *"You know, I am a little embarrassed. I was hoping that you might be willing to let it go for around $7,500."* Then add quickly. *"And I'll give you a check right here, today."*

At this point the owner is going to say that there is no way he or she can part with the car for that price or that what you're offering is below book value, etc., etc.

This is where you make your exit. Act I is over. However, as you leave, you want to firmly plant the idea that you're going to see if you can come up with some additional money.

Act 2

Now you start calling . . . as a friend. Tell the seller that you've done some research and discovered that the wholesale value of the car is $9,100. Say that you have scraped together some more cash and can offer them $8,765. Don't quote a round number. It should sound as if you've really scraped together the cash from your piggy bank. This conveys the impression to the seller than you're about as far as you can go financially and that if he wants to get rid of the car, he's going to have to deal with you in that range.

Candidly, the seller may simply turn you down and revert to the $12,000 figure. If so, be prepared to walk away. However, if this person has had the car on the market for a week or more, he or she will be very anxious to sell it. And unless it's a high-demand car, they may wonder if you're the last potential buyer they will see. Plus, now that they know the wholesale value is only $9,100, the need to make a deal may well motivate them to continue to negotiate.

"Look," the seller might say, *"if you can come up to $9,300, we have a deal."*

You can counter with $9,100 or $9,200 to be sure that you're not spending any more than you have to. Let's assume for this discussion that you settle on $9,300. It's time to pay for the car.

Act 3

After you've gone over all the papers and the title and checked the vehicle identification number (VIN) against the one on the car, you're ready to part with the money. You give the seller a certified check or money order for $8,800.

"We agreed on $9,300!" might be the response.

At this point you pull out the mechanic's checklist and your note that the seller has agreed to deduct the $500 for repairs.

If the seller gets upset, just point to the note on the inspection sheet. If he or she lives up to the agreement, fine, you've done well. If the seller tries to back out, you can either offer to absorb part of the $500, or you can walk. If you walk, do so slowly and after showing a lot of disappointment and sadness. As you start to leave, make it clear that you'd still like to make a deal and if the owner should have second thoughts, you're only a phone call away. This is one of those situations that requires you to play it by ear.

Not your style? No problem!

Again, while this may not be your style, you can see via this example how having a pre-purchase buying strategy can work to your advantage. A variation on this scenario might also be helpful in dealing with used-car salespeople. Especially if you're dealing at the end of the month.

10. Before Closing the Deal

Taking Delivery—What to Check

Before you sit down to complete the paperwork, it's a good idea to take a walk around the car. Check to see if there any new dents or dings. Then take the car out for one last test drive. Make sure that nothing has happened since you last saw it.

Open the hood and check to be sure that no oil leaks have developed.

If repairs or maintenance were to be performed, ask for proof that it was done as agreed.

Checking for the Proper Title

Always be sure that the seller has the title. Ask to see it and compare the vehicle identification number (VIN) on the title to the one on the car. In recent years the VIN numbers have been placed so that you can read them by looking through the windshield on the driver's side. If the numbers don't match, say good-bye.

BEFORE YOU SIGN

1. Read everything . . . twice!
2. Be sure that anything you sign has all the blanks filled in.
3. Be sure that the wording on any agreement, bill of sale, and/or warranty is specific, clear, and exact in its meaning.
4. An Odometer Mileage Statement must be provided stating that, to the best of the seller's knowledge, the odometer has not been tampered with. The odometer statement can be made part of the bill of sale. (In some states this is part of the title.)
5. Be sure you fully understand and agree with the warranty—if it has one. (See explanation of warranties in Chapter 2 of this section)
6. Bill of sale should include the following items:
   - Date of sale
   - Year, make, and model description
   - Tag number and state of registration
   - Vehicle identification number
   - Odometer reading
   - Amount paid for car and type of payment

- Conditions of the sale, if any
- Seller's and buyer's names, addresses, and phone numbers

7. Be sure that the title has the correct VIN on it.
8. Examine the title to be sure that the seller has clear ownership of the vehicle. Determine if there is a bank lien against the car. Is there a co-owner? Is the name of the seller the same as on the title?

PRE-CLOSING CHECKLIST

Be sure the seller gives you:

Title with VIN corresponding to car ❑
Odometer statement ❑
Warranty agreement or service contract ❑
Owner's manual ❑
Maintenance books and records ❑

Be sure to:

Register vehicle ❑
Pay sales tax ❑
Get state inspection if required ❑

11. When to Walk Away from a Used Car

There are no hard and fast rules about when to walk away from a used car, but here are some guidelines that we suggest you consider:

It's Time to Take a Walk . . .

1. Anytime you feel that the seller has misrepresented the car in terms of its mileage, history, or condition.
2. Anytime you find evidence of potential engine problems like blue or white smoke or evidence of oil leaks.
3. Anytime you sense that the car is "just not right."
4. Anytime there is evidence that the car has been in a major accident.
5. Anytime the seller refuses to allow you adequate time to test-drive the car or refuses to let you have the car inspected by a mechanic of your choice.
6. Anytime you discover that the title is incorrect or seems to have a problem.
7. Anytime the deal seems to be just too good to be true (it probably is).

III

About Leasing

To Lease or Not to Lease

1. Introduction

Question: Does Leasing Make Sense for You?

The answer: Unfortunately, it's an inconclusive "it depends."

The only way for you to answer the question satisfactorily is to understand how a lease works, how the payments are determined, and how to estimate your total out-of-pocket costs over the term of the lease.

A note: If, as you read this section, you get the impression that Automotive Consumer Information Service, Inc. is anti-lease, that is not the case. What we are is for knowing the facts. Unfortunately, in today's market many of the advertised leases are simply "come-ons" designed to get you into the dealership. Once in the "dealer's lair," you may find there are more out-of-pocket costs than the advertisement would have you believe. You may even find that the vehicle in the ad isn't available.

Having made that point, understand that leasing can be financially very beneficial in many situations. For example: A recent ad from Ford Motor Company offered a three-year lease on a $12,345 car for just $1,000 down and $169 per month. To buy that same car with $1,000 down and a three-year loan at 8 percent would cost just over $320 per month. Even were you to extend the loan to five years, the payment would be about $35 more per month than the lease. The only difference, of course, is at the end of the lease, you don't own the car.

Leasing Is Growing

Currently, over 1.7 million people are opting to lease vs. buy. And with the growing popularity of used-car leasing, the number should grow substantially. The keys to smart leasing—the decision to lease and the structure of the lease deal—are not much different from a purchase situation. The informed auto lessee makes it a point to know as much about leasing as possible and then to make decisions with the benefit of that knowledge and information.

2. Leasing Terminology

If you're going to play their leasing games, you'd better speak their language.

Base Monthly Payment The base payment is the amount being applied to the depreciation of the car over the term of the lease plus the amount being applied to the lease company's fee. (This "fee" is often mistakenly considered to be "interest." It is not. It is exactly what it says it is: a fee.)

The final lease might incorporate other charges, costs, taxes, and fees spread out over the term. But those are not part of the base.

"Cap Cost" or Capitalized Cost The equivalent of the selling price.

Cap Cost Reduction A discount off the list price. Often when the manufacturer is subsidizing a lease, you'll see a statement like: "Based on 90 percent of the capitalized cost." What this means is that the lease is figured on the list price less 10 percent. Or you might see it expressed this way: *"MSRP $42,000 including destination charges. Monthly payments based on a capitalized cost of $37,000."* You can read that as a $5,000 discount off the list price.

Down Payment The down payment is the amount of cash that the lessor may ask the lessee to pay upon signing the lease agreement. In most leases this down payment can be factored into the monthly payments if you so desire. It can also be negotiated.

The effect of the down payment is both to reduce the "perceived" amount of the customer's monthly cost and to put more money in the lessor's hands up-front.

Deficiency The difference between the amount owed on the lease and the actual cash value of the car. This is the amount that a customer who wishes to terminate the lease early must pay.

Early Termination Ending a lease before its term has run, which, we would add, can be very expensive.

Equity The difference between what a vehicle is worth at any given time and the amount owed.

Gap Insurance An insurance policy designed to cover the "gap" between what conventional replacement insurance will pay for—should the car be stolen or wrecked—and the amount owed on the lease.

> If you lease a car, van, or truck, gap insurance is a must. If it is not provided by the lease company, then you should arrange for it on your own.
>
> Here's why: Let's assume that your leased vehicle is stolen or that a tree falls on it and totally wrecks the car. Your normal vehicle insurance should reimburse you for the value of the vehicle at the time of the loss. However, in all probability, the insurance coverage or payment to you will amount to less than what it will cost you to terminate the lease. This gap can represent several to many thousands of dollars.
>
> To reiterate: The gap insurance covers the difference between the vehicle's value and the amount owed on the lease.

Lease There are basically two types of leases. The most common—and the only one you should probably ever consider—is the closed-end lease. The other, which we'll cover in a moment, is the open-end.

The *closed-end* lease is an agreement in which the customer has the right to walk away from the vehicle at the end of the lease with no additional charges except for excess mileage or excess wear and tear.

At the end of the majority of closed-end leases, the lessee is given the opportunity to buy the car for an amount equal to the residual value of the car as stated in the lease contract. If the residual value is higher than that actual current wholesale market value, the lessee can simply walk away with no other obligation. If the residual value is lower than the current wholesale market value of the car, the lessee might want to buy the vehicle and try to sell it for a profit. This doesn't happen very often, but it does on occasion and we'll cite an example later.

> Typically, a lease permits the lessee to drive an average of 15,000 miles per year without a mileage penalty. Every mile thereafter is charged to the lessee at a "cents per mile" rate, which should be clearly stated in the lease contract. Always be sure that you know exactly how many free miles are allowed and what the penalty will be for excess mileage.

The *open-end* lease contract is one in which the customer shares in the resale value of the car at the end of the lease. If the car is worth more than the guaranteed residual, the customer receives the profit. If the car is worth less than the residual, the customer has to come up to the difference. For that reason, one of the primary advantages of the closed-end lease is that the lessee walks away from the car at the end of the lease and is not responsible for making up the difference between the current market value and the projected residual. We advise you to think long and hard before agreeing to an open-end lease. It is a gamble.

Lessee The person (you) who leases the car.

Lessor The leasing company.

Mileage Allowance The number of miles you can drive a leased car per year without penalty.

Money Factor A money factor is simply a number used to determine the fee that a lease company will charge you for "renting" their car.

The lower the money factor, the less of a fee the lessor is taking. One way to make an easy comparison between the money factor charged for a lease and the interest rate that you'd be charged in a purchase finance agreement is to multiply the money factor by 24.

A money factor of .0026 × 24 equals 6.2, which in percent is approximately the equivalent of a 6.2 percent finance interest rate. A money factor of .0065 × 24 would be the approximately equivalent of a 15.6 percent interest rate.

While these are not exact percentage equivalents, they are very close. Close enough to make a quick determination as to whether or not the lease "fee" is competitive with the interest rates charged for loan agreements. When comparing or analyzing lease payments, you should always ask for the money factor and use it as the basis for comparison.

Normal Wear and Tear The amount of physical deterioration to the car that would normally be expected to occur over the period of the lease.

> It's a good idea to have "wear and tear" explained to you in advance of signing. Mercedes-Benz, which many regard as the class of the industry, defines excess wear and tear as follows: *"Consists only of mechanical failure of and/or required replacement or major repair to the major drive line components (engine, transmission, differential) not covered by warranty and existing substantial structural or body damage."*

Residual Value The wholesale value of the car at the end of the lease period as estimated by the leasing company at the time the lease is originated.

Single Payment Recently, manufacturers have been offering *single-payment* leases. These leases permit the lessee to pay the total amount of lease payments (plus any down payment, fees, etc.) up front in one single payment. The lessor often tosses in a small discount as an added incentive. This has, it would seem, only marginal value. If you have money sitting around earning low interest, and the single payment, less the discount, is equal to or higher than the interest that money would earn, the single payment might make sense. If you're interested in this type of lease, we advise you to discuss it with your accountant.

Subsidized Lease When the manufacturer lowers the lease rate or reduces the cap cost of the car to make it more attractive to the customer.

Upside Down A term the industry uses to describe a customer who owes more on the car—be it financed or leased—than the car is worth in actual cash value.

3. The Basics of Leasing

The Case For and Against

In a general sense, the case *for* leasing is that you are paying for only that depreciable portion of the car you use. The case *against* leasing is that you never own the car, van, or truck. The case *for* leasing says that you are not tying up as much of your capital as you would were you to finance the vehicle. The case *against* leasing says that once you've committed to a lease, you are truly *committed* because it can be expensive to terminate early.

From the dealer's perspective, the case for leasing is that leases generally are more profitable to the dealership than other financial agreements. Furthermore, as one manufacturer's spokesman was quoted in *Business Week*, "Leasing provides camouflage for price increases."

Two of the great allies of car salespeople are "the uninformed customer" and the customer's "ego-driven fear" of appearing not to understand the various components of the deal. Since most people don't want to look stupid in the eyes of a salesperson, they let themselves be intimidated out of asking questions and of asking for—even demanding—a simplified, step-by-step explanation of all the factors that go into making up a lease payment. Possibly no other transaction creates the opportunity for more confusion.

Sometimes, the desire to drive an exciting car for a low monthly payment clouds a person's better judgment. As a result, more often than not they:

1. Fail to recognize that, except where a discount is advertised, lease payments are based on the full list price of the vehicle.
2. Fail to recognize that virtually everything about a lease is negotiable.
3. Never stop to analyze the total out-of-pocket costs they will be responsible for over the life of the lease.
4. Never stop to consider the penalties for terminating a lease early.

Keep in mind that your ultimate objective is to drive a good vehicle and have a pleasant ownership experience. Too many people are so focused on the payments that they forget to make a sound and intelligent evaluation of the car and its ability to satisfy their needs. As you negotiate your lease, keep one very important thing in mind: *"You will not be driving a 'payment' off the lot."* You will be driving a car, van, or truck that you're going to have to live with for the length of your lease agreement.

Typically, the Leasing Advantages Are . . .

- **A lease can be tailored to your particular financial requirements.**
  A lease can be written for any number of months. You can virtually negotiate every component of a lease agreement and, if you and the seller agree, come up with a payment program that best suits your needs.
- **Lease payments are usually lower than finance payments.**
  If you look at a comparison between leasing and financing the same car for the same period of time (assuming similar down payments), you will find that the monthly lease payments are lower because you are paying for only that amount of the car's depreciation you intend to use.
- **Because of the lower lease payments you are not tying up as much money.**
  You have the option of spending or investing the difference as you see fit. Often salespeople use the argument that a lower monthly payment frees up your money for some other investment. If you actually were to take the difference and religiously put it into a safe, high-interest-earning financial instrument, there's little question that in most cases you'd actually be ahead of a straight finance deal. Keep in mind that the *difference* is easy to spend, but investing requires a discipline some of us just don't have.
- **Leasing offers the opportunity to drive a more expensive car.**
  Because lease payments for the same car are lower than finance payments (again assuming the down payment, if any, is the same), you can elect to drive a higher-priced car for essentially the same monthly payments as would be required to finance a lesser vehicle.
  Example: If a monthly finance payment totals something in the neighborhood of $600 for a top-of-the-line Toyota, you could very well lease a mid-luxury car, like a C220 Mercedes Benz, an Acura Legend, or a BMW 530i, for about the same amount.
  So the argument that you can drive more car for the same money is true. But remember, you end up owning nothing.

- **Most closed-end leases permit the lessee to buy the vehicle at the end of the lease for the residual value, which might be lower than wholesale value.**
  Here's an example: A man leased a car for his daughter. The car was given a residual value of $4,525 at the time the lease was signed. At the end of the lease, the car was well below the mileage allowance and the used market for the car had skyrocketed. The man was able to buy the car for $4,525—under the terms of the lease—and then sell it privately for $8,500. In this case, the lessee made out very well. Please note, however, this is the exception.
- **Businesses can often realize certain financial advantages with leases over a purchase agreement.**
  With a purchase, the IRS limits the amount that can be depreciated each year. With a lease, that portion of the car which is used for business can be deducted as a business expense. (As regulations change frequently, you will want to confirm this with your accountant.)
- **Other than paying for excess miles and more than normal wear and tear, the lessee has no responsibility to the car or lessor at the end of the lease.**

But be warned: You should know the mileage limitation and have a clear understanding of the wear-and-tear clause *before* you sign the lease.

The Disadvantages of a Lease Are . . .

- **At the end of your lease your payments have bought you nothing.**
  You have, in fact, been a renter.
- **Once you've contracted for a lease, it's very expensive to terminate early.**
  The reason is because under the terms of the lease contract you are obligated for the full number of payments. Let's say that you have a four-year lease and you're paying $488 per month to the lease company. At the end of two years you want out, but you still owe the lease company $488 × 24 months or $11,712. This is called "being upside down in your lease." This is why when you decide to lease, you want to be sure that you're going to stay with it.

Here's a more detailed look at the "upside down" problem.

The sticker or capitalized cost of the car was	$28,000
The lease company set the residual at	−9,240
The sticker less the residual equals the depreciation	$18,760
Each month your depreciation payment is	$ 391
The lease fee based on a .0026 money factor is	$ 97
Total monthly payments are	$ 488*
Over the 48 months your total outlay will be	$23,424

After two years, you decide you want out:

After 24 months your total payments amount to	$11,712
You'd have to pay the other half to get out of the contract	$11,712

By anyone's book, that's a lot of money to pay because you don't like a car. What's worse, if you were to pay the $11,712, you'd still be without wheels.

"*Ah!*" you say. "*I know what I'll do. I'll pay off the lease and buy the car for the residual and then sell it.*"

Let's see how that works:

The amount you paid to get out of the lease	$11,712
The residual you paid to buy the car	+ 9,240
The amount you paid to get out of the lease	$20,952

Now you put the car on the market. The wholesale value of the car—assuming it's in good condition and the market is good—would be a generous $14,300. Let's assume you follow all the instructions in Part VI of this book, "About Selling Your Car," and get a whopping 20 percent markup of $17,160. How did you do?

The amount you paid to get out of the lease:		$20, 952
The amount you received for you car		-17, 160
The cost of getting out of the lease	*Your Loss*	$ 3,792

Still a lot of money. And remember, we're being optimistic about what your car would bring on the used market.

There are two lessons here:

*For purposes of this illustration we are not including sales tax, acquisition fees, or any other changes that you may elect to have amortized in the lease.

1. If you decide to lease, plan to stay with it.
2. If you think you might tire of the car, select a shorter lease period. It will cost you more in monthly payments, but you'll be able to get out sooner.

- **Leases generally require very good credit ratings.**
  If you've been late on payments with any of your credit sources in the past, this may disqualify you. You might want to do some pre-checking so as not to embarrass yourself.
- **If the car is stolen or wrecked, you not only owe the lessor the cost of the replacement value of the car, but also the difference between the replacement cost and the amount owed on the lease.**
  Thus the need for "gap" insurance. Some leases build this in as a cost. If it's not in the lease, then it must be considered an additional expense.
- **If you lease a *lemon*, you're out of luck.**
  While even a lemon will have a manufacturer's guarantee for a given period of time, it could be that major problems will occur after the coverage runs out. As with a financed car, van, or truck, the repairs and maintenance come out of your pocket until the end of the term.
- **You never experience the last payment and ownership.**
  But then, in truth, how many finance buyers ever experience the last payment? Think about it: If you finance a car for four years, it's the bank that actually owns the car. If you decide you want a new car after three years, you can sell the car and pay off the loan (assuming you have positive equity in the car) and finance a new one. And guess what, you don't own that car either; the bank does until you pay off the loan. With financing, you have more flexibility when it comes to terminating your agreement with the lending institution.
- **You must pay for excessive mileage and wear.**

Skip This If You Dare

If you fully understand how leasing works, you might be able to skip this section. But in truth, not one customer in a hundred really understands how to look at a lease and make an informed decision as to whether or not a specific lease deal makes financial sense for their particular circumstances.

The purpose of this segment is to provide you with a fundamental understanding of leases, how they work and how they're sold. We'll conclude with the outline of a strategy that you might want to consider as you shop for a lease.

Leasing Unraveled

By definition, leasing is essentially "renting." (Or as some financial people put it, leasing is an alternative way of financing.) In either case, what is actually happening is that the dealer is selling the car to a finance company—frequently the manufacturer's finance arm—and that finance company turns around and "rents" the car to you. As a *lessee*, you are paying to use the car for a set period of time. Typically that period will run anywhere from 24 to 60 months. The amount you pay per month is determined by several factors. (We'll look at each in detail later.) Using a hypothetical 36-month lease as an example, the primary factors that make up a lease are:

1. The Residual Value

This is what the leasing company projects to be the wholesale value of the car at the end of the lease period. For example, a car that lists new for $25,000 might have an anticipated residual value equal to 45 percent of its original list price at the end of 36 months.

$25,000 List price
× 45%
$11,250 Residual value of car after 36 mos.

The $11,250 represents what the lease company projects as the wholesale price of the car after three years. The *depreciation* is the difference between the list price and the residual. As the lessee, you are paying that difference. Or to put it another way, you are paying for that portion of the car's original value that you use up during the 36-month period.

$ 25,000 List price
−11,250 Residual value
$ 13,750 Amount of depreciation you will pay for

The lease company then divides the $13,750 depreciation by 36 months and comes up with a monthly payment of $381.94. (For purposes of simplicity, we'll round that off to $382.) To this they add a "fee" for the use of the car. (See #2 below.)

All depreciation is not equal

Residual values will vary from car to car. For example, currently the Japanese have strong residual values in part because of their quality image. As a result, you may find that a Japanese car with a sticker price of about $22,000 will, after three years, retain about 47 percent of its value while a similar domestic car has a depreciation of 43 percent.

One of the keys to a low lease rate is to find a car that retains a higher percent of its original value. Thus the higher the estimated residual value, the lower the amount of depreciation. Since your lease is based on the *amount of depreciation* over the course of the lease, you benefit from a high residual.

Some residuals are inflated

Sometimes the residuals are purposely set artificially high by the manufacturer. By inflating the residual figure, they are lowering the lease payments and thus hoping that the prospect of a "low, low monthly payment" will attract more customers. This is good news for you. But it could be a problem for the manufacturer in the long run. Once the lease expires, the manufacturer and their leasing operation will find themselves with a car whose residual value is well above the market value of the car.

Several years ago a major New York bank decided to get into the car-lease business. Quite unintentionally, we suspect, they inflated the residuals only to find that they were holding the bag at the end of the lease. All too often lease companies have found that eating the difference is like letting someone else "eat their lunch"—financially speaking.

To illustrate the lease company's problem—not that anyone cares about their problems—let's say that today a car company puts a certain model's residual at $16,500. Furthermore, let's assume that they know the chances of that car being worth $16,500 at the end of a 36-month lease are somewhere between slim and none. Sure enough, the lease period is up and the market puts the car's value at $15,000. The leasing company is faced with a $1,500 loss if they wholesale the car. If you exercise your option to buy the car for its residual value, you're going to make a whole bunch of folks real happy. You will have saved their bacon. If your mission in life is to do social work for the rich—buy the car. Otherwise, you may be better off walking away. However, if you are really, really in love with those wheels, consult the chapter titled "End of Lease" in this section. There's a hidden opportunity here.

We've got to move these "off-lease" cars.

The reality is that manufacturers are not selling as many of their "end-of-lease" cars to the original lessees as they'd like. So what have they done? They've created the "used-car lease." They're cleaning up these "off-lease cars" and putting them back on the lot for a second lease go-around. This strategy gives them a much greater opportunity to recoup the $1,500 and to recover much of the remaining cost they have in the car. We'll talk more about used-car leases later.

2. The Lease Company's Fee

Clearly, leasing companies are not doing social work, so they charge you a fee over and above the depreciation for letting you use their vehicle. This fee becomes their profit, and it is based on what, for many, is looked upon as a voodoo number called the "money factor," which is expressed as .0025 or .0031 or .0040, etc. The money factor is what determines the fee the lessor charges you for the use—i.e., the rental—of their vehicle. In our example we're going to use a money factor of .0026. The fee is often referred to as "implicit interest." In fact, it is not interest at all, just a *fee for use*.

However, in order for you to have some basis for comparison, it is possible to convert the money factor to a nearly equivalent interest rate. As we noted earlier, all you have to do is take the money factor and multiply it by 24. Example (.0026 × 24 = 6.2%) Now, at least, you have a figure to which you can easily relate.

How do they calculate the fee?

As one salesman admitted, this is something that they would really rather you never find out. We're going to tell you why this is one of those things a dealer will never tell you. It's very simple: If you were to finance a car, the interest you'd pay would be based on the amount you financed. The lease fee, on the other hand, *is not based* on the depreciation, i.e., the amount of the car you use. Rather, it's determined by adding the capitalized cost of the car to the projected residual value and then multiplying that number by the money factor.

Is this illegal, immoral, or fattening? No. It's simply the method they use to come up with the lease fee. They could probably arrive at the same number by creating some other formula. Here, then, is how you would calculate the monthly payment for a $25,000 car with a residual after 36 months of $11,250.

The capitalized cost of the car	$ 25,000
Plus the residual	+ 11,250
Total	$ 36,250

Total of cap cost and residual	$ 36,250
Times the money factor	× .0026
Equals a monthly lease fee of	$ 94

Add this to a $382 monthly depreciation figure, and you have a monthly lease payment of $476.

Monthly depreciation	$ 382
Lease company fee	+ 94
Monthly payment	$ 476*

An exception

One exception to this formula is Ford Motor Credit Corporation. In their case they apply one money factor to the capitalized cost and a second to the residual value. Their money factors also include an administration fee which ends up adding from 1.5 to 2% to the interest rate they quote you.

Usually, because they must be as competitive as everyone else, the lease fee or implied interest ends up about the same. One potential plus on Ford's side is that they have become very aggressive in both their new- and used-car leases by adding subsidies that can add up to real savings.

If you'd like a computer software package that will perform all the calculations for you, you might want to call Chart Software at 1-800-418-8450.

3. The Down Payment

Dealers and lease companies realize that the higher the advertised monthly payment, the lower the attractiveness of the lease. One way to reduce the monthly payment is to ask the customer to pay a certain amount in the form of a down payment. This is really nothing more than an advance payment against your share of the depreciation. In our example a down payment of $2,000 reduces the monthly payment by just under $70 per month.

*Some leases will include sales taxes, acquisition fees, disposal fees, luxury tax, and other charges that the buyer and seller might agree to amortize over the period of the lease.

Here's the math:

The capitalized cost of the car	$ 25,000
Less a down payment to reduce the cap cost	− 2,000
New capitalized cost	$ 23,000

New capitalized cost	$ 23,000
Less the residual	−11,250
Equals the depreciation	$ 11,750

The depreciation (amount to be used by lessee)	$ 11,750
Divided by 36-month lease term	÷ 36
Equals monthly depreciation payment of	$ 326

New cap cost plus residual	$ 34,250
Times money factor	× .0026
Lease company fee	$ 89

Monthly depreciation	$ 326
Lease fee	+ 89
Monthly payment	$ 415

4. Factory Subsidy and/or Dealer Contribution

Another way to lower the monthly payment is for the factory to offer a discount off the list price of the car. This is called a "capital cost reduction" or a "dealer contribution" or a "list price discount" depending on who is making the reduction and what sounds best in the advertising.

Let's say, for purposes of illustration, that the factory is reducing the list price of the car by $1,500. You will see this reflected in the small print of the ad with words something to the effect of:

> **MSRP of $25,000. Monthly payment is based on a capitalized cost of $23,500.**

This reduction is the same as having the dealer offer, or having you negotiate, a $1,500 discount off the price during a purchase transaction. Here's what this discount plus the customer down payment does to the monthly figures in a 36-month lease:

The capitalized cost of the car	$ 25,000
Less the factory price reduction	− 1,500
Less a down payment to reduce the cap cost	− 2,000
New capitalized cost	$ 21,500

New capitalized cost	$ 21,500
Less the residual	−11,250
Equals the depreciation	$ 10,250
The depreciation (amount to be used by lessee)	$ 10,250
Divided by 36-month lease term	36
Equals monthly depreciation payment of	$ 285
New cap cost plus residual	$ 32,750
Times money factor	.0026
Lease company fee	$ 85
Monthly depreciation	$ 285
Lease company fee	+85
Monthly payment	$ 370

Summary

Here's a summary of how the monthly payments are impacted by the discounts and down payments.

Reductions	Monthly Payments
1. No discount, no down payments	$484
2. Customer down payment ($2,000)	$415
3. Down payment and dealer/factory ($1,500 capital cost reduction)	$370

KEY TIP

Here's an important fact to keep in mind and one that we'll talk more about later: Many people fail to recognize that the MSRP—i.e., the sticker price or capitalized cost of the car—*is negotiable*. If the factory is not discounting the car—and even if they are—there is no reason you can't negotiate a discount.

Clearly, an advertised price of $370 per month looks a whole lot more attractive than $484 per month. Unfortunately, many people never look beyond the $370 advertised figure. As you'll discover in some examples provided later, the actual out-of-pocket cost of this lease over the 36 months—i.e., the total amount that you'd have to pay—could easily average out to an additional $100 or more per month. Even at that, this deal may still make good financial sense for you. Our goal is not to make recommendations, but rather to help you make better-informed decisions. Remember this bit of ultimate truth: *If you venture in unprepared, you will leave lighter—in the pocketbook.* But be not alarmed. If you stick with us to the end, you'll be able to determine the true out-of-pocket costs.

5. Other Charges

Depending on how you end up structuring the lease, the other costs will be paid up front as one lump sum, paid at the end of the lease, or factored into the monthly payments. These may or may not include an "acquisition fee," an end-of-lease "disposal fee," a security payment, sales tax, license, and tags. Depending on the price range and fuel efficiency, there might also be a luxury tax and a gas-guzzler tax. In addition, the dealer may try to tack on some charges of his own (little services and extras which you should avoid).

Mileage Allowance

Finally, the lease will give you a set number of miles free per year—15,000 is very typical, although some offer fewer free miles. Every mile over that will cost you about anywhere from $.10 to $.25, again, depending on the lease agreement.

In a moment we're going to show you how to "unravel" a lease by reading the fine print—or "mouse tracks," as the industry calls them—that appears at the bottom of a typical lease ad.

What to Take from This Chapter

Those factors which have the greatest impact on your monthly payments are:

- The amount of money the manufacturer or dealer is putting into the car to reduce the cap cost (or the amount of money you are able to negotiate *off* the cap cost).
- The amount of down payment required. This too is negotiable.
- The money factor. The closer to .0000 that they quote, the lower the payment.
- The residual value of the car. The higher the residual, the lower your payments, all other things being equal.

There are some other items that impact your total out-of-pocket costs over the period of the lease, and we'll deal with those later in the book.

4. Reading the Lease Ad

One of the keys to reducing the confusion that often surrounds lease ads is to know how to read the fine print. Many lease ads tout monthly payments that, at first glance, seem almost too good to be true. Unfortunately, many are exactly that. When you get beyond the low monthly payment number that jumps out from the ad and start to read the fine print, you may well find that when you factor in all the costs, the actual monthly average of all the expenses can be much higher than the ad would have you believe. Even when the lease is being heavily subsidized to help make the lease appear to be a particularly good deal, the average total out-of-pocket costs are almost always higher than the come-on figure advertised in bold print.

Lease This Car
for Just $399 a Month
36 MOS. $1,999 Down*

*Available at participating dealers **(1)** to qualified lessees approved by the manufacturer's finance corporation. **(2)** Subject to availability. **(3)** Advertised lease rate of $399/month is for a 36-month closed-end lease for the automatic (with available leather-trimmed interior). MSRP plus destination charges equal $36,485. **(4)** Taxes, title, license and registration, insurance, and optional equipment and services not included. **(5)** Advertised rate based on a consumer payment of $1,999 as a prepaid rental reduction (down payment), and **(6)** a dealer capitalized cost reduction of $2,876.75 ($3,227 in IL, IN, KS, ME, NY, OK, and UT, where no security deposit is required); condition of dealer participation may affect actual rate. **(7)** Due at lease signing are consumer's $1,999 down payment, first month's lease payment, refundable security deposit equal to one month's payment rounded to the next highest $25 increment (except where security deposit not collected), title, license, and registration fee, and tax to the extent applicable. Total of monthly payments is $14,364 (plus tax as applicable). **(8)** Option to purchase at end of lease for purchase price of $19,701.90 plus applicable tax and official fees except in MS, NY, and SD, where no purchase option is available. **(9)** Lessee pays for maintenance, insurance, repairs, and service, any and all taxes related to the vehicle or the lease, registration renewals, and excessive wear and use. **(10)** Mileage charge of $.15/mile over 15,000 miles per year due at end of term. **(11)** A disposition fee of no more than $400 is due if vehicle is not purchased at the end of lease term. **(12)** MSRP, dealer capital cost reduction, and option-to-purchase price subject to change. See your participating dealer for details. **(13)**

To determine the true cost, all you need to do is sit down with a selection of lease ads from the newspaper and spend a few minutes studying the fine print.

1. Your dealer may not be participating in this particular lease.
2. There is no guarantee that you will qualify. In fact, it's usually more difficult to qualify for a lease than a finance agreement. Your credit record usually has to be pretty good.
3. If the car as described isn't available, the dealer is not obliged to order it for you. However, you can be sure that they will certainly try to lease you another car. Switching you to another car could impact the lease payments plus or minus.
4. This simply gives you the monthly payment and the capitalized cost of the car, which, as you will discover later, represents a dealer discount off the list price.
5. Lots of potential costs in this statement. You should have them all itemized before you sign any agreement.
6. You must make a down payment of $1,999 to get the rate. Keep in mind that this payment can usually be factored into the lease payment. It can also be negotiated, especially if inventory is building up on the lot.
7. This is what the dealer puts into the deal to reduce the list price of the car and to help make the monthly payments more attractive. When the factory or dealer reduces the price via a discount, this is called "capitalized cost reduction," and it produces a figure which becomes the "capitalized cost of the car." This number is important when it comes to determining the lease company fee.

   Note that the fine print says "condition of dealer participation may affect rate." What this means is that if the dealer decides he doesn't want to give up all the profit, he doesn't have to. If he wants to give up more, great. You'll want to know exactly what the dealer is putting into the deal. By the way, remember that the dealer's contribution is not always the sacrifice that it appears to be. Frequently, what is never mentioned is the fact that the factory is providing a factory-to-dealer incentive (financial support) and that the factory has a dealer hold-back program which results in an additional payment amounting to between 2.5 and 3 percent of the list price. So don't let salespeople give you the impression that they are doing social work for their customers.
8. The actual amount of the check you write upon signing the lease will vary according to where you live. Typically, all

applicable sales taxes are added to each lease payment. You will pay tax on just that portion of the car's value you use during the lease. You do not pay sales taxes on the entire car. However, you will have to pay the entire luxury tax and gas-guzzler tax should they apply. That's the penalty for being the first "user" or owner.

9. The option to purchase the car at the end of the lease is not available in certain states. Frequently this is due to state laws which require certain disclosures that the manufacturer would prefer not to have known.
10. You are responsible for these costs in the same manner as if you had purchased the car. The "excess wear and tear" charges are assessed at the end of the lease and could represent a significant amount if the car has been abused or damaged.
11. This is what you'll pay if, over the three years, your total mileage exceeds 45,000 miles or an average of 15,000 miles per year.
12. This is an extra fee that comes out of your pocket at the end of the lease if you decide not to buy the car. In some states, this fee is lower because of state laws.
13. A nice way of saying that the deal may be totally different by the time you arrive.

Adding it all up

When you put your calculator to this ad, you find that the approximate out-of-pocket costs of the entire lease averaged over a 36-month period become:

$399 × 36 mos.	$14,364
Customer down payment	1,999
Refundable security deposit	400
Disposition fee if you do not buy	400
Luxury tax	160
Total	**$17,323**
Approx. out-of-pocket cost—36 mos.	**$481**

Add to the $481, the sales tax, any options, or services purchased at the time of signing, plus title and registration fees, and the figure will hover around an actual out-of-pocket cost, averaged out over the 36 months, of about $500—unless you negotiate the price. (See Chapter 7.)

This may still be a very good deal when compared to a financing arrangement or to similar cars without factory support. And since the IRS won't let you deduct interest payments, the ability to write off some or all of the lease expense to your business may make this a very attractive alternative. Again, review this with your accountant or a finance professional.

Making Your Own Analysis

In order to help you better analyze the fine print and to determine the approximate out-of-pocket costs that you can expect over the life of a lease, we've created the following checklist to help you better identify and understand the hidden costs in ads.

LEASE ANALYSIS CHECK SHEET

Competitive Lease Information

Make and model of car ____________

Money factor: ________ as a percentage (24 × money factor) ________

Term of lease: ________ Monthly advertised payment: $ ________

Clarification Questions

- Has the offer been confirmed during a visit to the dealership? Yes❑ No❑
- Is this number fixed or is it conditional on dealer participation? Yes❑ No❑
- Will the factory warranty last as long as the lease? Yes❑ No❑
- How much of the maintenance is lessee's responsibility? ________

Financial Questions

1. How much down payment is required? $ ________
2. What is the total of the advertised monthly payments (payment × number of months)? $ ________
3. How much is the acquisition or bank fee? $ ________
4. How much is the security deposit?* $ ________
5. How much is the lease termination or "disposal" fee? $ ________
6. Does the lease offer 15,000 free miles? Yes❑ No❑
   a. If not, what is the cost of the additional miles? $ ________
   b. Excess miles likely to be added each year mi ________
   c. Excess per mile cost × estimated excess miles $ ________
7. What is the cost of any additional equipment/services? $ ________
8. Does the lease include gap insurance? Yes❑ No❑
   If not, how much does it cost over the term? $ ________
9. What is the cost of your insurance? $ ________
   (Certain cars have very high rates.)

*Even though the deposit is conditionally refundable, it's still money out-of-pocket that does not earn interest.

10. Are the luxury taxes factored into the lease? Yes❑ No❑
    If not, how much are they? $ ________
11. Gas-guzzler taxes if applicable $ ________
12. Cost of registration, license, and sales tax $ ________

13. TOTAL (add up all the costs) $ ________
Divide by the number of months in lease, and compare to advertised monthly payment. $ ________**

**This is the approximate projected out-of-pocket cost that you will be paying over the life of the lease less applicable sales taxes, license, registration, and fees.

Putting the Analysis Check Sheet to Work

Using the check sheet, take a look at the "mouse tracks" of this BMW ad. Understand that by the time you read this, the offer will probably have long since been withdrawn. We offer it for illustrative purposes only, and no conclusions or inferences should be assumed.

BMW 540i $479 per month*

*Actual lease price determined by dealer. Offered to qualified customers by BMW Financial Services, N.A., Inc., through participating dealers. Estimated monthly payment of $479 for a 1994 BMW 540i is based on a suggested retail price of $48,950, including dealer prep and destination charge less dealer contribution, which could affect final negotiated transaction, with a down payment of $5,000, for a 42-month closed-end lease. First month's payment of $479, plus $500 refundable deposit or last month's payment to be paid in advance, and the down payment for a total of $5,979 is due at lease signing. Title, taxes, and registration fees may be due at lease signing. Title, taxes, registration, license fees insurance, maintenance, and option are the responsibility of the lessee and are not included in the monthly lease price of $479. Total amount of monthly payment is $20,118. At the end of the lease, the lessee pays an excess mileage charge of $.15 per mile over 35,000 miles at lease termination, a charge of any excess wear and tear as defined in lease contract, and a termination fee of $250. End-of-term purchase option is available for an estimated price of $24,965, plus applicable fees and taxes. Lessee acquires no ownership rights in the vehicle unless purchase option is exercised. Subject to credit approval. Offer effective until February 28, 1994. See your participating BMW dealer for details.

Reading the Mouse Tracks

As stated, the lessee is being asked to make a down payment of $5,000 and pay a termination fee of $250. Add this to the total of $20,118 in monthly payments and then divide by 42 months, and you find that the average out-of-pocket costs to the consumer as averaged over the term of the lease actually amount to about $604. (Note: A BMW salesperson agreed to factoring $5,000 into the lease payment, thereby eliminating the down payment but, obviously, greatly increasing the monthly payments.)

$20,118	($479 × 42 months)
5,000	Customer down payment
250	Termination fee or disposal fee
$25,368	Or approximately $604 per month

But that's not all. Luxury cars have a luxury tax based on 10 percent of the amount over $32,000. (In this case $48,950 − 32,000 = 16,950 × 10% = $1,695 in luxury tax. Did you see any mention of that being included in the monthly payments? It wasn't. Plus, the BMW lessor must pay a gas-guzzler tax because its average fuel mileage did not at the time of this ad meet set government standards. That's $1,000 the customer has to pay, and there's no mention of that either. So add another $2,695 to the tab. The fine print also notes that the lessee must give the lease company a $500 refundable security deposit or the last month's payment in advance. Guess who gets the benefit of the interest for 42 months?

Finally, there's one more potential expense that the customer should consider factoring into the analysis. The fine print notes that the lease gives the lessor only 10,000 free miles per year. There is a charge of $.15 per mile for every mile over. Which means if the customer should drive 15,000 miles—and the average driver puts between 12,500 and 15,000 per year on a car—they will have to pay another $750 per year. Ah! But there was an interesting twist here. At the time the ad was published, BMW was willing to increase the free miles to 15,000 for an additional payment of approximately $30 per month. What a nice add-on sale opportunity.

"Mr. Customer, if you think you might drive over 10,000 miles a year, you might want to protect yourself and buy the extra 5,000 miles per year. Just think, for only about $360 a year you can potentially save yourself $750 ($.15 × 5000 additional miles)."

Put that into the total, and the out-of-pocket dollars paid by the customer averaged out over the life of the lease becomes $720.

$25,818	Total payments
2,695	Luxury tax/gas-guzzler tax
500	Security deposit refundable in 42 months
+1,260	(Purchase of 5,000 free miles $30 × 42 months)
$30,273	New total or $720 per month for 42 months.*

Whoa! So what happened to the advertised payment of $479? It doesn't look all that attractive when you add in all the out-of-pocket costs. And by the way, don't forget we're talking about a 42-month lease here.

Leasing When "They're Giving Them Away"

Some leases are so heavily subsidized via discounts and low money-factor fees that it can be said, with some degree of truth, that the manufacturer is paying you to lease their car. If a manufacturer is putting a major chunk of their money into the car, you may well find that the lease, as it stands, represents a very good deal. However, keep in mind that car dealers don't live in big houses because they give cars away. As a case in point, the lease ad below might, upon first glance, appear to be a case in which the dealer is taking a bath.

> Now Lease a New Seville SLS $539 Mo.
> 24 Months $2,200 Down Payment
>
> First month's lease payment of $539, plus $575 refundable security deposit and consumer down payment of $2,200, for a total of $3,324 due at lease signing. Taxes, license, title fees, and insurance extra. You must take retail delivery out of dealer stock [and it gave a date that limited the offer to about 5 weeks]. GMAC must approve lease. Example based on a 1994 Seville SLS: $43,243 MSRP including destination charge. Monthly payment is based on a capitalized cost of $36,788 for a total of monthly payments of $12,936. Your payments may be higher or lower. Option to purchase at lease end for $29,017. Mileage charge of $.10 per mile over 30,000 miles. Lessee pays for excessive wear and use. See your participating dealer for qualification details.

*Obviously, this figure does not factor in such things as cost of money, potential interest lost, or the return of the full $500 deposit.

In this ad, the car shows a $6,455 discount to $36,788. What's particularly interesting is that at the time of the ad, the "published" invoice cost was $37,462. At first you might assume that the dealer was ready to deal under his costs. Ah, but look again.

$43,243	The list price, which includes several options
$37,462	Less the "published" invoice price
$ 5,781	Leaves what would appear to be the dealer's profit if the car were sold at full list

But the ad indicates that the list price is being reduced. The capitalized cost—that is, the price on which the dealer is basing the lease—is quoted as $36,788. What the ad and the dealer won't tell you is that there is a 3 percent dealer hold-back on this car which does not show up on the invoice. This is money that the dealer receives after the car is sold or leased. That hold-back amounts to about $1,297.

$ 5,781	Visible profit
+ 1,297	3% dealer hold-back (also profit)
$ 7,078	The profit were dealer to sell car at full list price

If we take the list and subtract the profit, we come up with the approximate invoice price of the car to the dealer.

$43,243	List
− 7,078	Markup including dealer hold-back
$36,165	Actual invoice price—cost to dealer

Now, subtract the capitalized cost, as quoted in the ad, from what we know to be the true cost of the car to the dealer.

$ 36,788	Quoted as capitalized cost—the discounted price of the car
−36,165	True dealer cost (invoice)
$623 *Profit*	Difference between cap cost and dealer cost
+ 2,200 *Profit*	Consumer down payment
+ 551 *Profit*	1.5% of cap cost paid to dealer by lease co.
$ 3,374 *Total*	Dealer profit in the deal as presented

There is yet another source of significant profit in this deal for the lease company. It appears that their money factor is about .00327 or the equivalent of a 7.8 percent (.00327 × 24) interest charge. At the time of this comparison, other manufacturers were subsidizing their leases and offering money factors in the .002 range or lower (.002 represents an equivalent interest rate of 4.8 percent).

The facts:

Of the total of $12,936 payments over 24 months:

$7,771 is for depreciation and
$5,165 is the lease company's fee*

We're almost giving the cars away as it is!

Chances are, if you were to suggest negotiating the capitalized cost of the car or try to reduce the $2,200, the dealership would eventually bring out the invoice and, pointing to $37,462, try to make you believe that your paltry little down payment of $2,200 represents a profit of only about $1,500 or about 4 percent. Expect to hear something to the effect:

"I know you want to be fair and I think you'll agree that a 4 percent profit is not a lot of money. Keep in mind that the 4 percent has to pay for the salesperson's commission, it has to pay for some of our overhead, the interest I have to pay the bank, and I've got to make at least a little profit for the dealership."

You might want to be sure you have a handkerchief to wipe away your tears. In fact, the dealer's profit in this deal could amount to just over 9 percent or even more if the dealer is participating in the lease.

Now, considering that the dealer's floor plan—the interest he pays a bank or financial institution which finances his inventory—might amount to something less than $250 a month, this is a pretty good return on a very minimum investment.

The positives in the lease are the fact that there was no gas-guzzler tax. The luxury tax on the low capitalized cost would have amounted to only $419 and the $.10 a mile penalty for miles driven over 30,000 during the 24 months is well below what other lease companies tend to charge. Further, if you had financed or leased with GMAC in the past, they would waive the security deposit.

Here's the bottom line

While the ad touted a monthly payment of $539, the actual out-of-pocket costs averaged over the 24-month lease would have amounted to about $670 per month. The key question, of course, remains: is this a good deal? The manufacturer is putting his own money into the car to make it more attractive. The free mileage allowance is good and the penalty of $.10 is low. All that's to your benefit. However, the money factor is high. If you like the car, we suggest you

*If the dealer is participating in the lease with the finance company, a portion of this fee will also become dealer profit.

work on reducing the down payment and the money factor. If the dealership says they can't or won't negotiate, talk to their competitors. One thing you can generally count on when it comes to car dealers is that while they may be selling the same brand, they are fierce competitors. Chances are, a little time on the phone or in your car will turn up someone ready to negotiate a better deal.

Deceptive Ads

Clearly, the whole purpose of these highly attractive lease ads is to get you in the door. Fair enough, so long as you have a reasonable opportunity to lease the car that's been advertised. Sometimes it's virtually impossible to lease the advertised car.

As a case in point, one of the most deceptive ads we've ever seen was placed in the paper by a dealer advertising two luxury cars for a monthly payment of $145. It seemed too good to be true, and it was. When you read the lease you discovered that the $145 was for the first 18 months and then the monthly payment jumped to over $800 a month. Plus there was a $5,000 down payment required.

A somewhat less deceptive ad, but nonetheless misleading, suggested you could lease a car with an MSRP of $14,040 for $172 per month. That looked pretty attractive until we discovered that the featured car did not have a radio or an air conditioner. It was what is known in the industry as a "stripper." When the car was finally priced with what proved to be a minimum of extras (i.e., radio and A/C) the customer's down payment, including the acquisition fee, security, and disposal, the monthly payment had grown to $269 plus taxes, license, etc.

Here's another one with built-in confusion.

> Equipped, Not Stripped! $2,000 Off MSRP
> Automatic, Air Condition, AM/FM cassette
> Special $139 per month
>
> 4dr. 4 cyl. P.S. P.B. automatic, tinted glass, R/defrost, bucket seats, console. Optional: Air condition, AM/FM cassette w/speakers, floor mats, Stk.#RO388, VIN#RE182736. MSRP $16,277. Closed-end lease based on 42 mos. 10K mi/yr, must pay bank fee. 1st mo & last mos. sec. required. Residual $8,780.

What Does This Ad Really Say—and Not Say?

Well, it says the car has four doors and four cylinders, power steering, power brakes, automatic transmission, tinted glass (most cars have this), a rear defroster (which is required in most states), bucket seats, and a console, which means there's something between the seats and hopefully it has some storage space in it.

Here's where confusion sets in: The headline would suggest that the automatic transmission, air conditioning, and AM/FM cassette radio are part of the deal. But then, in the fine print, we see "Optional" followed by those same items. It appears that what the headline suggests the small print denies. Also notice that the dealer includes a sticker number and VIN number, which means that this ad applies to one and only one car. Odds are when a customer comes in and asks about the car he or she will hear something to the effect:

"Too bad, that specific car, the one in the ad, the only one in the entire world *that would fit that description, just drove out the door."*

How many times have you seen a great advertised price on a product only to find that they're sold out long before you get to the store?

"Ah, but we have a much, much better unit over here for just a few dollars a month more."

Bait and switch, anyone?

Referring back to the ad, you can see that it is structured around a 42-month lease which allows only 10,000 miles per year with who knows what kind of cent-per-mile penalty. There may well be a bank fee, which is probably about $400, and a security deposit. What they also don't mention is that the deal is contingent on the lessee making a $2,500 down payment. To be fair, the factory appears to be cutting the list price by $2,000. This in turn brings the capitalized cost down to the invoice. However, there is so much confusion and misdirection in the fine print that one would do well to take a long, long look at the deal before making a decision.

One more bit of reality: Even if this specific car is on the floor when you arrive, you can bet they will do their very best *not* to sell it to you. Believe it or not, there are dealerships in which it is made very, very clear that the prize for the salesman who sells the advertised car is that he loses his job.

While it's very easy for us to find and focus on the ads with built-in deception, don't assume that every ad with a low payment is going to carry major—note, we said "major"—hidden expenses. There are good deals out there, and you can make them even better with a little effort. Still, the key lesson to be taken from this chapter is to always study the fine print and understand exactly what your true out-of-pocket costs will be over the term.

How Long Should Your Lease Term Be?

Ask yourself: *Is it in my best interest to get involved in a lease that runs 42, 48, 60, or even 72 months?* True, the longer the lease, the lower the monthly payments. But it's also true that you'll experience higher out-of-pocket costs. Plus, the longer the lease, the longer your commitment. If you have a 60-month lease and get tired of the car after three years, it's going to cost you a good deal of money to terminate. Plus, if you've got what you consider to be a lemon, you're going to have to live with it. Usually the shorter the lease, the lower the total cost to the lessee. Consider that once the factory guarantee expires, all the repair costs are on you. If you lease a car with a 50,000 mile warranty and drive it for three years at an average of 15,000 miles per year, you will still have some guarantee left when you turn the car in.

5. Finding the Bottom

One of the keys to negotiating a lease is to "find the bottom," the lowest payment that a dealer will go before losing money or, more important, the point at which the lease company decides that there just isn't enough money in the deal to make it worth their while to take your lease. Here are two strategies for determining that figure.

"Give Me Your Best Lease"

One of the most difficult customers for a salesperson to deal with is the one who makes it very clear that (1) they are going to lease a car "soon" and (2) that they are going to shop other dealers and take the best offer. Let's assume that you've figured the difference between the advertised lease price and the total out-of-pocket costs. You've spent enough time so that the salesperson knows you're for real, and he or she has offered the car at just a little below the advertised lease price with a down payment of $1,500. Be very pleasant, but very firm and say something to the effect:

"You've given me a lease price. But I'm afraid if we are to do business, you'll have to do much better than that. Here's what I'd like to have you do: I want you to go back to your calculator and work out your lowest lease price with the down payment factored into the monthly payments. Because it would really be a waste of both your time and mine to get involved in a long, drawn-out negotiation, I will give you only one opportunity to bid for my business. I am now going to pay a visit to three other dealers. Because you have given me so much of your *time, I would certainly*

be inclined to give you my business, if your deal is competitive. *Thank you and I hope to hear from you this evening."*

And then leave and go visit the other dealerships and deliver the same speech. If the car or truck you are intending to lease is in abundant supply, if you've timed your shopping to the end of the month, when dealers are more likely to need sales to make their monthly numbers, you're going to get competitive bids. You will, however, want to look at each lease agreement very carefully to make sure that they haven't tried to slip in a lower number of free miles or quoted you a payment with a high money factor or, worse, a payment which is based on a cap cost that is actually higher than the MSRP. Yes, it does happen.

Getting the Lowest Payment

If you're interested in doing a little homework, you can use the lease formula to calculate what the very lowest lease payment would be were the dealer to actually figure it on the true invoice price of the car. Keep in mind, however, that while a dealer might be anxious to move some vehicles off his lot, the lease company may reject the lease because there is not enough profit in the deal. Possibly the key benefit of knowing the bottom is that it provides you with the information necessary to develop an aggressive negotiation strategy.

How to Calculate the Bottom

This exercise will reveal what your payment would be if you were able to negotiate the price of the car down to the *invoice cost*. The point of this exercise is to give you an idea of the point at which the dealer would begin to lose money and would refuse to negotiate.

Facts you need to know

1. The suggested retail price and the invoice cost of the car, including options
2. The money factor (call several different dealerships that sell the car you want to lease to see if they all quote the same money factor. Factors may differ if the dealers are using different lease companies or if they are adding a few points to the factor as another source of profit)
3. The number of months you plan to lease
4. The residual value

Where do you get this information?
Call a dealership, tell them that you're thinking about leasing, and that you want to do some figuring before you come to shop. They'll usually give you the money factor they're using and the residual value of the car. Most salespeople will assume that this is just a ploy and that you really have no idea of what you're talking about. The invoice cost you can find in a recent copy of an auto price magazine like *Edmund's*, or you can call a service like the Car Price Network's 800 number. For a fee they will send you the prices you need.

A Hypothetical Case

Let's assume that a dealer is selling a $24,000 car. To entice buyers to come in, he uses factory-to-dealer incentive money to enable him to offer a $2,000 cap-cost reduction. Let's also assume that the dealer is working with a money factor of .0023. This would permit him to advertise a 36-month lease for $387, not including taxes, license, and any other fees they might tack on.

Your research tells you

- The advertised monthly payment is $387.
- The car has a suggested retail price of $24,000.
- It has an invoice cost of $20,000.
- The dealer is using a money factor of .0023.
- The car has a 36-month residual value equal to 45% of the suggested retail price.

Calculating the "bottom" monthly lease payment
The formula:

1. Suggested retail price	$24,000
2. Times the residual value percentage	× 45%
3. Equals the residual	$10,800
4. The invoice (net capitalized cost*)	$20,000
5. Minus residual	−10,800
6. Equals depreciation over 36 months	$ 9,200

*To figure the bottom we're using the actual cost (which reflects the 2.5 to 3% dealer holdback) as the net capitalized cost of the car, i.e., the dealer's cost.

7.	Divided by the number of months	÷ 36 mos.
8.	Equals the monthly depreciation payment	$ 256
9.	Net capitalized cost	$20,000
10.	Plus the residual	+10,800
	Equals	$30,800
11.	Times the money factor	× .0023
12.	Equals money factor payment portion	$ 71
13.	Monthly depreciable payment	$ 256
14.	Plus money factor payment portion	+ 71
15.	Bottom monthly lease payment	$ 327**

Were you to get a price below this, it would be because the manufacturer was supporting the price of the car with a factory-to-dealer incentive. In other words, if the factory was anxious to move inventory, you could expect that they would incent the dealer to sell the cars. In this case, let's assume that the incentive amounts to $1,500, which would bring the dealer's true invoice down to $18,500. Many major libraries carry a weekly magazine called *Automotive News*. In the back of each issue you'll find *factory-to-dealer* and *factory-to-consumer* incentives listed. You'll also find that various car-buying services will publish bimonthly reports on factory and consumer incentives on CompuServe and America Online. You can also get this information through a special service offered by *Consumer Reports*.

Line 15: What does it tell you?

Unless the dealer is ready to deal below invoice (and this would happen only if there is a factory-to-dealer incentive assuring the dealer of a profit), this figure gives you what might well be the lowest per month cost for a 36-month lease based on a money factor of .0023. (This equates to a percentage of 24 × .0023 = 5.5%.) To get the monthly payment lower without a down payment, you'd either have to find a lower money factor or get the seller to agree to a capitalized cost under the invoice price, i.e., a further price reduction.

Let's assume for the sake of illustration that you negotiated a lease price of $397 per month. While what amounts to about a $2.00 a day savings over the term of the lease doesn't seem like much, when you total it up (36 months times $2 per day) you find that you're saving $2,190 over the three-year period. So you can see the value of trying to negotiate the lease payments.

**This is a base figure. An actual lease would include sales tax and other fees which you might want to spread over the term of the lease. Further, if the lease called for, and you agreed to, a down payment of say $1,000, that would be deducted from line 6.

Keep in mind that one of the keys to getting a good deal is your personal commitment to walk away if you don't get what you want. Remember, the key to negotiation from the sales side is to make you really want the vehicle and then to wear you down until you simply give up and agree to buy. To be successful as a negotiator, you've got to want the deal more than the car.

Leasing vs. Financing

At some point you may want to compare the cost of leasing vs. the cost of financing. Once you have all the terms and payments on both the lease and finance, you multiply the payments by the number of months to arrive at the total costs. The leasing monthly payments will be lower. However, to get to the bottom line in terms of whether you're financially ahead or behind, you have to factor in the residual value.

Scenario 1
Finance rate 7% and money factor .0029 (equivalent 7%)
Sticker price: $36,500
Negotiated price: $35,000 (represents cap-cost reduction of $1,500)
Residual value: 33% of sticker ($12,045)

48-MONTH LEASE

		Finance	Lease
Down payment	(1)	$ 5,000	$ 1,500
Total monthly payments	(2)	$34,464	$27,774
TOTAL	(3)	$39,464	$29,244
Your equity at end of period	(4)	$12,045*	0
Line 3 minus line 4			
Your Cost of Driving		**$27,419**	**$29,244**

*Assumes you sold or traded the car for this amount. Keep in mind that your ability to trade or sell your car for this amount depends on the condition of the car, the market, and your ability to market your car.

If you were comparing a finance rate and lease rate which were essentially the same, the finance option would result in a lower cost of driving over the four years. However, in most cases you will find that the money factor, when converted to a percentage, will be substantially lower, as shown in the next example.

Scenario 2
Finance rate 8% and money factor .0020 (equivalent 4.8%)
Sticker price: $36,500
Negotiated price: $35,000 (represents cap-cost reduction of $1,500)
Residual value: 33% of sticker price ($12,045)

48-MONTH LEASE

		Finance	Lease
Down payment	(1)	$ 5,000	$ 2,000
Total monthly payments	(2)	+35,136	+25,296*
TOTAL	(3)	$40,136	$27,296
Your equity at end of period (Based on estimated residual)	(4)	$12,045**	0
Line 3 minus line 4 **Your cost of driving**		**$28,091**	**$27,296**

*One of the things several manufacturers have done over the past few years is inflate the residual rate in order to help create a more attractive monthly rate. In this scenario, if they had inflated the residual to 40%, the lease payment, after a cap-cost reduction of $1,500 and a $2,000 down payment, would be $479 for a total of $22,992. While the car company makes less money with this strategy, they hope to make it up by attracting more customers. You, on the other hand, also benefit in that the higher the residual, the lower your payments—assuming the money factor stays the same. In this case you would have saved over $2,200 in monthly payments. The message here is to always know both the residual and the money factor. Plus, you'll want to check any of the additional costs, which could bring you right back to the $25,248.

**Assumes you sold or traded the car for this amount.

Scenario 3

Finance rate 8% and money factor .0020 (equivalent 4.8%)

Sticker price: $19,900

Negotiated price: same

Residual value: 47% of sticker price ($9,353)

36-MONTH LEASE

		Finance	Lease
Down payment	(1)	$ 3,000	0
Total monthly payments	(2)	$20,832	$12,672
TOTAL	(3)	$23,832	$12,672
Your equity at end of period (Based on estimated residual)	(4)	$ 9,353*	0
Line 3 minus line 4			
Your cost of driving		**$14,479**	**$12,672**

*Assumes you sold or traded the car for this amount

What you'll find is that the cost of driving will vary greatly depending on: the number of months, the finance rate or money factor, the negotiated price, and the residual value. You should also consider that if you were to finance and sell the car at the end of the period, you may be able to sell it for more than the residual value. On the other hand, it may be worth less than the projected residual. All this comparison can do is give you a rough idea of the projected difference.

Getting all the numbers

Recently we saw an article extolling the savings one could realize via leasing. On the face of their example, it made leasing appear to be the only rational choice.

24-MONTH TERM

	Finance	Lease	Lease $ Plus or Minus
Price	$35,025	$35,025	
Down payment	$ 1,500	$ 1,500	
Monthly payment	$ 1,546	$ 666	$ 880
Monthly payment total	$37,104	$15,984	$21,120
Residual value %			53%
Equity at end of term	18,563		0
Lease versus buy			$ 2,557
Lease savings earning 3%		$21,741	$ 3,178

On the face of it, this would seem to be a very strong case for leasing. It appears that you'd be about $5,700 ahead on a 24-month term. However, what they don't tell you in this example is that the finance is based on about 10 percent interest rate and that the money factor is about .000082 or the equivalent of about 1.9 percent interest. If you were to find this much spread, then certainly the lease could be your best option and you would potentially save $2,557.

They also show you what the $21,120 difference would earn if you were to invest it. As noted earlier, to invest the difference takes discipline. Further, many people choose leasing because they don't have the additional capital either for the car or to invest.

What this example shows is, again, the importance of having all the numbers when you make your analysis.

LEASE VS. FINANCING WORK SHEET

Sticker price: ________

Negotiated price: ________

Residual value: ________% of sticker price. Residual $ ________

Purchase finance rate ________% Finance monthly payments ________

Lease money factor ________ Lease monthly payments ________*

______ MONTH LEASE

		Finance	Lease
Down payment	(1)	______	______
Total monthly payments	(2)	______	______
(TOTAL)	(3)		
Your equity at end of period (Based on estimated residual)	(4)	$______	______0
Line 3 minus line 4 **Your cost of driving**		______	______

Plus taxes and other after sales costs to which you might agree.

*For formula to determine monthly lease, review chapter 3.

6. Leasing Strategy

How Salespeople Sell Leases

One of the more important pieces of information salespeople can learn about a customer is how they intend to buy. The moment sellers discover that the prospect is a lease buyer, they will do their best *never* to mention the list price of the vehicle. Rather, they will talk only in terms of monthly payments and focus solely on what the prospect feels he or she can afford on a monthly basis. Once they know that number, their job is to structure the lease to fit the payment.

Let's say, for example, that you tell the salesperson that you can afford $250 a month. The salesperson will usually try to bump you up a few dollars and then, having agreed that $265 is "in the ballpark," the salesperson has several ways to structure the lease to fit the payment:

1. He can lower the cost of the car by giving the you a cap-cost reduction.
2. He can ask you to make a down payment—against the depreciation figure—up to several thousand dollars so that the monthly payments will look better.
3. He can take your present vehicle on trade and use its wholesale value as a down payment.
4. He can stretch the lease to 48-, 60-, 72-, and yes, there have even been 84-month leases. The more months in the lease, the lower the payments, but the higher the cost of driving over the term of the lease.

The manufacturer can lower the cost:

1. They can use a lower money factor, which is one way for them to subsidize a lease.
2. They can boost the residual value of the car and write that into the contract. The higher the residual, the lower the amount of depreciation. Of course, at the end of the lease the lease company may have a car with a residual value higher than the market value, and that can present them with a problem.
3. They can offer their dealers financial incentives to deal.

Unfortunately, there are so many customers who literally can see nothing beyond the monthly payments that they end up with a lease based on the full list price of the car and/or they end up with a lease that locks them into the car for far too many years.

As we've noted earlier, the higher the residual, the lower your payment. At times a car will have a rebate attached. You're entitled to that rebate even though you're leasing the car. The question is, should you use the rebate as a means to negotiate a higher residual, or just apply the rebate as a cap-cost reduction? Remember, if you think you might want to buy the car at the end of the lease, anything that increases the residual makes this a less attractive option. Our advice is to look at the figures carefully before you decide.

Developing Your Strategy

As we noted above, most lessees get stuck on the monthly payments and fail to recognize that they should be negotiating virtually every aspect of the agreement.

Further, as we've explained, if the salesperson marks you as a lessee, he or she will adapt their sales strategy accordingly. We suggest that you consider the following:

1. Do not reveal your intention to lease prior to the negotiation.
2. Negotiate the price as though you were going to buy.
3. Once you have agreed to a price, then announce that you'd like to "tailor" a lease to that price.*

Remember, the lower the price of the car—i.e., the capitalized cost—the less the difference between the capitalized cost and the residual. That difference is the depreciation you'll be paying for.

When to Lease

Generally, it's best to lease during the early part of the model year. As you get close to July, August, and September, you'll find that the residual value of the car is less than it was at the beginning of the model year, which will increase your monthly payments.

Much of the leasing strategy we are going to outline is similar to that of buying a new car. If you've read "About Buying New Cars" you may be able to skim over most of the information covered in Steps 1 through 5.

*We had a salesman tell us that when he discovers a customer wants to create a lease deal on the negotiated purchase price, the salesman goes back to his calculator and performs some mathematical sleight-of-hand and out pops a lease deal which, for all intents and purposes, produces a profit equal to that which is in the regular lease. The unwary customer looks at the monthly fee and never stops to analyze the calculation. By knowing how to figure a lease payment and having done so in advance, you'll be able to spot a bogus payment the moment it's offered.

Step 1. Pre-Shopping Preparation

Take time to do some research on the make and model you'd like to lease. What do the car magazines say about it? What kind of rating does it get from *Consumer Reports*? What do current owners have to say? If you're concerned about the safety performance of a particular model, you can contact the Insurance Institute for Highway Safety at 1005 N. Glebe Road, Arlington, VA 22201 (703-247-1500). They can provide crash-test reports and cost-of-repair information. Keep in mind that those vehicles with better safety records usually have lower insurance rates.

Step 2. Evaluating the Vehicle

Visit a dealership and ask for a test drive. Make it clear that you are not interested in buying a car, van, or pickup that day, but that you will be shortly. The fact that you're a future prospect should get you some cooperation. Of course, you may also find that the salesperson will make an effort to convert you from "looker" to "buyer" before you leave.

Your objective is to spend some time behind the wheel and really get a feel for the car. Below you'll find an evaluation sheet to help you assess how a particular make and model satisfies your needs.

LEASED-CAR EVALUATION CHECKLIST

1 Poor, 2 Fair, 3 Okay, 4 Good, 5 Excellent

General Quality Impression	1	2	3	4	5
Exterior (fit, finish, paint)	❑	❑	❑	❑	❑
Interior (workmanship, fit)	❑	❑	❑	❑	❑
Comfort					
Ease of entry front and back	❑	❑	❑	❑	❑
Headroom front	❑	❑	❑	❑	❑
Headroom back	❑	❑	❑	❑	❑
Legroom front	❑	❑	❑	❑	❑
Legroom back	❑	❑	❑	❑	❑
Seat support/comfort	❑	❑	❑	❑	❑
Ease of access to controls, dash buttons	❑	❑	❑	❑	❑
Visibility	❑	❑	❑	❑	❑
Trunk space	❑	❑	❑	❑	❑
Ride and Handling					
Acceleration	❑	❑	❑	❑	❑
Passing acceleration	❑	❑	❑	❑	❑

Ride and Handling	1	2	3	4	5
Hill climb power	❑	❑	❑	❑	❑
Cornering	❑	❑	❑	❑	❑
Steering response	❑	❑	❑	❑	❑
Road feel—bumps	❑	❑	❑	❑	❑
Braking	❑	❑	❑	❑	❑
General Impression					
Interior noise	❑	❑	❑	❑	❑
Rattles/Squeaks	❑	❑	❑	❑	❑
Sound system	❑	❑	❑	❑	❑
Convenience features	❑	❑	❑	❑	❑
Safety Equipment					
Air bags—driver	❑	❑	❑	❑	❑
passenger	❑	❑	❑	❑	❑
side	❑	❑	❑	❑	❑
ABS brakes	❑	❑	❑	❑	❑
Traction control	❑	❑	❑	❑	❑
Total Rating—Each Column	__	__	__	__	__

Sum Total of All Five Columns
(135 is highest possible score) ________

Step 3. Getting the Retail Numbers

Even though you plan to lease, you still want to know the true invoice cost of the car and the true cost of the options the manufacturer charges the dealer. This becomes important when you begin to negotiate your lease agreement. For that reason, before you leave the dealership, copy down the information shown on the manufacturer's price sticker. Put down the price of the car and the price of all the options, plus all of the extras the dealer may be tacking on to the car.

Make ________ Model ________ VIN# ________

	MSRP—List Price	Invoice/Dealer cost
Car	$________	$________
Destination charge	$________	$________
Options		
________	$________	$________
________	$________	$________
________	$________	$________
________	$________	$________

Dealer charges

________		$________
________		$________
________		$________
TOTALS	$________	$________

Step 4. Determining the Invoice Cost

Buy the most current copy of a new-car price guide like *Edmund's New Car Prices* or *Consumer's Guide—Auto Series* and find your car. Compare the list prices with those you've copied from the window sticker. If the figures don't match you may have an older book.

Using the work sheet on the preceding page, list the dealership's prices for the car and the options in column 1 and the actual cost of each item in column 2.

When you add up the invoice/dealer cost figures, you'll know what the manufacture is charging the dealer for the car.

Then add the dealer's charges for transportation, advertising, gas, and oil. Some dealers will add a charge for dealer prep. Since every manufacturer we know includes this in the base price of the car, challenge them on this figure.

Factory-to-Dealer Incentives

Frequently, manufacturers—often called "the factory" in car parlance—will offer dealers incentives on certain cars in order to help move inventory. Essentially, the incentives serve to lower the cost of the car to the dealer and make it possible for the dealer to offer deals, negotiate deeper discounts, and generally provide the customer with the opportunity to buy the car for a lesser price. You may find that these incentives will show up as capital-cost reductions in a lease agreement. The key here is to know how much financial support the manufacturer and dealer are putting into their cars.

The industry magazine *Automotive News* is a weekly publication from Crain Communications. You can often find copies in your library. In the back you'll usually find a section called "Incentive Watch," which shows current dealer and customer incentives. In one issue we found dealer incentives ranging from $200 up to $5,000. Obviously, the higher the retail price of the car, the higher the factory incentive.

Consumer incentives ranged from $300 to $3,000. Understand that these incentives are likely to change frequently.

Step 5. Appraising Your Trade-in

Many people considering a lease don't think about the role of a trade-in. However, a trade-in is "money," and that money can be used to cover your down payment—if such is part of the deal—and at the same time serve as a cap-cost reduction to help reduce your monthly payments.

If you plan to use your trade-in (and let's assume that it's only two or three years old and is in reasonably good condition), take the car to three different dealers and tell them that you are interested in selling the car and that you'd like their best price. No matter what price they quote, show some pain and tell them that if they want the car, they're going to have to do better than that. When they want to know how much better, respond by asking for another ten or fifteen percent. You can be assured that they will probably shake their heads and say that the car isn't worth that much. If they don't make a counter offer, they've probably quoted you what they believe is a price just below that which a wholesaler will pay them. Remember, this is a business, and if someone takes your car in on trade with the idea of selling it to a wholesaler, they want something in return. On the other hand, if they plan to put it on their lot and sell it, chances are their offer will be nearer wholesale. If your car is really in top condition—and they know that *you* know it—they may even go slightly above wholesale. Because of the competition for really good used cars, dealers will let themselves be drawn into a bidding war for a true cream puff.

All of this is another way of explaining why you need to visit three different dealerships. Use the highest offer as the basis for what your car is worth on the wholesale market.

Book Prices

The industry uses any of several books as price guides: the *NADA Official Used Car Guide*, *National Auto Research Black Book*, *Kelley Blue Book Auto Market Report,* and *Galves Auto Price List*. These books purport to reflect the average wholesale prices that various cars are bringing across the country. The only problem is that they don't agree. Compare the suggested wholesale prices for a 1991 Chevrolet four-door Lumina from the same month:

Kelley Blue Book:	$7,500 (tends to reflect West Coast prices)
NADA:	$6,750 (combination of auction and dealer reports)
Black Book:	$5,650 to $8,850 (reports from dealer auction sales)

Your objective is to find out how your local market values your car, and the only way to do that is to have it appraised by the people who are putting up the cash. You may find that certain vehicles will be worth more at certain times of the year. A convertible will probably bring more in the spring. A station wagon will bring more as vacation time approaches and the market for family cars increases. A four-wheel-drive vehicle might do better in the north as winter approaches. The bottom line is that you won't know until you test the market.

Selling Your Car Yourself

If you've got a car that's in good condition, most used-car dealers would rather take it in on trade than let you sell it yourself. The reason is simple: Most dealerships make more money with their used-car business than they do with their new cars. And why not? Most new car markups fall in a range between 12 to 20 percent, while used-car markups have virtually no top.

If a dealer believes your car will sell quickly for a good profit, he will try to convince you that the hassle of selling the car yourself is just not worth it. They might even point out that if you trade your car, you pay sales tax only on the difference between the trade-in allowance and the price of the vehicle. True, but keep in mind that it will be you, and not the dealership, who will be pocketing the profit and that profit should more than cover the additional sales tax. (See Part VI, "About Selling Your Car.")

Step 6. Shopping for Your Lease

To begin, you should understand that there are basically two kinds of leases: those written by manufacturers and those offered by independent leasing companies and banks. If your credit is good, you will have your choice. Most often the manufacturer's deal will serve you best. Keep your eye out for leases that are both heavily promoted and heavily subsidized by the manufacturer. You'll see this reflected in cap-cost reduction or low/no down payments, etc. And don't assume that these discount leases can't be negotiated even lower. They can.

These discount offers are usually worth looking at closely. When times are tough and there are more cars than buyers, all kinds of deals will begin to appear. Read all the fine print to make sure that they aren't trying to make up for the lost profit by hitting you with you extras on the back end.

The Independents

Many independent lease companies tend to like longer contracts. We've seen them up to 80 months. And why not? They make more money that way. Usually, if the salesperson at a franchise dealer appears to be pushing you toward an independent lease company, it's because there is money in it for the dealership—more than they'd get from the manufacturer. By the way, keep in mind that lease companies do pay a fee or commission to dealerships for bringing them lease business.

Another thing we've discovered about some independents is that they write leases based on prices well over the actual MSRP. What they do is add an extra 10 percent or more on top of the price, base the lease on six-, seven-, or even eight-year terms, and offer you a terrific-sounding price of just $199 a month. The poor sucker who signs on to that one ends up paying over $19,000 for a car with an invoice of about $10,000.

Also, if your credit is shaky, beware of any lease company that says they'll take you on and help you restore your credit. This will end up costing you a bundle.

Check on the Money Factors

While money factors of .002 and .003 don't appear to present that great a difference, they represent hundreds of dollars over the course of a lease. If you decide to lease through the dealership's financial arm or through one of their sources, keep in mind that if the dealership can get you to sign a lease based on .0035 instead of .003, they keep the difference as profit. So don't be reluctant to challenge the money factor.

If you plan to lease through a dealer, always shop other sources so that you will know the going market rate in your area for leases. Also, be sure to negotiate the price of the car before you reveal that you are thinking about leasing—more on this below.

Planning Your Lease Shopping

Before you start shopping, take a look at your credit history. If it's good, then you should be able to qualify for a lease. Here are some tips that you might find well to consider.

1. **Decide on a comfortable monthly payment.**
   It is probably in your best interest to limit yourself to a 36-month lease. If you opt for a longer lease, consider the downside of the longer commitment before you finalize your decision.

2. **Use your lease-analysis form to determine what the total out-of-pocket cost, averaged over the term of the lease, would be were you to accept their deal without negotiation.**

   If the average of the total out-of-pocket costs is higher than your monthly payment, set your sites on negotiating the lower payment.
3. **Call several lease companies and ask them to "design you a lease" based on the car you intend to buy.**

   The key facts you want to know are:

   a. The money factor

   b. Any fees, charges, penalties, etc.

   This information will be useful when you get into the negotiation.
4. **Once you have a fix on your finances, start to shop.**

LEASE WORK SHEET

As a reminder, here are some of the figures you'll need for your calculations.

MSRP	$ ________
Dealer invoice	$ ________
Your target capitalized cost— i.e., the price on which your lease is based	$ ________
Money factor	$ ________
Term of lease	$ ________
Depreciation amount (what you're paying for)	$ ________
Residual value	$ ________

Step 7. Shopping for Your Vehicle

Plan your visit for one of the times listed below at the dealership where you'd prefer to do business. Let the salesperson take you through the entire presentation process. Have him or her present the car and take you for a demo drive. Remember, time is the only thing a car salesperson has and the more of it you consume, the more anxious they are to make sure that the time spent results in a commission.

The Best Times to Buy or Lease a New Car

End of the month

Car dealerships and car manufacturers work on a month-to-month basis. Virtually every car dealership is under end-of-the-month pressure to meet sales forecasts. If you've done your homework and are ready to lease, there's probably no better time than the end of the month.

End of the year

Dealers are under pressure to move out the current year's inventory at the end of each year. At the same time, many manufacturers will offer dealers incentives to motivate them to offer bigger discounts and move the cars off the lot. Chances are, since you're making your deal at a time when the car is probably being discounted to make way for the new cars, the residual value will probably be less than it would have been several months earlier. The reason is because once the calendar rolls into the next year, you're driving a year-old car even though you will have owned it for only a month. Clearly, this is a time to make your own deal.

Rainy days

If the weather has been bad, you can assume that business in the dealership will be a little slow. Slow periods make sales managers very nervous because their general manager and/or dealer is probably pressing them to move some cars. After all, the interest on their floor plan doesn't know it's raining.

When car sales are slow

If business is bad and a dealership is really scratching for sales, you should be able to negotiate a good deal.

Targeting the Best Opportunities for Deals

In Part I we talked about the realities of supply and demand. If a vehicle is in high demand by buyers and there is limited supply, the chances of making a great deal are reduced.* However, if the dealer has a large inventory and if that inventory has been sitting on the lot for several months, you will be in a position to deal. Keep in mind that every day a car, van, or truck sits on a dealer's lot, the bank is collecting another day of interest.

*One recent exception: Mercedes-Benz introduced the C-Class in 1994 with a $29,900 price on the C220. This car was hot from the get-go, and dealers were pleading for more cars to capitalize on consumer demand. In most cases, buyers who asked for a discount were turned down because the dealerships knew that other buyers were waiting to pay full price. And yet even in the midst of all this demand, some dealers were still discounting the cars up to $1,500. Why? Ask one of their competitors. The point is that if you shop around, you may find that even high-demand cars can be leased or bought at a discount. Note: Part I— "About Buying New Cars" has more detail on shopping strategies, and we suggest that you take time to review it.

For that reason, one of the key pieces of information you'd like to have prior to negotiation is how long the car has been sitting on the lot. One clue to the answer is to open the driver's side front door and look for the metal identification label, which will tell you the date the car came off the assembly line. If you assume that it took about a month to get the car from the factory to the dealer, you will have an approximate idea of how long the car has been in inventory.

Step 8. Negotiating the Deal

One and Only One Opportunity

There are any number of ways to negotiate a lease deal. Possibly the best way to cut through all the hassle is to simply pick three or four dealerships and, after you've settled on the car you want, walk in and in a friendly, but very firm manner, tell the salesperson what you're looking for, that you plan to lease, and that you'll accept a car from their stock. Keep in mind that their stock, or inventory, is costing them interest. Then give them the one bit of news that they certainly don't want to hear:

"I am going to give you one and only one chance to quote me your best lease deal. If it is competitive, I will do business here. However, understand that I will give two or three other dealerships the same opportunity."

Again, be very pleasant and very businesslike. You'll find that the better salespeople will begin to work very hard to find reasons to build a rapport and to help you understand why you should lease from them. Listen as long as your tolerance factor lets you. Then suggest that they get their pencils out and develop a bid.

Now, smart dealers don't want to let you out with a number that you can shop to other dealerships because they know that someone will probably beat their offer. You must be very firm. If they want your business—and make it clear that you're going to make a deal within the next 48 hours—they have to play the game your way. Most will at least take a shot. Especially if it means another "sold unit" before the end of the month.

Negotiate the Price First

This tactic will require more of your time, and it may not produce any better results than the one outlined above. However, if you'd like to deal with one particular dealership or if your choices of dealerships are limited by your willingness to shop distant locations, then this might be an approach worth considering.

Consider These Steps

1. Shop as you would were you fully intent on *buying* the car. After the presentation and the demo drive, go back to the salesman's office and announce, in a nice way, that you'd like to see if you can make a deal and that you hope the two of you can come to some agreement within the next half hour because you have an appointment at another dealership. (Salespeople like to use a time-pressure ploy on their customers. This is one way to turn it back on them.)

   Also, inform the salesperson that if you aren't satisfied with the deal, you will shop other dealerships, and the one with the best price on the new car and the best offer on the used car will get your business. Said with conviction, this will strike fear into the salesperson's heart. You will be in control.

   Maintain that control by telling the salesperson that you have carefully calculated the actual price of the new car and that you are prepared to offer the dealership a price that reflects a profit of X. (You should decide ahead of time what that figure will be.) As a rule of thumb you might begin with a profit margin that amounts to about 2 percent of the true cost and be prepared to up your offer once—and only once—to a figure that amounts to 3 percent.

   The salesperson will either show great pain and suggest that management won't accept your offer or he or she will agree to write up the order and take it in to see if it can be approved. If the salesperson hesitates to write up the order, insist that your offer be taken to management. If they resist, tell them that you have no other choice but to leave.
2. At some point during the demo drive, ask the salesperson to tell you about their leases. Suggest that you really don't think a lease is for you, but that you'd like to know something about what they offer. Make it clear that you have some knowledge of leases so that when you begin to hit them with depreciation and cap-cost reductions and money factors, they won't feel as though you've set them up. Your ploy will be to suggest that it was the salesperson's influence, not your intent, that has made you interested in exploring the lease option. Be sure to ask for the money factor. Depending on how knowledgeable the salesperson is, he or she may or may not know it.
3. Once you arrive at a price, you might say something like:

   "You know, I've been thinking about what you said in the car about leases. Maybe you're right. I probably should

at least take a look at what a lease would cost based on the price that we've just agreed upon."

Your sudden desire to "look at a lease based on the negotiated payment" is *not* going to win you any new friends. Your challenge is to remain pleasant, unaggressive, but very firm in your desire to explore leasing. When the salesperson comes up with a number—usually a monthly payment figure—ask to be taken step by step through the math. Use the process that we outlined above. If you need to look at your "notes," ask the salesperson to go get you a cup of coffee or a soda. That will give you time to do your calculations without his discovering that you've come into the dealership *very* prepared.

Bring on the F & I Guy

Don't be surprised if at this point they turn you over to an F&I (finance and insurance) manager. Don't try to outmaneuver this guy. He knows his numbers and could produce a calculation that would make 2 + 2 add up to 6.3. Just stick to your guns and say that you negotiated a price and now you want to create a lease based on that price. If he says that the lease company will not accept the deal, he may or may not be telling you the truth. If you suspect he is telling you the truth—and there is no way of knowing—you might go to the strategy outlined earlier and tell him and the salesperson that you do not wish to get into a drawn-out negotiation. They should figure their best lease price—you will give them one *and only one* opportunity to do so—and call you. Make it clear that you are going to shop other dealerships.

If the F&I manager agrees to develop a lease based on your numbers, be aware that he might try to plug all the profit back into the monthly price by giving you monthly payment figures that he hopes you'll find a good deal.

Once he gives you his number, pull out your own calculations. If you're up for the theatrics, you might have written them on the back of an envelope so that the F&I man will think that these are the figures you worked out while talking to the salesperson. They really don't like to deal with people who actually know what they're doing because that reduces their ability to control the sale.

By using the formulas that we've provided in this book, his lease figures should be very, very close to the ones you will have precalculated. If they're off a little, that could be because he's figuring in taxes and titles. If they're off a lot . . . guess what? He's tap dancing on his calculator, and you might be well advised to refuse to dance.

4. If, as we suspect, you find the F&I guy is dancing you around, cut it short. Give him the ultimatum speech:

   "Your salesperson and I agreed on a price, and I assume it was agreed to by the sales manager. While I was on the demo ride, it was suggested I consider leasing. I have. And now I want a lease payment based on this price. If you don't want to create the lease at this price, that's your option. I appreciate your time. I really would like to have done business here, but I'm afraid I'll just have to see what I can do at another dealership."

   And say it without emotion. Don't give the people in the dealership an outward reason to get openly angry. It's very, very hard to argue with a pleasant person who keeps smiling and agreeing and saying nice things, but just won't give an inch.
5. At this point, unless they actually structure the lease at your negotiated purchase price, shop other dealers. Keep in mind that if a strategy backfires at one dealership, you can always walk out and adjust your strategy for the next dealership. Happily, there are always more dealers and more vehicles for you to shop.

Taking Delivery

Once you've made your deal, read all the fine print in the lease. Take it apart just as you did the mouse tracks. Be sure that there is nothing in the lease that you don't understand or that you have not agreed to. Follow the guidelines set down in "About Buying New Cars."

Leasing Inside Tips

1. In many states standard lease documents are not required to disclose the capitalized cost. That doesn't mean you can't ask. If they won't tell you and put it in writing, then it's best to walk away. They are out to gouge you.
2. Always be sure that your lease agreement clearly states that you have the option to purchase the car for its stated residual value or to walk away.
3. Get the facts on wear and tear. Have them explain how they determine excessive wear and tear. Who makes the decision and how do they estimate the costs?
4. Have the salesperson explain what happens should you need to "get out early." Don't fall for *"we'll work something out."* Ask to have the clause in the contract pointed out to you and then read it aloud. You'll find that getting out is neither easy nor cheap.
5. There are literally hundreds of lease scams. To be safe, stick with the manufacturer or your bank.
6. A trade-in on a lease can be a license to steal. The dealership doesn't have to show what they gave you for your trade-in on the lease contract. But you should ask and insist on being given a figure.
7. There are times when a dealership will try to renege on giving you a factory rebate if you decide to lease. Don't let them. The factory is giving that money to you.
8. When you're using a payment or a trade to lower your capitalized cost, ask to see it reflected in the paperwork. In fact, make the seller list all of the figures on a separate sheet of paper and then compare it to your own worksheet. If they aren't within a couple of dollars of one another, find out why. Yes, it could be your error, but it could also be that someone is trying to up the profits.
9. Don't get dazzled by the monthly payments. Take the time to figure your true out-of-pocket costs over the life of the lease.
10. Never sign anything under pressure. Read all the fine print. And, if you're up to it, read it aloud and make your salesperson listen. It's probably the first time he or she will have heard it. If you have questions, ask.
11. If they offer you an extended warranty, rustproofing, and life insurance, just say "No, thank you."

7. End of Lease

Let's say you come to the end of your lease, and the lease company has set your residual value at $15,500. You now have the option of buying the car for that amount. Or, if you prefer, you can simply walk away. Now, let's further assume that the leasing company made a mistake and that they missed the residual by two thousand dollars. (In a few cases the leasing company has been off by as much as $5,000.) Or possibly, at the time you leased the car, they were quoting high residuals—i.e., supporting the lease—to help reduce the payments and make the price more attractive.

For illustration, we'll say that the car has an actual wholesale value of $13,500. Understand that when you signed the lease, the leasing company based your monthly payment on the residual. You paid only for what they estimated would be the depreciation of the car—assuming it is kept in good condition—over the term of the lease. The leasing company intended to wholesale the car for a price equal to and maybe even slightly higher than the residual value to recoup their investment and make a profit.

But what happens if the wholesale value is under the residual estimate? Very simply the leasing company is out the $2,000. They're going to have to wholesale it for the going price and eat the loss. Plus, they're going to have to pay to have it picked up at the dealer where you turn it in and transport it to the auction. That costs money, which only adds to their loss. If you like the car and think you might want to buy it or think that you may be able to sell it yourself, you're in a perfect position to offer the leasing company the current wholesale price. Chances are they will jump at the chance to have you take it off their hands. At the very least, they will save the time and money associated with having to take it to auction.

Selling Your Leased Car

If you're thinking about selling your leased car at the end of the term, you might want to consider the following:

1. Two months before the end of the lease, have the car appraised by three different wholesalers to see if the car has fallen below its residual.
2. Call the lease company and tell them that you'd like to buy the car, not at the residual figure in the lease agreement, but at the current wholesale price. If they agree, and chances are they will, you're free to market the car aggressively. By starting the

process two months before the end of the lease, you will have ample opportunity to sell the car without investing any of your own money—other than a nice detail job.

3. Advertise the car. (See "About Selling Your Car.") Put a price on it that is about 20 to 25 percent higher than the original estimate of the residual.
4. Once you have a buyer, write up an agreement and ask for a deposit. After all, if the dealers can ask, so can you. Tell the buyer it's good-faith money to hold the car until the close.
5. Should the car sell before the end of the lease, call the lease company, make your final payment, and make arrangements to buy the car. If necessary, you can help finance your purchase by arranging a short term—30-day—loan at your bank. They can hold the title for collateral.
6. On closing day, have the buyer bring a certified check, cashier check, or cash to the bank. Have the bank recertify that the check is good and then sign over the title. Once the buyer leaves, pay off the bank and pocket the profit.

The Upside and Downside

The Upside

1. You potentially make a profit.
2. The profit could be applied to your next purchase or lease.

The Downside

1. You have to find a buyer, which means advertising and showing the car.
2. You have to arrange to buy the car before you can sell it.
3. The buyer may back out at the last minute.
4. You have to declare the profit as income.

IV

About Buying at Auction

So You Want to Try Your Luck at the Auction?

1. Introduction

About Auctions

So you'd like to try buying a car at auction. Our advice is "Don't." Most industry auctions are restricted to dealers. Those that are open to the public are often best suited, in our opinion, for people who truly know cars and who either know how to fix them or have access to a low-cost maintenance facility. At those auctions open to the public you can walk around and look at the car, open the doors and look inside, note the mileage and look at the engine, but you will not be allowed to drive it. Indeed, the chances are great that you will not even be allowed to start the car.

In most cases, full payment is required at the time of purchase, all sales are final, and they come "as is," which means there is no guarantee or warranty. This is a high-risk proposition, and while there are some good deals to be had, we suggest that you have an expert along to help reduce the risk.

But You Can Buy So Cheap!

As many of the ads for auction information suggest, it *is* possible to buy a great used car for an unbelievably low price. However, the ads should probably add the word "sometimes" and maybe even "rarely."

Having said that, let us quickly add that there are good deals to be had at auctions. The trick is to know what's a *deal* and what's a *disaster.* Candidly, that takes some expertise that most of us simply don't possess. Even the experts can get fooled. As the old adage puts it:

"You pays your money and you takes your chances." We know of a situation in which a luxury car dealer who was attending a wholesale auction asked one of the manufacturer's field representatives for his opinion on a particular used car that was about to be auctioned. The field representative, whose business is inspecting cars, looked it over and told the dealer that it looked like a good buy.

The dealer bought the car and sold it to a customer. A month later the customer discovered—via a mechanic who was rotating his tires—that the car had been in a major accident and that someone had straightened the frame, welded on a new floor pan, and repainted it.

The customer was irate and returned to the dealer, who, to his and the manufacturer's credit, took the car back, returned the customer's money, and offered him an extremely attractive deal on a replacement car.

In another situation a used-car dealer admitted that he'd bought what he considered to be a good deal at an auction only to discover once he got it on the rack in his shop that the rear end had been "clipped," meaning that the rear of the car had been replaced with the rear of another car.

The point is that even people whose business is buying and selling used cars can occasionally be fooled. In the "About Buying Used Cars" section of this book we give you some tips that may help you spot a car that has been in a major accident.

I still want to try buying at auction

Okay, as long as you keep this basic fact in mind: The average car buyer can get hammered at an auction. However, if you're determined to try your hand at an auction we suggest that you do the following:

2. How to Survive Car Auctions

A Strategy

1. Go to the pre-auction preview and select one or two cars, vans, or pickups that appeal to you. As you begin the inspection process, try to remain inconspicuous. Don't give advice, unless it is to your benefit to do so. Don't try to make friends with other bidders. Keep in mind that they are the competition, and auctions can be a little cutthroat.
2. To the extent possible, perform the inspection checks outlined in this book. Unfortunately, you will not be permitted to drive the vehicle, and there may be other restrictions that will limit your inspection. As you inspect, keep in mind that there is

much to be learned from your competition. If you listen carefully, you may learn what more experienced bidders feel a car is worth, and you may hear them identify flaws that you overlooked. At the same time, you should be aware that some bidders will "talk down" a car in hopes of discouraging competitive bidders. Listen, evaluate, and then make up your own mind.

3. Write down as much information as you can about the car: make, model, number of cylinders, mileage, optional equipment, and the condition of both the exterior and interior.
4. Then call three used-car dealers or wholesalers and pretend that you have a used car to sell. Tell them that you must sell your car and that you're trying to get some idea of what it's worth. Describe the car that you've inspected, giving them all the details. In most cases a used-car dealer will quote you a price over the phone. Usually, this price is just below what he assumes is the wholesale value. Call a total of three used-car dealers so that you can establish an average value.
5. Knowing the wholesale-market value of the auction car, you can adjust your bidding accordingly, i.e., keep your bid under the wholesale price so that, in a worst-case scenario, you can probably sell the car back to a wholesaler. Your objective should be to try to buy the car below what you know to be its current wholesale value.
6. Again, keep in mind that buying at auction is a gamble. Yes, you might get lucky, but then again . . . ? Remember whose money you're putting at risk!

Some Stuff to Know or Find Out

If you're going to an auction, here are some things you'll need to know.

Inspection Period

Find out when and where it is and take advantage of it. Perform as thorough an inspection as they will allow.

Terms of the Sale

Inquire about the terms of the sale. Find the answer to these questions:

1. Do they require a deposit before permitting you to bid?
2. How will they accept payment? Personal check? Credit Card? Cash? Cashier check? Traveler's checks? Find out!
3. How will you get the car from the auction lot home? Be wary of people selling temporary registrations at auctions. In most cases, you're going to have to tow or flat-bed the car off the

auction lot. Generally, you'll find various tow services offered at the lot. Be sure to check their fees ahead of time and factor that into your cost analysis.

In addition

Find out how they handle any possible liens against the car and who is responsible for paying the lienholder.

Understand that most auction houses will make no warranty either expressed or implied as to the condition, roadworthiness, and condition of any vehicle they auction.

Remember that you will be required to pay sales tax. You might want to check to see if your state charges you on the actual monies paid or the current wholesale price.

Tips on Bidding

1. Predetermine the maximum amount that you are willing to bid on any given car and stick to it. The number should never be higher than the wholesale price and ideally 10 percent or more below what you know the car will bring should you have to turn around and sell it to a wholesaler.
2. Sit in the back so that you can survey the action.
3. Try to pick out any dealers or wholesalers in the crowd. They will have a better idea of what to bid on, and they will generally bail out at the wholesale price. If you see bids for a car go beyond the wholesale price, then you may be bidding against dealers who already have a buyer for the car and know that they can make a profit even if they pay above its wholesale value. Or you may be bidding against buyers who have no idea of what they're doing and have let themselves get caught up in the excitement of the process.
4. Just because an auctioneer calls for an opening bid of $1,000 does not mean that you can't lower the bid by being the first one to speak up.
5. Don't let yourself get caught up in the frenzy of bids. If you have never had auction experience, don't be surprised if your adrenaline flows and your heart starts to beat faster. Again, have a maximum figure and never let your emotions carry you beyond your limit. Remember, there are more cars on the lot and many more auctions to come.
6. Be patient. In fact, it would be a good idea for you to attend an auction or two before you start seriously bidding. The more you can learn, the better your chances of reducing your risks.

Who Holds Auctions?

1. General Services Administration
2. U.S. Customs Service
3. IRS
4. U.S. Postal Service
5. Your local police department (state, county, and city)

To find out what auctions are being held in your area, check your newspapers and television. Also consult notices posted in public buildings, post offices, city halls, and county and state administration buildings.

About Car-Buying Services

An Alternative Buying Strategy

1. Introduction

What Are Car-Buying Services?

Car-buying services offer a buying alternative. For a fee these services can provide a range of services—depending on the company—that will make it possible for you to buy a car at a very good price. Generally, car services claim that they can get you a price well below what the average buyer will get and without the hassle. In fact, most car-buying services will tell you that with but a few exceptions they can help you buy a car for a price ranging from a few hundred dollars over invoice to hundreds of dollars under invoice. We'll explain how they are able to do that below.

Like car dealerships, some deliver as promised. Some, unfortunately, may not be all that they represent themselves to be. In fact, it has been shown that some are actually little more than fronts for car dealerships. As a result, some states outlaw their services.

Brokers, Car-Buying Services, and Information Providers

It's important to understand that these middleman services vary in terms of what they provide and how they operate. Ofttimes "car-buying service" is used as a generic term and does not necessarily represent what a particular firm offers.

Car Brokers

By definition a car broker is different from a car-buying service. Generally, a broker is someone who buys a car from a seller and then resells it to a buyer. There's nothing wrong with this. In fact, stockbrokers do it with stocks every day. In the stock market a broker gets a fee or commission from the seller and one from the new buyer. This is called "stripping both sides of the deal." In the car business, brokers do essentially the same thing, although there are many variations as to how they work.

A broker may buy a car from a dealer at one price and then sell it to a buyer at another price and pocket the difference between what he paid and what he received. In some cases the broker also tacks on a fee for his services to the buyer. There are also cases in which brokers are acting as a front for certain dealers. They represent themselves as a car-buying service and charge a fee for that service, but in fact serve as a "funnel" into specific dealerships who pay them a fee for having sent them a customer.

Brokers are often shunned by manufacturers because they do not represent themselves for what they really are, i.e., a reseller of cars. Keep in mind that once a broker has purchased a car, he becomes the original owner, and when he resells it, the customer is, in fact, buying a second owner or used car.

This does not mean that there are not times when a broker can be of value to you. What it does mean is that you need to fully understand with whom you're dealing, who's paying the seller a fee, and for whom he's really working.

Car-Buying Services

Car-buying services, by definition, provide an advocate service in that they become the agents for the buyer. For an up-front, set fee, they will do some or all of the following depending on the extent of their service. They will help the buyer decide on a car, locate that car, make the deal and establish an all-in price with the dealer, check all the paperwork, and then arrange for the customer to take delivery at a nearby dealership or, in some cases, have the car delivered to the customer's home or office. While the customer pays the car-buying service a fee—usually a few hundred dollars—the actual payment for the car, in most cases, is paid by the consumer directly to the dealer.

Reputable car-buying services are paid only by their clients and receive no compensation or commission from the dealers. If you find that they are getting a fee from the dealer, look out!

Car-Buying Information Services

There are also services which primarily provide consumers with car-buying information. These range from simple price quotes to services that will solicit bids for a specific car from several dealerships in the buyer's area and then provide the buyer with the information and dealer price quotes to do with as he or she pleases. In other words, once the customer has the information in hand, he or she is on their own to select the dealership, go in, and conclude the deal.

How They Buy for Less

The first question most people ask when considering a car-buying service is how they can help you buy a car for prices that are just above or even below the factory invoice. The answer gets to the heart of the car business. The name of the game is to "move inventory."

Here are some of the reasons why car-buying services can help you buy at a low price. Keep in mind as you read this, that with persistence, you can probably accomplish the same objective.

They Deal with Fleet Managers

Many dealerships have fleet managers whose job it is to sell multiple numbers of cars at one time to people like taxi companies or police departments or corporations that have a fleet of company cars. While the new-car sales manager is measured on the number of units sold, he is also responsible for the amount of total overall profit margin that those units bring the dealership. The fleet manager, on the other hand, is responsible only for the number of units he sells, not the profit margin. For that reason he is always looking to move another unit and is therefore more than happy to deal with a car-buying service, which might represent a multiple of units over the course of a year.

While the fleet manager does in fact earn a small profit for the dealership on each unit sold, generally the factory provides an additional financial incentive to the dealer for these sales. In their heart of hearts factories are primarily interested in moving inventory. Of course, they want their dealers to remain profitable enough to keep their doors open, but keep in mind that most dealership profits come from their service operation, used cars, and the back end of new-car sales.

"Turn and Earn"

In keeping with the above, factories commonly incent their dealerships to sell more units with "turn and earn" programs. Translated, this means that the more units they turn, or sell, the more they will earn from the factory in terms of bonus payments. Again, the factory needs to keep the flow of cars moving off the production line, through the dealerships, and into buyers' garages.

One car-buying service reports that it's not uncommon to find a dealer who will part with a car for a price well below invoice because he needs the unit to help him qualify for a bonus and incentive trip. Think about it: If moving just one more car meant a $5,000 bonus and a trip to some Caribbean destination, you, were you a dealer, might be more than happy to sell the unit at cost.

Credit Against Allocation

Another variation on turn and earn is the practice of rewarding dealers with high numbers of unit sales with a larger allocation of new cars and a better selection of the hot, or in-demand, cars. The key here is that a dealer needs a large inventory in order to satisfy diverse customer requirements. The dealer that can provide a customer with a car in stock has a greater opportunity of closing the sale.

Found Money

Car dealers deal with car-buying services because the profit, small as it may turn out to be, represents "found money." Chances are the car service is bringing the dealer business he would never have had otherwise. The small profit and the added unit are considered plus business. As one of the car-buying service executives put it, "What we're doing is giving the dealer the opportunity to sell my client a car at my client's best price or to give his competition the opportunity to sell my client a car." As we noted earlier in this book, car dealers have two enemies: the customer and the competitive dealer who they "know" will always try to undercut them. Yes, Virginia, this is a cutthroat business.

Linkage

When a factory happens to have a particularly hot-selling, much-in-demand car, they will use the car to leverage the dealers into accepting more of the factory's slow-selling models. It's as if they are saying, "We'll give you some of these hot-selling cars if you'll agree to take two of these slow-selling slugs." If the dealer agrees and is able to move out the slugs, then he is in a position to go back to the factory and ask for another one of the hot sellers. What some smart car-buying services do is help the dealer get more of the hot cars by taking the slugs off his hands at rock-bottom prices. Furthermore, having helped move the slugs they are often in a position to demand one of the hot cars at a low price. Anytime a car-buying service can help a dealer unlock a hot car by helping him move other inventory, that car service earns a favor which he can pass on to his clients.

New Dealership Allotments

When a new dealership opens, the factory gives them what they call an "open allotment" for several months. What this means is they can get any and all of the cars in the model line just for the asking. During this period of time, they have the ability to "suck" hot-selling cars out of allotments that were originally slotted for other dealers. During the "open allotment" time frame, the new dealership is looking to establish itself as a major player in the eyes of the factory. Therefore, the more unit sales they can show the factory, the more cars they will be allocated once they go off the open-allotment period. To be a success, a dealership needs a diverse inventory so that they can attract more prospects and deliver more cars off the lot without having to order from the factory or work a trade with another dealer.

KEY TIP

Note: You may not be familiar with the term "dealer trade." When a customer comes into a dealership looking for a specific car that they do not have in inventory, the dealer can either order it from the factory—which takes time—or call other dealers and, in effect, trade a car they have in stock for the car the customer wants to buy. Generally, dealers will cooperate with one another because sooner or later the dealer *with the car* will become the dealer *in search of a car.* Dealers who refuse to trade, or who trade and then don't reciprocate quickly, get on the "no-cookie list."

When a car service can help these new dealers move units, they are in turn helping them earn larger allotments. Sure, the dealers know that they are "giving away" these cars to car-buying services, but earning a larger and more attractive allotment is of utmost importance. Plus, they know that they will have enough customers who will pay something near the sticker price to assure that their monthly bottom line is in the black. Because most people don't have a clue about how much profit a dealer is making on the sale, dealership are able to profit even when they give you the impression that they're losing money. The less the consumer understands about the car-selling business, the happier most dealers are.

2. Six Different Buying Services

In order to provide you with a better understanding of how car-buying services work with their customers, we selected six national car-buying services and interviewed the president or a top executive of each. In what follows you will read the results of those interviews. Our intent is not to endorse any of these services or even to recommend this method of car buying. We present this information as it was presented to us so that you can make your own evaluations. It's our hope that the information we've gathered from these organizations will prove of value should you decide to explore these or any of the many car-buying services that exist today.

Again, we do not intend nor imply any endorsement of the services we are presenting. If you want to know more, give them a call.

AUTOMOBILE CONSUMER SERVICES, INC.
Cincinnati, OH
1-800-223-4882
Tarry Shebesta, President

How Does Your Service Work? "Our service is personalized. The major difference between us and other car-buying services is that when we get a price or a quote from a dealership, we don't just send our clients to the dealer. When someone calls us wanting to buy a particular car, we discuss all the options with the customer until we understand exactly what they want. We locate that car in their area and negotiate the lowest price with a dealer. Then we present the purchase options to the customers in terms of what's available and, if the customer approves, proceed to set up the deal through a local dealer in the customer's area.

"We get a buyer's order from the dealership that has everything totaled out, including tax, registration, and license. The order has the VIN number of the car. We get a copy and give one to the client before they go into the dealership. That basically guarantees that nothing else can be added to the deal. If you don't do it that way, if you just give people a dealer's name, they go in and find themselves in front of an F&I guy who is trying to sell dealer prep, rustproofing, extended warranties."

What Does It Cost? The fee for having ACS find and negotiate a car is $295 for a car in stock. If the car has to be ordered—and they do that through a dealer—the fee is $249 in most cases. If you enlist their services you are asked to pay a $75 retainer, which is credited against the total fee.

The client writes a check for the amount that ACS has negotiated. The final figure—and all the details supporting that figure—appears on the order form that the client receives and approves. The check is made out directly to the selling dealer, and ACS states that they do not collect any fee or commission from the selling dealer.

Other Services ACS will help you through a lease agreement and show you how to negotiate the best terms and what to look for in the contract. They also provide a monthly payment quote based upon the best lease sources available. Their fee for this is $99 per vehicle.

If you prefer to do your own negotiation ACS will provide you with a target number based on the invoice plus the rebates. Fee is $29 per quote sheet.

Can You Deliver Any Car at or Below Invoice? They work nationwide and cover all makes and models with the exception of Saturn. They claim they can deliver most domestics at invoice and some cars even lower. It depends on the dealer rebates.

"Suburbans are $750 over and I can get them. Many imports we get are at invoice."

What Guarantees Do You Offer? "If someone is unhappy with our services, we offer a complete refund. This rarely happens. Much of our business is referral and repeat, which means that people understand we honor our guarantee." Their written guarantee reads as follows:

"Automobile Consumer Services, Inc., agrees to refund all service fees, upon client's proof of a signed buyer's order from a new car dealer for an identical vehicle at a selling price less than the ACS selling price, dated prior to the ACS quotation."

In addition, the buyer also gets the full factory guarantees just as he or she would had they not used ACS's service.

What Advice Would You Offer the Consumer Shopping for a Car-Buying Service? "Make sure if you're ordering the car and if you make a deposit on it, that it goes to the dealer and not to the buying service.

"The main thing is to be sure that the company is a buying agent or service and not a car broker. There is a small association called the National Auto Buyers Association, which is working to help enact laws in each state that will force brokers to represent themselves as a broker and not as an agent. They did get a law passed in California. ACS is a member of this association. NABA can be reached at 415-721-7741 if you'd like more information."

AUTOADVISOR
Seattle, WA
1-800-326-1976
Ashley Knapp, President

How Does Your Service Work? "We feel that an ultra-personal service is needed. We believe there are many people out there who like to negotiate and enjoy educating themselves. But they don't have the time to gather all the facts they need to have. So we decided to be that source. We even will 'coach' someone through the process. We get them all the prices and hidden money and become a *buyer's service.* Like an accountant or doctor we work exclusively for our clients and do everything we can to save them every penny.

"After we have done our locate work, we then look at what dealer has the biggest cash-back deal with the manufacture, or what dealer may need a couple of cars to put them over a certain sales target.

"After we have gotten a price and reviewed the car with the customer, we ask them, 'Do you want the car?' We give them a chance to go out and shop our price to see if they can beat it. Some do shop, most don't. The reason is because when customers go into a dealer and say they have a price that's $200 under invoice, most dealers won't believe them.

"So we select the dealer and make the final arrangements with the customer and dealer to be sure that the car is exactly what the client wants and that the price is understood by both the dealer and the customer.

"As a rule, we like to have the car delivered by a factory-authorized dealer so that the client can establish a direct relationship with the factory and the local dealers. Most of the cars and trucks are bought by our clients below invoice. We also will look out for them in terms of lemon laws."

This company likes to think of themselves as "research nuts." If they, in fact, have access to all the information they claim they do, then they may well have a better information network than the dealers themselves in terms of the ability to locate cars around the nation.

"The reason we're able to guarantee the lowest price is that we research where every one of the cars our clients request is to be found anywhere in the country. Plus, we have to know which dealers to work with. If, for example, a car is in Ohio and the customer is in Florida, we know which dealer in Florida will buy the car from the dealer in Ohio and agree to sell it to the customer at the price we've negotiated."

What Does Your Service Cost? Autoadvisor's fee depends on the level of information and service you select. It can range from $300 to just over $400 per customer. The price is the same no matter what the cost of the car.

They will also work out the price for any of the additional services that the customer might want—extended warranty, credit life, etc.

Can You Deliver Any Car at or Below Invoice? Autoadvisor claims that they can locate any make of car in the U.S. with the options you designate—assuming that the options are offered by the manufacturer—and have it sent to a local dealer for delivery within an agreed-upon time deadline and at the lowest price.

What Guarantees Do You Offer? Money back if not satisfied.

What Advice Would You Offer the Consumer Shopping for a Car-Buying Service? The following are the questions that Mr. Knapp feels that someone considering his or any car-buying service should consider:

1. Many companies will provide a quote. Is there a car to go with the quote?
2. Are you a car-buying service or are you a broker or a lease company who is using leasing to disguise the fact that you are really a broker?
3. Are there automotive experts at your service who can answer your questions about the car itself?
4. What percent of your clients buy their vehicles below dealer's cost?
5. Does your company make more money if I buy a more expensive car?
6. What is your price guarantee?
7. Can I lease my car through you? That is, can you help me get a good lease and shop it to various lease companies to assure that I get the best deal?
8. Where do I take delivery of my car?
9. If I purchase through you, are my car and my purchase protected by my state's lemon laws?

10. Will the car be titled as a new car, and will that title come from the manufacturer?
11. Do I directly receive all rebates and warranties on the car?
12. Am I obligated to buy the vehicle if, at the time of delivery, I find that it is damaged, dented, scratched, or otherwise in less than showroom condition?
13. How many years have you been in business?
14. What is the cost of your service?
15. Do you have a trade-in service and, if so, how does it work?
16. Can I go to my local dealer for free warranty service no matter where the car was purchased?

AUTOVANTAGE
Houston, TX
1-800-876-7787
Bruce Jakubovitz, VP, Industry Marketing

How Does Your Service Work? "We are not in business to be a car-buying service. We are in the auto information business. We make our money through our membership fees, and the car-buying services we provide is simply one of the benefits of that membership."

Autovantage offers consumers a car membership program which serves a variety of car owner needs. In some respects they are more like AAA than a car-buying service. In order of usage their services include:

- A car emergency 24-hour road and tow network with 12,500 tow providers nationwide.
- Car-maintenance and repair discount network with 25,000 locations nationwide where you can show your membership card and get from 10 to 50 percent discounts off retail prices. In about half of the establishments you can get from 5 to 10 percent off the lowest advertised sales price.
- Car summaries. These are 8- to 10-page reports on each car sold in the U.S. This report offers objective data on road-test evaluations, price information, National Highway Traffic and Safety Association information on safety performance, and information on estimated annual operating costs.
- Used-car evaluation service. You call and describe the car you want to buy or sell, and they will give you the wholesale and retail numbers. They base their figures on national auction results.
- *Car Buying Service.* While this is the least used of their

services, they still help their members buy over 24,000 cars and trucks each year.

The Car-Buying Service—How It Works If you become a member and decide to use the car-buying service, Autovantage contacts one of its contract dealers in your area and tells you for how much over—and sometimes under—the invoice price the dealer is prepared to sell you the car of your choice. That price typically is no more than $100 to $150 over invoice. In some cases it will be under invoice. Foreign car prices tend to be about $300 or more over invoice.

They work through their network of dealer fleet managers. Once they've located a car, they confirm the price and then ask that you go to the dealership and look at the car. After you've inspected the car, you call Autovantage to confirm the price and have any price-related questions answered. If you change what you want in the way of services, they will refigure the quote and confirm the new price.

Because the dealers that Autovantage uses are under contract to them, Mr. Jakubovitz assured us that this prohibits them from trying to hit customers with extra charges and back-end expenses. If any of their contracted dealers in their network don't live up to their commitment to Autovantage, they are taken out of the network. Apparently, that rarely happens.

What Does Your Service Cost? Cost of joining is $69 per year to take advantage of all their services or $49 if you do not want the road and tow network service. Currently, they have about 2,000,000 members, which, after doing a little multiplication, tells you how they make their money. They are a public company, have been in business for 23 years, and they do not take any fees or commissions from dealers.

What Guarantees Do You Offer? Full money-back guarantee on the membership fee if not satisfied with their services.

What Advice Would You Offer the Consumer Shopping for a Car-Buying Service?

1. Look out for anyone who charges a lot of money up front.
2. Be wary of a service that doesn't have a money-back guarantee.
3. Look for someone who has a history of being in the consumer business.

CARBARGAINS
Washington, D.C.
1-800-475-7283
Robert Ellis

Carbargains is run by the Center for the Study of Services, which is a consumer group based in Washington, D.C. It was founded with support from Consumers Union and the U.S. Office of Consumer Affairs. They operate on the philosophy that the car-buying consumer needs to have a good deal of information prior to purchase and that market competition is what really works to the consumer's advantage so long as it's truly competitive. Carbargains tells us that they have structured their service to facilitate this competition. The company is totally self-funded. They accept no money from dealers or advertising.

How Does Your Service Work? "The customer tells us the make model and style of the vehicle they are shopping for, and then we get at least five dealers in their area to bid against one another above or below invoice cost. This falls in line with the Center's philosophy that market competition is the key to getting the customer a fair deal. Once the bidding process is done and we feel that we have five competitive bids for the area, we get the lowest bidders to confirm those bids in writing and then give our client all the bid information along with an invoice printout on the vehicle and all options. We also provide a fairly lengthy discussion of things they might or might not want in addition to the car, such as extended service guarantees. Once they have this information, they are free to do with it as they please. They can buy from one of the bidding dealers or use it to negotiate with another dealer."

Can You Deliver Any Car at or below Invoice? "Any car? No. Cars that have large factory incentives will sell well below invoice price. But supply and demand is the key. For some low-supply, high-demand vehicles, $1,000 to $1,500 over invoice might be a great price. Our goal is to get the *lowest* prices, not a *specific* price."

How Does the Customer Know He Won't Get Hassled by the Dealer? "We closely monitor what happens to our customers, and they are very good about giving us feedback. So if they encounter dealers who are chronic problems in that they try to up-sell the customer or try to switch them to another car after they have submitted a written bid, they're deleted from the database and don't get a chance to bid. We are very up-front with the dealers and tell them that if we find that they are playing games with our customers, they are out of the bidding pool. We've found that the process is very stable. Once we give the customer the bid and they have all the facts, we really don't have many problems."

What Guarantees Do You Offer? "Our guarantee is to get our clients the lowest price. So if they are able to beat our price without taking our bids into a dealer and using it to leverage their price down, then we'll refund their fee."

What Is the Cost of Your Service? Our fee for the service is $150.

What Advice Would You Offer the Consumer Shopping for a Car-Buying Service? "If the service gives you only a price without the backup, you really don't know how good your deal is. You want as much support and backup information as possible. 'At invoice' may sound great unless there's a $2,000 dealer incentive that you don't know about. Our view is that the consumer needs information in all areas, and that's what we provide.

"Second, I'd be leery of anybody who requires a lot of up-front money, especially if you're dealing directly with a broker."

CONSUMERS AUTOMOTIVE
Fairfax, VA
1-800-WE SHOP 4U
Jim Boerger, President

How Does Your Service Work? "The client tells us the make, model, and options, and we go out shopping for that car or cars and give them quotes on a couple of different cars so that they can make a comparison. For example, they may find that car A has a slightly higher price than car B. But because car A has a factory-to-dealer incentive, the actual purchase price, as negotiated by Consumers Automotive, may be less.

"Once we have found the car, we give the customer a breakdown of all the prices, including the car itself, the options, additional add-on services, taxes, and tags. This is, to my knowledge, completely unique from any other car-buying service. We're different because many, or even all, of the other services end up sending the consumer into the dealership to take delivery of the car. Once they're in the dealership, the consumer is on their own, and there is no one there looking out for them or protecting them. What we do is shop for the car and give them the price on the car after we've negotiated the lowest possible price. We then have the dealer supply us with a copy of the paperwork. We must see and approve the paperwork before the car is delivered. This eliminates any opportunity for the dealer to come back with additional back-end charges. Few consumers understand that it's at the back end where dealers make much of their profit.

"Keep in mind that while the purchase price of a car is one cost, the add-ons, or back end, is another. When people agree to buy extended warranties, paint protection, fabric protection, undercoat, health and accident insurance, finance packages, and agree to pay dealer handling, and prep, etc., the additional costs could add up to several thousand dollars more than the purchase price. You could get buried on the back end, if you don't know how to protect yourself.

"After I've seen the paperwork, we do something else that's different. We have the car delivered right to the client's front door. What this means is that the customer never has to go into a dealership.

"For example, I'm buying a car today from a dealer in Louisville, where I've got the lowest price—cheaper than in any other area for that car—and I'm having it delivered to a client's front door in Nashville.

Editor: "What's the delivery cost going to be?"

Jim: "Nothing. It's part of the purchase price."

Editor: "I presume the dealer has to have one of his people drive it down to Nashville and deliver it. And he pays for that?

Jim: "Yes. Naturally, I don't tell the dealer that until we've negotiated the price, and then I say, 'By the way I need to have this delivered to my client's front door.' And 99 percent of the time they go along with that. The reason we do that is to protect the consumer. By having the paperwork approved ahead of time and having my client know to the penny what the price of the car is going to be, when it shows up, if there's anything different, my client can say, 'No, take it back, that's not what I agreed to.' The dealer doesn't have the opportunity to get the person in the back room because they are delivering it to the person's house. To my knowledge, no one else does that. If we can keep the consumer out of the dealership, we have kept them out of harm's way."

How is the Car Paid For? "The consumer pays the car dealer, so that you're in control until you approve the car as delivered. All the paperwork is done, and all you have to do is go over the car to be sure that it's proper.

"The real difference between us and other services is that we help our clients buy or lease cars, we don't help dealers sell them. I don't represent the dealer. I don't take any back-end money from the dealer.

If you have someone taking money from a dealer, how can they represent the consumer?

"The other thing we do for the consumer is handle leases for them. If my clients want to consider leases, I help them be sure they are getting the best deal. It is not unusual at all for me to save a client $1,000 over the dealer's best price on a lease or purchase."

What Does Your Service Cost? "The cost of the service is based on the sticker price of the car. Cars with a manufacturer's suggested retail price—sticker price—up to $15,000 is $195. Cars between $15,000 and $30,000 MSRP have a fee of $295. And for cars over an MSRP of $30,000 the fee is $395."

What Guarantees Do You Offer? "If the consumer has a lower price than Consumers Automotive has found, we'll refund the fee."

What Advice Would You Offer the Consumer Shopping for a Car-Buying Service? "The customer should find out: Who the service is really working for. Who is paying their phone bill and who is paying their overhead. If it's coming from a dealer, then you really can't assume that they are representing you."

NATIONWIDE AUTO BROKERS
Southfield, MI
1-800-521-7257
Stephen Weinberg, President

How Does Your Service Work? "Customers call and tell Nationwide what they want, and then Nationwide sends them a computerized printout of the car or truck, all the options, and the dealer invoice. Once the customer has reviewed all the material, specifies what he or she wants, and gives approval, Nationwide orders the car from a local dealer in the Detroit area. Essentially we serve as the middleman in the deal between the consumer and the dealer.

"We require a $100 deposit if the customer plans to pick up the car in Michigan or a $500 deposit if you plan to have the car shipped to a dealer in your area. The deposit is strictly a good-faith deposit for ordering the vehicle, and this comes off the final price paid for the car.

"We then order the car through a local Michigan dealer. The customer submits the names of three dealers in his or her geographic area from whom they would be willing to accept delivery. We contact those dealers and make a decision as to which one will handle the customer's delivery.

"The drop-ship charge for having the car delivered to the dealer will run from $75 to an average high of $300. In some areas it may run more because the delivering dealership may want a higher fee to handle what we call a 'courtesy delivery fee.' "

As discussed, this is found money for the dealer. More important, the expectation is that the new owner may become a service customer. Your check is made out to the original ordering dealer back in Detroit, and that dealer pays Nationwide a commission for having brought about the sale. You will pay anywhere from $50 to $125 over dealer invoice to order the car through Nationwide, plus whatever the dealer is charging for the delivery fee. Customers know these numbers in advance.

"We are unique in that we can sell you the car at the price we quote. Some services only quote you prices and then send you off on your own. But we can actually deliver the vehicle at the price we state on the quote sheet."

Nationwide also offers a quote service. You pay $11.95 for the quote and $9.95 for additional quotes.

How Does a Customer Know He or She Won't Get Hassled by the Dealer? "All the paperwork comes to the local dealer. There is a document from the Manufacturer's Statement of Origin. This is the original title documentation, and a dealer cannot sell the vehicle without that document. That vehicle can't be titled to anyone without that document."

Mr. Weinberg has that document in his possession. When the car arrives in the local dealership, the dealer notifies the selling dealer in Michigan, who notifies Nationwide, who in turn calls the customer to say that the car is in. Nationwide has a contact at the dealership, and they tell you to go over and take a look at it. They give you the vehicle or VIN number so that you can check to be sure that you're looking at the one Nationwide has arranged for you to buy. You verify the number and check over the car to be sure that everything is okay. You then call Nationwide and tell them that everything is okay—or not okay—and Nationwide gives you the final figure. You then express mail or Fed Ex the certified check. Nationwide pays the dealer and then calls the local dealer and informs them that it's okay to release the car.

Nationwide collects all the money except for the sales tax, license, and title fees. That gets paid locally. Nationwide in turns sends a courtesy payment to the delivering local dealer. The safety latch here is that the local dealer cannot sell the car without the paperwork that Nationwide is holding.

The benefit to the dealer is that they hope you'll bring your car in for warranty and regular maintenance work. In this way you become a source of added revenue to the dealership and who knows, maybe you'll buy your next new or used car from them. The dealer might end up buying your used car and selling it at a profit.

Nationwide can also arrange to have the car delivered to your home for an additional fee.

What Guarantees Do You Offer? If you are not happy with the vehicle, you don't have to accept delivery. They stand behind the product. If you are unhappy with the quote service, they will refund the money. Of course, they'll want to know why.

Plus, all vehicles carry a full factory warranty.

What Advice Would You Offer the Consumer Shopping for a Car?

1. Get references from people who have used the service.
2. Find out if the service is licensed by the state department of motor vehicles.
3. Ask if they represent a particular dealership.
4. Check with the Better Business Bureau.

Other Car-Buying Services and Brokers

For other buying services, you need only turn to your yellow pages.

Ask Questions First!

If you decide to explore a car-buying service, you might want to call and ask the following questions before you make your decision to proceed:

1. What makes your service different from other car-buying services—i.e., why should I choose you over your competitors?
2. Are you able to deliver me any car on the market at invoice price or lower?
3. What does your service cost me?
4. How and where do I take delivery of the car?
5. *(If you take delivery through a dealer)* How do I know that the dealer won't try to hassle me into paying more or claim that the car I wanted was "just sold"?

6. How much, on average, are your prices over or below the dealer's invoice? How can you prove it?
7. What guarantees do you offer and how do you back them up?

Are They Really a Good Deal?

Certainly, there are any number of people who have been very pleased with their car-service experience. If this buying option appeals to you, get on the phone. Talk to the various services. Ask for referrals and then make up your own mind. As long as the car has a manufacturer's guarantee and as long as you don't hand over the check until you're completely satisfied, this may be something you'll want to explore.

VI

About Selling Your Car

How to Get More for Your Car by Selling It Yourself

1. Introduction

Okay, so you've decided to sell your car privately rather than trade it in or sell it to a used-car wholesaler. With that decision you find yourself with certain advantages and certain disadvantages of which you should be aware.

The Disadvantages

In short: the time, the effort, and possibly some hassle.

1. You have to deal with the "lookers," the "tire kickers," and all manner of other potential buyers on a one-to-one basis.
2. You have to endure phone calls.
3. You have to be sure that you're paid in cash, certified check, or bank check.
4. You must be aware of your personal liabilities as the seller and protect yourself from any future recourse by the buyer.

The Advantages

Basically: potentially more money for your car.

1. You stand to make more on the sale of your car to a private party than you will trading it in or selling it outright to a car lot or wholesaler.
2. There is no middleman.
3. You can price your car under the going dealership prices and

still make money because you don't have to deal with overhead or commissions.

The bottom line, then, is that while it takes more effort and time, by selling the car yourself you create the opportunity to make more money.

The Used Market

The used-car market is huge, with estimates ranging up to 40 million used-car, van, and light truck transactions every year. In addition, the percentage of first-time used-car buyers has been increasing steadily.

Virtually every make, model, and condition of used car is marketable or, to use the maxim of the trade: "There is a buyer for every car!" Even junkers or cars that don't run will have value to someone as a "fixer-upper" or as a source of spare parts. It can be said with a high degree of certainty there is always a buyer for your car. The question—and the most important from your perspective—is, at what price?

Keep in mind that even if your car has problems, be they cosmetic, mechanical, or electrical, those shortcomings may simply serve to make the car more affordable and therefore attractive to a certain kind of shopper. Thus, a high-mileage car, a bit long in the tooth and a little beat up *but reliable*, may be the perfect car for the college student seeking basic transportation or the person looking for something that "runs." You'll also find that those parents who opt to buy a car for their kids will be drawn to an older, larger car because it is likely to be safer than a bargain-priced econobox and because the price and the insurance will be lower than a more recent, mint condition model.

There is only one car like yours

Almost any used-car salesperson will tell you that the one major advantage they have selling a used car is that there is no other car exactly like it. Even another car of the same make, model, and year will not be exactly the same as the one the seller is offering. The mileage will vary, the type of driver who drove it most will vary, the body condition, the wear and tear or lack of it will vary, the care that was put into the car will vary, the tires will vary, and so forth and so on.

Unlike new-car buyers, the used-car buyer looking at your car can't shop for exactly the same car anywhere else. Nobody else has your car. And that's exactly the attitude that good used-car salespeople use.

Of course, they can shop for a similar model elsewhere. But what you're going to do is sell your used car on the basis of its uniqueness. And what constitutes uniqueness? The condition of the car is one thing. In addition, certain accessories will help make a car unique. Certain after-market items—yes, even special decorative paint jobs—will appeal to certain buyers. Having the service records helps make the car unique, as would an evaluation report performed by a mechanic. (More on this later.)

What matters most to used-car buyers?
For most the condition, the mileage, the horsepower, seating configuration, and the existence of options such as an AM/FM radio and air conditioning tend to be deal makers or breakers. Color and special trim packages tend to become less of a factor in the used-car market.

The record of past performance
Another advantage you may have is that your make and model car will have a performance record. Consumer guides such as *Consumer Reports* track owner opinions of reliability, the frequency of problems and repair costs. If your car has been rated well in one of the consumer magazines, you have yet another key selling point.

When to sell
Given the size and composition of the used-car market, if your car is priced right and properly prepped (more about that later), just about any time is the right time to sell. However, there are probably some selling times to avoid if you possibly can. For instance, between Thanksgiving and Christmas people usually have other plans for their money than they do during the high vacation periods of July and August.

2. Getting Your Car Ready to Sell

Assessing Your Car

Before you start thinking about setting a price or advertising, your first step should be to make a complete assessment of your car. You need to make an inventory of both its selling points and its weak points.

Step 1
Using the forms on the next pages that we developed for you to use when evaluating a used car, put yourself in the position of the buyer

and make a cold, detached assessment. See your car for what it really is. The purpose of this exercise is twofold:

First, it will give you an opportunity to look for those features that can be used as sales points. In other words, it will help you identify those features and aspects of the car that may appeal to potential buyers. Second, you should know your car's problems and shortcomings so that (1) you won't be surprised when a prospect points them out; and (2) you can make a decision as to whether or not you want to make a pre-sales investment in some repair and reconditioning work.

INTERIOR CHECKLIST

(The items with "$" indicate potentially expensive repair costs.)

Books and Records	**Yes**	**No**
Owner's manual	❑	❑
Maintenance records	❑	❑

General Appearance	**Excel.**	**Good**	**Fair**	**Poor**
Upholstery wear/stains	❑	❑	❑	❑
Rug wear/stains	❑	❑	❑	❑
General impression of interior	❑	❑	❑	❑
Front seats—check how they move/adjust	❑	❑	❑	❑
Window cranks (manual)	❑	❑	❑	❑
Smell (mildew, oil, gas, etc.)	❑	❑	❑	❑

Mechanical	**OK**	**Problem**
Glove box door	❑	❑
Ashtrays	❑	❑
Center armrests	❑	❑
Exterior rearview mirrors	❑	❑
Inside rearview mirror	❑	❑
Inside door handles	❑	❑
Seat adjustments	❑	❑

Electrical	**OK**	**Problem**	
Headlights—high/low beam	❑	❑	
Parking lights	❑	❑	
Taillights	❑	❑	
Brake lights	❑	❑	
Turn signals	❑	❑	
Emergency flashers	❑	❑	
Wipers (washers)	❑	❑	
Heater/Blowers	❑	❑	$

	OK	Problem	
Defrost	❑	❑	
Air conditioner	❑	❑	$
Radio/Stereo	❑	❑	$
Lighter	❑	❑	
Glove box light	❑	❑	
Interior dome light	❑	❑	
Rearview mirror adjustment	❑	❑	
Rear defrost	❑	❑	
Horn	❑	❑	
Power windows	❑	❑	
Power seats	❑	❑	

Instrument Panel Indicator Lights/Gauges	**OK**	**Problem**	
Oil pressure	❑	❑	$
Temperature gauge/light	❑	❑	
High beam/Low beam indicator	❑	❑	
Turn signal indicators	❑	❑	
Battery charging system (light/gauge)	❑	❑	
Speedometer	❑	❑	
Tachometer (RPM indicator)	❑	❑	

Trunk	**Yes**	**No**
Spare tire (Full spare or space saver)	❑	❑
Jack	❑	❑
Lug wrench	❑	❑
Other tools	❑	❑

EXTERIOR CHECK SHEET

(The items with "$" indicate potentially expensive repair costs.)

Exterior Body Condition	**Good**	**Fair**	**Poor**
Body condition (i.e., signs of rust)	❑	❑	❑
Finish and paint condition	❑	❑	❑
Door fit/open & close	❑	❑	❑

Tires	**Yes**	**No**	
Good condition	❑	❑	$
Pass "penny" test	❑	❑	
Even wear	❑	❑	
Matched set of tires	❑	❑	

Shock Absorbers	**Yes**	**No**	
Good condition	❑	❑	$

Exhaust System	**Yes**	**No**	
System appears well secured to car	❑	❑	$
Pressure test is good	❑	❑	$

Engine	**Pass**	**Fail**	
Smoke from tailpipe	❑	❑	$
Engine idle	❑	❑	
Knocking sounds	❑	❑	$
Engine runs hot at idle	❑	❑	$
Signs of oil on engine	❑	❑	$
Coolant low	❑	❑	
Oil is low	❑	❑	
Transmission fluid is orange	❑	❑	$
Transmission fluid smells burnt	❑	❑	$
Signs of leaking fluids under car	❑	❑	

TEST-DRIVE EVALUATION

(The items with "$" indicate potentially expensive repair costs.)

Brakes	**Pass**	**Fail**	
Straight-line stopping	❑	❑	
Brake pedal firm	❑	❑	$
Parking brake holds	❑	❑	
Acceleration			
Hill test	❑	❑	
Acceleration	❑	❑	
Highway speed test (sounds/overheating)	❑	❑	$
Car at idle (overheating test)	❑	❑	
Alignment and Suspension			
Rough road at 25 MPH test—holds straight line	❑	❑	$
Rattles or squeaks	❑	❑	
Steering—veer/drift test	❑	❑	$
Transmission			
No unusual sounds	❑	❑	$
Shift quality	❑	❑	$
Back and forth test—no clanks or thuds	❑	❑	$
Standard Transmission			
Shifting test—smooth, no grab, slips, or chatter	❑	❑	$
Hill test—clutch does not slip	❑	❑	$

Test Items	Pass	Fail	
Driving Evaluation			
Highway speed performance test	❑	❑	
Shimmy and vibration test	❑	❑	$
Steering			
Steering input—no sloppiness	❑	❑	
Wheel turn test—car stopped	❑	❑	
Turn wheel hard left/right and check for squeal	❑	❑	
Retest the Accessories			
Accessory retest—turn everything on	❑	❑	
Charging system	❑	❑	
Cruise Control			
Holds speed	❑	❑	
Disengages at touch of brake	❑	❑	
Engine Restart Test			
Engine restarts without hesitation	❑	❑	$
Recheck the Fluids			
Oil level	❑	❑	
Coolant level	❑	❑	
Transmission fluid level	❑	❑	
Evidence of drips or leaks underneath	❑	❑	$

Notes:

Step 2

As you can appreciate, one of the keys to successful selling is trust. And one way to establish that trust is to be able to present the potential buyer with a third-party assessment of your car's mechanical condition. What we suggest is that you use the Mechanic's Evaluation Checklist (see next page) that we introduced in "About Buying Used Cars" and have a mechanic go over the car, estimate the cost of the repairs, and then sign the evaluation sheet and attach his business card. This will make it easy for the potential buyer to call and verify the estimate. You might also want to make a deal with the mechanic to the effect that if the new owner brings the car in for repairs—or even if you do it—he'll give a discount on the repairs. The benefits of the evaluation form are:

1. It gives you a third-party evaluation that becomes a strong selling tool.
2. If the repairs are minimal, your honesty in presenting the sheet to the buyer will help build his or her trust in you.
3. You can use the mechanic's estimate in your negotiation as a means of dropping the price without appearing to have caved in on your asking price.

Of course, if the mechanic tells you that it's going to cost you more to fix the car than the car is worth, you can burn the evaluation sheet and let the car speak for itself. Remember, even a car that looks to be just one left turn from a junkyard will be of interest to someone.

Note: Below we have included a form for the Professional Mechanic's Evaluation. On the following page you'll find a "Personal Inventory Evaluation" form. This form was designed to let you look at your car on paper and to give you an opportunity to weigh its assets against its liabilities.

PROFESSIONAL MECHANIC'S INSPECTION

Test Items	**OK**	**Needs Repair**	**Est. Cost**
Brake check	❑	❑	$ ________
Engine test	❑	❑	$ ________
Charging system	❑	❑	$ ________
Cooling system test	❑	❑	$ ________
Spark plugs	❑	❑	$ ________
Emission level test	❑	❑	$ ________
Drive axle	❑	❑	$ ________
Suspension	❑	❑	$ ________
Alignment	❑	❑	$ ________
Tires	❑	❑	$ ________
Shocks	❑	❑	$ ________
Exhaust system	❑	❑	$ ________
Brake lines/Fuel lines	❑	❑	$ ________
Underbody rust	❑	❑	$ ________
Accident damage	❑	❑	$ ________
Total Repair Costs			**$** ________

Odometer accuracy ❑ Appears accurate

______________________________ ______________________

Professional Mechanic Date Inspected

PERSONAL INVENTORY EVALUATION

In your opinion, does each of the following represent a liability or an asset in terms of a potential buyer's interest in your car? Remember, even a bucket of bolts might be an asset to someone looking for parts. The purpose of this evaluation is to help you identify those features which can help sell the car or potentially kill the deal or force you to take less for your car. Recognizing your car's assets will also be useful in writing your classified ad. As you'll note, we've tried to suggest some guidelines for assets and liabilities. The guidelines are just that and subject to your personal evaluation.

Item	Liability	No Impact	Asset
Exterior Appearance			
Body condition	❑	❑	❑
Glass—no stars, cracks	❑	❑	❑
Bumpers	❑	❑	❑
Interior Appearance			
Mats and rugs	❑	❑	❑
Gas and brake rubber pedal covers	❑	❑	❑
Upholstery	❑	❑	❑
Door trim pieces	❑	❑	❑
Dashboard surface	❑	❑	❑
Headliner (cloth/plastic cover inside roof)	❑	❑	❑
Maintenance Costs			
What do your records show?	❑	❑	❑
How does *Consumer Reports* rate your car?	❑	❑	❑
Performance			
Pickup	❑	❑	❑
Mileage (odometer reading)			
10,000 per year or less is asset	❑	❑	❑
15,000 and up is liability	❑	❑	❑
Gas Mileage	❑	❑	❑
Safety Features			
Seat belts front/rear—asset	❑	❑	❑
Air bag(s)—asset	❑	❑	❑
Other—full-size car, crumple zones	❑	❑	❑

Item	Liability	No Impact	Asset
Accessories—assets			
Air conditioning	❑	❑	❑
Radio AM/FM	❑	❑	❑
Stereo	❑	❑	❑
Cassette player	❑	❑	❑
CD player	❑	❑	❑
Phone	❑	❑	❑
Power seats	❑	❑	❑
Power windows	❑	❑	❑
Other ________	❑	❑	❑
Trunk Size	❑	❑	❑
Tires			
Under 10,000 miles—asset	❑	❑	❑
Over 30,000—liability	❑	❑	❑
Spare Tire			
Full size—asset	❑	❑	❑
Space saver—no impact	❑	❑	❑
Jack & tools	❑	❑	❑
Records & Ownership History			
Maintenance records—asset	❑	❑	❑
All warranties and car-related records	❑	❑	❑
One owner—asset	❑	❑	❑
Previous owner—liability	❑	❑	❑
Mechanic's Assessment			
Under $300 repairs—asset	❑	❑	❑
Over $300—liability	❑	❑	❑

Assessing Your Evaluation

Look at your evaluation sheet. As you do, remember that as "seller" you are now a "marketer." As with anyone selling a product, you want to promote the product's assets and minimize its drawbacks or weak points.

The assets, then, should be considered for mention in your ad (more on that later). These are the points that you'll want to be sure a potential buyer sees and is made aware of. When it comes to the liabilities, you have a decision to make: Is it worth the time and money investment to have them repaired? Obviously, only you can make that decision. But to help you in making that decision we offer the following for your consideration:

General Appearance

Your car's general appearance may be the single most important factor in selling your car. If it needs repairs, pulls to the left, idles roughly, or has a hundred other problems, you very well may never get a chance to explain the problems or offer a price adjustment if the car is dirty or looks like a teenager's bedroom. Even if you decide to sell it as is, "as is" has to mean clean.

Every visible defect will weaken your negotiating position. You'll have to decide whether the repairs are worth the investment. Also, keep in mind that while some items may seem to be only cosmetic, *they may cause the car to fail state inspection.* For example, in some states a chipped windshield or a seriously cracked glass in any of the windows will fail inspection. Many windshield "stars," or chips, as they are called, can be repaired inexpensively by a new special process. (Visit an auto-parts store or look in your yellow pages under Auto Repair—Glass.) Otherwise, a new windshield may be required, and you should make note of the probable cost.

Exterior conditions

Rust If it is extensive, you are probably better off leaving the exterior pretty much as is except for a wash and wax. If body rust is minor and superficial, you may want to consider applying touch-up paint or, depending on the extent, a complete repaint. Be cautious about where and how this is done because, unless it is done carefully, the repaint will raise "What is this hiding?" questions in the mind of the buyer. Here again, you've got to calculate cost vs. possible return.

Paint If the paint is dull but not badly scratched, dented, nicked, etc., a good wash and wax will restore its luster and sales appeal. Small blemishes which are rust free are probably better left alone. Whatever touch-up work you do, *do it before waxing* because paint will not adhere well to a newly waxed surface.

Tires Your tires are a kind of diary of the age, suspension, alignment, and front-end condition of your car. Tires with uneven wear or a scalloped, cupped, or severe tread wear pattern tell a story of either neglect or problems. Old-looking, graying walls on otherwise healthy tires will also make a terrible first impression. Any auto-parts store will stock products to dress up your tires.

It's very important that all the tires match. They do not all have to be the same brand, but they should all be of the same ply design—radial or bias. For safety reasons, you can't mix and match these.

While you do not have to have four identical tires all around, you should have matched sets on the front and rear axles respectively.

Be sure to check the spare. Does it match your other tires, and do you have all the necessary tools (which came with the car) to change a flat?

Is the tire pressure correct in all four tires and the spare? If it isn't, it will lead to premature wear.

Interior Mats, rugs, and pedal pads can be washed, shampooed, or even replaced at a nominal cost. Upholstery may simply need a good cleaning with any of the many products available at an auto-parts store. If it has seriously deteriorated, you may want to consider seat covers. Again, cost vs. return is the principle.

Engine, Transmission, Brakes, Exhaust System These are all major items which should be thoroughly checked by your mechanic when he does your estimate. However, there are certain checks you can run yourself to discover possible problems in these areas.

Leaks With the car parked on a dry, non-absorbent surface, look underneath for any of the following:

1. *Thick black stains.* This is engine oil. It could be something simple like a loose oil pan bolt; however, it could represent much more serious and expensive trouble. This is a must for your mechanic's inspection.
2. *Red or orange stains with an oily texture.* This is most likely transmission fluid. Again, it could be a loose pan bolt or leaking gasket—relatively simple and cheap to fix. Very often it is more serious and has to be diagnosed by an expert.

Incidentally, either of these conditions should remind you to check the fluid level indicated by the stain. You may have had these leaks for some time and run the risk of engine seizure or transmission failure.

Engine oil should be checked only after a car sits idle for a few minutes so the oil can run back into the pan and enable you to get an accurate reading.

To check the transmission oil, the engine must be running and warm. In this case, you should check the level *and* the color. The fluid should be red. If it is brown or orange, you may have serious problems. The reading is done with a dipstick. Refer to your owner's manual for location. If you prefer, have it checked the next time you get fuel.

Finally, look under the engine for green or greenish white stains. This indicates a coolant leak. Check the coolant level. Unless your car is old, there is probably a plastic coolant tank with high and low indicator marks.

Hoses and Belts Once you have the hood up, carefully inspect all the hoses and belts. They are fairly inexpensive to replace but can cause catastrophic damage if they fail. Hoses should be firm and tightly anchored. If they are soft to the touch or badly oil-stained, change them.

Engine belts should not appear badly worn or frayed and should be properly adjusted.

Exhaust While you're peering under the car, note the condition of the exhaust system. Is it hanging by one rubber strap? Is it perforated with holes? Has it been making a great deal of noise or have you been smelling exhaust fumes inside the car? It is very possible that you have an exhaust leak of which you are unaware. Be sure to have this checked at the shop.

Paperwork You must have all the essential paperwork. This is not just the title, which you must make sure is properly filled out, but also a bill of sale, which you've bought at a stationery store, and the owner's manual. If you no longer have an owner's manual, order one from a dealer. They are cheap enough, and having one sends a good signal to a buyer.

A copy of your service records can make or break the deal. They show a history of care and maintenance and will instill confidence. If you have had your car serviced but did not keep the records, bear in mind that many repair facilities keep copies. Likewise, any warranties for tires, batteries, or mufflers should be at hand.

In the spirit of every little bit helps, if you think the prices from the used-car guides will strengthen your position, have copies available.

Other items Depending on the condition, make, and model of your car, van, or pickup there may be other items to consider as well. You might want to review chapters 4 through 8 in "About Buying Used Cars" for other things to consider in your personal evaluation.

3. Putting a Price on Your Car

There are two basic components of determining the asking price of your used car. First, you need to know its true wholesale value in your market and the going retail dealership price of cars similar to yours.

Second, you need to be aware that, like most of us, the person who buys your car wants to think he or she has gotten a deal. What you've got to do, then, is price your car so that your prospective buyer is motivated to close before someone else comes along and beats them to it.

We'll deal with each of these components separately.

Determining the Wholesale Price

Your first task is to find out what your car is worth at wholesale in your area. Yes, you can look at the car books, but in truth, it's the local market and not the books that ultimately determine worth. For example, we've seen many examples where a car is given one price in the national price books, but actually commands more in a specific market. There are any number of reasons for these variations. However, keep in mind that "Why?" is not as important as "How much?" Here are the steps that we suggest you take.

Step 1. Sell Your Car—But Not Really

Have your car detailed—cleaned up inside and out—so that it creates a positive first impression. Take it to three different used-car lots, tell them you want to sell it and that you're looking for a fair price.

When the used-car appraisers give you a price, you can assume that in most cases they are quoting you a figure that will be from 10 to 20 percent below the price that they believe the car will bring at auction. We had one used-car dealer tell us that if a car has an auction or true wholesale value of $12,000, he will always quote a figure 20 percent below. If the customer balks or suggests that he or she is going to get other bids, he'll begin to come up in hopes of closing the deal and dissuading the seller from visiting a competitive lot. If the used car is really in good shape—and understand that used-car lots are always in the market for cream puffs—they may even quote you a price above the wholesale figure, knowing that they can still put a good markup on the car and sell it retail.

No matter what price you're given, shake your head sadly and tell them that you really have to get more than what they've quoted. If the used-car lot buyer begins to come up, you know that he has indeed been testing your knowledge of what the car is really worth. If he refuses to come up, then you know that either he is at the top of what he believes to be its wholesale price or he simply isn't in the market for your car and would buy it only if the price was well below wholesale. (In that case, he'd simply call on one of his wholesalers and "flip" the car for maybe $500 and consider it a good hour's work.)

> Make note of all that the used-car dealer finds wrong with your car. Don't worry that they'll tell you because they want to lower your price expectations. Write this down, because you'll want to use the information later.

Step 2. "Buy Your Car"

Let's say you have a 1992 Ford Taurus with AM/FM radio, air conditioner, power seats, and power windows. The car has 47,000 miles on it, and it's in pretty good condition. Get on the phone and begin to call the used-car operations of your local Ford dealers as well as several independent lots. Ask for a salesperson and say something like the following:

"I'm in the market for a used car, and I would like a Ford Taurus. Probably a '92 would be in my price range. I'd like it to have an AM/FM radio and air-conditioning. And if it had some other options like power seats and windows, that would be great." At that point . . . stop. Let the used-car salesperson respond.

"What are you looking to spend?" will almost certainly be their response.

"Well, it all depends on the condition of the car. Have you got any '92's on your lot?"

At that point he or she will go get their inventory book and begin to look for a '92 Taurus. As they scan their inventory, you might expect to hear questions like: *"How soon are you looking to buy?" "Have you been shopping?"*

Tell them you're in the market now and that, no, you thought that before you ran all over town, you'd begin with the phone and that this is the first place you've called. Always tell them they are the first place you've called. It creates a false sense of security, and they will work a little harder, thinking that you're a virgin prospect.

Have them quote you prices on all the 1992 cars in their inventory. Be sure to ask for the mileage and the equipment (radio, AC, power seats, window, etc.) on the car. By the way, notice how differently they talk to you when they think you're a buyer and when they think you're a seller. It's a wonderful lesson in human psychology.

The purpose of this exercise is to find out what the lots are asking for your car. Remember, of course, that no two used cars are alike. But by calling several dealers you'll get a feel for the retail market on the car.

Once the salesperson has given you several prices, ask how much of a discount they are offering. They may tell you to name your price if they think that will bring you into the dealership. And remember, at this point, if they think you're a live buyer, they will say anything to get you in. However, it doesn't hurt to find out if the market is in a discounting mood or if your car is in such hot demand that the dealers aren't having to discount it.

Looking at the Numbers

You now have a good idea of the true wholesale price and the true retail asking price of your car. If you want, you can compare it to the industry price books, but keep in mind that these tend to reflect national or eastern/western prices and do not necessarily reflect the realities in your particular market. You might also want to glance through the newspaper and the used-car tabloids that come out each week to see how private owners are pricing cars like yours.

What Has Your Research Told You?

1. You know what your car will bring if you trade it in.
2. You know what a dealer would ask for your car were he to buy it and put it on the lot.
3. You know what the private sellers are asking. Some will be too high and some will be too low.

You might also want to call some of the private sellers (of cars like yours) and ask them if they've had much action. If you find someone who tells you that they've sold the car, try to engage them in conversation and give them the impression that you're just a babe in the woods. Tell them that you really want a car just like the one they sold and wonder what you will have to pay. The intent is to motivate them to tell you what they actually sold the car for. Depending on their asking price, it will add to your knowledge of the current market.

Pricing Psychology

At this point you're about ready to set an asking price. But first, a lesson in pricing psychology. In his book *You Can Negotiate Anything*—which we recommend, by the way—author Herb Cohen tells the story of a couple who walked into an antique shop and saw a grandfather clock that they liked. It was priced at $500. Believing they were good negotiators, they decided to try to work the price down. So after some discussion they approached the shop owner and announced that they'd like to buy the clock and that they'd give him $250 for it.

The shop owner then did something that absolutely destroyed the couple. He said, "Okay." No resistance, no attempt at negotiation—just "Okay."

The couple took the clock home and hated it. Why? Because the shop owner had violated the one rule of negotiation: You must make the buyer feel like he or she's gotten a deal. That they've won. This couple left wondering if the clock was worth $250, much less $500. Why had he given in so quickly? Unless maybe he knew something they didn't. Now, had the shop owner attempted to negotiate, had he said he couldn't part with it for less than $400 and then settled at $375, the couple would have left believing that not only had they managed to "steal" the clock, but they had proved themselves able negotiators. The satisfaction would have been not only in owning the clock, but in the achievement of a negotiation victory.

Let the Buyer Think He or She Has Won

Keep this in mind as you price your car: You want to leave "victory" room. One of the great ploys of successful car salespeople is to make their customers feel that they have somehow won the negotiation and have gotten a deal. The salesperson lets the customer believe he or she has won as they laugh all the way to the bank.

In addition, people expect you to negotiate the price. That's part of the game, and if you deny them the opportunity to play the game, they may not buy your car. So the key is to put your price above that which you really want or need to get. If by chance someone pays your full asking price, then you really have done well.

The only exception to the tactic of creating negotiation room is in those situations where you have a truly unique, one-of-a-kind high-demand car. One that is so sought after you might find two potential buyers bidding up the asking price. Note, however, that these situations are rare . . . very rare!

Setting the Price

Here's what we suggest you consider:

Set your price about 5 percent below the highest retail price that you've seen a dealer ask for a car like yours, but not higher than 5 percent above the average of all the private-owner offerings that you've seen in the paper. Take the highest wholesale price your car will bring—as determined by the used-car appraisers—and decide how much *above* the wholesale price is the *lowest* amount you'll accept. Remember, your ultimate goal is to make more money on your current car than you'd get from a dealer. You be the judge of how much above the trade-in price makes this exercise worth your while.

You now have an *asking price* and you know the price below which you will not go. Keep something else in mind: When you trade a car in on a new car, you pay sales tax only on the difference. Let's say your car is worth $8,000 at wholesale and you trade it in on a $20,000 car. If your sales tax rate is 6 percent, with the trade you'd pay $720 in sales tax. However, if you took the cash from the sale and added it to a loan, you'd have to pay sales tax on the full purchase price. In this case that would amount to $1,200. Obviously, you don't want the sales tax on a new car to eat up your profit.

4. Advertising

Look at some ads found in your local classified newspaper ads and used-car books. Make note of those which do the best job in attracting and holding your attention. See if they don't reflect some of the suggestions below.

Sell the Assets

Go back to your evaluation assessment and look at those items that you believe are your car's strongest assets. These are the things you want to call out in your ad.

You'll want to use terms like:

Mint condition
Excellent pickup
Low mileage
One owner
Loaded with options
Very clean
Great ride
Low maintenance
Rated ______ by (name of consumer book)
Excellent fuel economy
Like new
Meticulously cared for
All service records
Professional mechanic inspection report available.
And even: Great source of spare parts

One word of caution: While all these are "selling words," they must relate to the facts. If you like the idea of dealing with hostile buyers, just make claims about your car that aren't true. To reiterate: The key is to look for the assets and make those assets the core of your ad.

Advertising Options

Put a for-sale sign in the car window
Park the car in your front yard
Put a sign on your bulletin board at work
Place an ad in the classifieds
    Daily papers
    Weeklies
    Used-car books
Consider a selling service
    Those that will take your ad for one fee until it sells

Writing Ads That Sell

One of the primary goals of an ad is to attract the right prospects. For that reason, in addition to hyping your car, you'll want to be specific enough so that the reader will know if the car is what he or she is looking for and if the price is within their range. So be specific.

Equally important, your ad should arouse interest. To do that you need to select at least one strong feature and surround it with selling words.

Generally, an ad should start with the make, year and model, color, the number of doors, and any other information that will help specifically identify the car for the reader.

Only 18K miles. Like new. All serv. records. Many options.

Then state the price: $9,700, give your name—you need not give your last name—and the best times to call.

$9,700. Bob 555-1234. Call betwn. 6PM–10PM

> Don't overabbreviate—people won't understand what you're saying, and if it's too hard to read they will just skip over it. At the same time don't under abbreviate. A sure sign of a green seller is someone who spells out everything. This will not only cost you more, but sends the wrong signals to knowledgeable used-car buyers.

What If Your Car Has Mostly Liabilities?

Don't pretend in your ad that it's a cream puff if it isn't. Rather, sell it for what it is: *basic transportation, a fixer-upper, or a great source of parts. Great first car for student, runs good, needs body work.* Assuming you've priced it right, you'd be surprised at how many people will be attracted to the car.

The rule, then, is accent the positive—the assets—don't lie about the negatives. This is not to say that you need to disclose all the problems. If it's got some dings and dents and the interior has some stains, that doesn't have to be in the ad.

Staying Legal—Your Exposure as a Seller

Don't lie. It could get you in trouble. While the laws will differ from state to state, you can assume that if you say that a car is in mint condition and it turns out to be a junker, or if you claim that it hasn't been in an accident and it's just come from the body shop, you could be liable for damages brought by the buyer after the sale.

While used-car dealers have more stringent requirements, most states recognize express warranties. These are the things you say about the car in writing, in conversation with the buyer, and things that you even imply.

If the car has been in an accident and repaired, don't lie about it. The buyer could come back and demand recourse at some later date.

Now, having said that, understand that the burden of proof is on the buyer. He or she has to prove that you said something untrue while showing them the car. If you lied in your ad, it will be easier to prove.

The main thing is to be that which you'd like a used-car salesman to be: *honest*. This doesn't mean you have to point out the cut in the upholstery on the backseat, or the stain on the headliner, or the fact that the cassette player sometimes eats tapes. But it does mean that you don't mislead the buyer in a way that could lead to his buying your car based on your word that you've never had any mechanical problems, when in fact you know the transmission is about to fall out.

Finally, if you failed to disclose something that you *know* represents a safety hazard and that would normally be discovered by a mechanic during a general inspection, you could be sued for either breach of contract or fraud or even worse.

Know that in today's environment, judges tend to look at car sellers more negatively than they do car buyers. Don't create problems for yourself.

When to Run Your Ad

A general rule of thumb is to run an ad two days in a row toward the weekend. There are those who feel that Thursday and Friday are good days because it gives the prospect an opportunity to call and make an appointment for the weekend. There are those who believe that Saturday and Sunday are best because that's when people have time to look at the classified ads. One way to assess the best time in your market is to look at the number of ads for used cars each day of the week.

5. Let the Selling Begin!

When They Call

Ask yourself this: If you were to call on a car, what would you like to hear? Probably a friendly, honest-sounding voice on the other end of the line. Remember, as a seller, first impressions—even phone first impressions—are important.

Here are some tips:

1. Be enthusiastic but not overly so. You don't want to create the impression that this is the first and only call you've had—even if it is.
2. Create the impression that you want to be open and helpful in answering the caller's questions.
3. Create the feeling that while you want to sell the car, you're not really in a hurry. Any sign of overanxiousness gives the caller the sense that he or she can buy your car at a price well below what you've advertised.
4. Remember who's in control. You are. While you want to be accommodating, you should decide when and where the car can be seen. Make specific appointments. You don't want to have the person tell you, "I'll be over sometime on Saturday." Make a specific time. You don't want several people arriving on top of each other.
5. Answer their questions forthrightly. Look at the list of questions that appear in Chapter 2 of the "About Buying Used Cars" segment of this book. That will give you some idea of what the more knowledgeable buyers might ask. Chances are, typical potential buyers will want to know:
   - Have you had any problems with it?
   - How long have you had it and are you the first owner?
   - Has the car been in an accident?
   - Is it in good condition and does it run well?

And, of course, you'll get a question about the price. Is it firm? Will you negotiate? And so forth. Remember what your objective is: You want *real* buyers with *real* money to come look at your car. At the same time, while you know that they expect to negotiate, don't give them the impression that you're ready to roll over for whatever they offer.

If they ask the price, just answer $9,700. And say no more. You may be greeted by a long silence. The clever caller will know that "he/she who talks first loses." If you're greeted with silence, you might be tempted to say, *"Of course, I'm prepared to negotiate"* or *"That's what I'd like to get"* or *"That's what I'm told it's worth."* If you say anything like that, you've lost round one.

If the buyer comes back and says, *"Well, I know that's your asking price, but I assume you're prepared to negotiate,"* your answer should be hopeful—from the caller's point of view—but vague. For example, you might say: *"That depends on the offer."* Or you might use a classic car salesman answer: *"Before we talk price, maybe you should come out and see if the car meets your needs."*

Don't fall into the trap of saying how much less you're prepared to take or that you might drop the price by X amount. The key is to leave the door open for negotiation, but not to reveal too much of what's behind the door.

If you have a knowledgeable car buyer on the phone who says nothing after you state your price, it could be that he or she is trying to induce you, via the silence, into talking first and revealing some clue as to how anxious you are to sell the car. To break the silence without compromising your price position, simply ask, *"Do you have any more questions?"* or *"Would you like to make an appointment to see the car?"*

Again, keep in mind your objective: *To get qualified buyers to come look at your car.* Don't try to sell the car on the phone. It won't work. As we say in the car business, "The only way to sell a car is to put them behind the wheel."

What Should You Ask?

While you want to motivate people to come see your car, you don't want everyone to come. The phone call is an opportunity for you to sort the tire kickers from the buyers. Here are some tips:

1. Don't create the impression that your price is so flexible that your $9,700 car might be purchased by the buyer looking for something in the $6,000 range.
2. Ask when they plan to buy.
3. Ask if there is anyone other than themselves who will want to look at the car. This will tell you if you're dealing with a

teenager who will need parental approval or with a person who will need to have his or her spouse involved.

4. In conversation find out where they live. This may give you some clue as to the ability of the person to pay your price. If you're selling a Mercedes for $32,000 and the caller is from an economically disadvantaged neighborhood (how's that for being PC?) you might well wonder if you're talking to a real buyer.
5. Find out what they're driving now and how they plan to use the car. If this is to be a second car and they've got a fairly nice, upscale car, it may provide a clue as to their ability to buy your car.
6. You might also want to check to see if they are a dealer or a wholesaler looking to buy used cars at a "price." Generally, if the person sounds very, very knowledgeable and is focusing on your price, you may have a wholesaler on the line. Ask.

Finally, be aware that, like you, some callers may have read this book and are calling to help *themselves* establish the asking price of the car *they* are about to sell.

When the Prospect Arrives

Most people have no idea of how to inspect a used car—unless they're experienced car buffs, mechanics, or have read this book. You'll be able to tell from the outset if the person has experience by both the questions he or she asks and the way they go about the inspection. Their tactic may be to point out and suggest that there are so many things wrong with your car that it's not worth the price. If you've followed all the steps that we've suggested, you'll know exactly what is right and wrong with your car. If they're right, you can acknowledge it and even quote them a price—based on your mechanic's inspection sheet—of what it will take to repair it. If they're wrong, you can calmly suggest that your mechanic might disagree.

If you've got an expert—someone who really knows cars—the best thing is to just let them conduct their inspection and answer their questions directly, simply, and without much amplification. If there are problems with your car, they'll find them without your help.

One potential advantage of dealing with more experienced buyers is that they don't expect a used car to be perfect. They will look at it in terms of what needs to be done to put it into good condition and make reasonable allowances for normal wear and tear.

The Novice

If, as is more likely the case, the buyer is a novice, you may find yourself confronting any number of situations:

1. Buyers who have no idea of what they're looking at. They kick the tires, start the car, look blankly at the engine, and then attempt to make a deal. Oftentimes the most difficult aspect of closing the deal with these people is that they are afraid to make a decision. This is where you play the role of the salesperson (more below).
2. The novice buyer may be looking for perfection and expect the car to have all the attributes and be in the same condition as a new car. These people have to be educated to the fact that a used car is just that. And while the used car may have some defects, it has benefits as well. (See Part II, Chapter 1, "Pre-Shopping Preparation.")

You as the Seller

With the inexperienced used-car buyer, you might find it helpful to take a page out of the professional salesperson's book. We call it "hot-button selling," and the key is to identify the buyer's number one priority or concern and then "sell" to that concern. A good professional salesperson will ask the prospect—usually after a good rapport has been established—a question like this:

"What would you say is your number one priority—other than getting a good price—when it comes to buying a used car?"

Potential buyers may be surprised at the question, but if you can get them to take a moment to consider their answer, you may find that they will reveal their "hot button"—i.e., the one thing that must be satisfied in order for them to make the purchase. Notice that we take price out of the equation. Everyone wants a good price. What you want to know is what *beyond* a good price will motivate them to buy.

In many cases you'll find that their answer will be "reliability." They don't want to deal with a lemon. Your opportunity, at that point, is to sell them your "reliable car." If they say they want a car with great performance, your job is to sell them your "performance" car. If "safety" is the hot button, then you'll sell them your "safe" car.

Let's say for purposes of illustration that they answer your question with "a reliable car." This is where all your research and preparation will pay off. This will be your opportunity to prove that not only has your car been reliable, but also that in all likelihood it will continue to be reliable. How do you do that? By showing them the following:

1. *Consumer Reports* owner survey of repairs and reliability
2. Your mechanic's evaluation of the car
3. Your service and repair records

You might also take this opportunity to establish yourself as someone they can trust by pointing out a major problem. In truth, the major problem might be a very minor one. But the fact that you have pointed it out to them will build trust and confidence in you as the seller.

The Test Drive

If you're in the role of a used-car buyer, you'd like to have the car long enough to put it through the test-drive checklist that appears earlier in this segment. You'd also like the opportunity to take it to your mechanic for an inspection. In other words, you'd like to have the seller leave you alone with the car for an hour.

As the seller, the shoe is on the other foot. You probably don't know anything about the prospect. Certainly, you don't want to give the person your keys and then discover that the car has found its way to a chop shop, where it's been hacked into resalable parts. Nor do you want to let someone drive your car who thinks that every road is the Indianapolis Speedway and run the risk of putting some nice dents into the side.

Understand that a knowledgeable prospect will want to put your car through its paces. This means acceleration, braking, and handling tests. Here's what we suggest:

1. If you feel uneasy about the prospect, insist on riding with him or her.
2. Check your insurance to be sure that if anything does happen, you are covered.
3. If you feel uneasy about the driver, tell him or her that your insurance company wants you to write down the name, address, and license number of anyone driving your car. Blame it on your insurance company. If the prospect balks, ask yourself, "Why?" and proceed with caution.
4. If you decide to let the person take the car for a test drive on their own, make sure they leave their car—it should be a comparable or more expensive one—and the car keys. If you have any doubts about the person, ask for the license—for insurance purposes—and then check the name against the registration of the prospect's car.

This sounds like a lot of effort, and in most cases you will probably feel it's not necessary. The main thing is always to look out for your own interests.

Preparing for the Negotiation

During the test drive you have an excellent opportunity to learn things about your prospects. Their occupation, where they live, what their interests are. The more you know about prospects, the better prepared you'll be for the negotiation. On the other hand, reveal little about yourself. The last thing a prospect should know is that you're short of cash, that you need to sell the car, or that you've got your eye on a new car and can hardly wait to unload the current car. Remember: Good negotiators know as much as possible about their opponents while revealing as little as possible about themselves.

Returning from the Test Drive

Once you return, listen for buying signals. If the prospect starts talking about price or asks when you'll be ready to close a deal, you're on the way. If, however, he or she remains noncommittal, you might want to take their measure with questions like:

"How would you rate this car?" or *"How does it measure up to what you were expecting?"* Notice that these are what we call open-ended questions. They cannot be answered with a simple yes or no. The reason you ask these questions is to find out:

1. If you have a hot prospect
2. If there is something about the car that the prospect didn't like that you can explain or that you should deal with before the next prospect comes along

If the prospect is accompanied by a spouse or friend, ask for their opinions as well. Remember, when the prospect brings others, you are probably going to have to sell everyone on the value and desirability of the car.

The Negotiation

Here are the keys to a good negotiation strategy:

Read Your Customer

Look for signals that tell you he or she has fallen in love with the car. Once potential buyers reveal their true feelings, you are in control. However, always assume that the prospect has done his or her homework. This is frequently *not* the case, but it's a good assumption to make until they prove otherwise. If you know your car and know the market, you'll be able to deal with any suggestions that your car is overpriced.

Make Them Offer First

Never drop your price before they make their first offer. Good negotiators will try to get you to reduce your price before they offer theirs. One of the tactics of a good negotiator is to know how to deflect questions about "dropping the price."

PROSPECT: *What are you looking to get?*
YOU: *I'm looking to get* (quote the asking price).

PROSPECT: *Are you willing to negotiate?*
YOU: *You're certainly free to make an offer.*

PROSPECT: *What's the least you'll accept?*
YOU: *That depends on what you're prepared to offer.*

PROSPECT: *Are you flexible on the price?*
YOU: *You're certainly free to make an offer.*

PROSPECT: *What other offers have you had?*
YOU: *Several. But please feel free to make yours.*

Sell the Value

Be ready to increase the perceived value of your car. If you've gotten a professional mechanic's inspection and it shows that your car is in excellent shape, you might want to reveal this fact during the negotiation as a means of demonstrating to the buyer the car is really worth your asking price. On the other hand, you might want to use it earlier in the process to establish your candor and to help support the value and condition of the car.

Create Competition

One of the things that used-car salespeople try to do is create a sense of urgency by telling you that someone else is interested in the car and that another potential buyer plans to return within the hour . . . *"so if you are really interested in this car, give me a deposit so I can hold it for you."* Sometimes car salespeople lack subtlety and you can see right through their ploy. You, on the other hand, can accomplish the same thing without being quite so obvious.

The ploy is ingeniously simple: Call them by the wrong name. If a person has come back for a second look, greet them warmly. But if their name is Brown, say: *"I'm glad you came back, Mr. Jones."*

When he corrects you, act embarrassed and apologize: *"I'm sorry,*

I just got off the phone with Mr. Jones. It's amazing what a single ad will do."

Or you can say: *"I'm sorry, I got mixed up. Brown is coming at three."* Then totally change the subject. The message that there is someone else interested in the car will have gotten through more effectively than if you had said: *"Someone else is interested in the car."*

Be Ready to Toss in an Extra

If you're close and the buyer has refused to up his or her bid, you can offer to add some things to the deal which have a low dollar cost to you but a high perceived value to the buyer. You can offer to pay for the repairs on the mechanic's checklist, especially if they are not high and if the mechanic will give you a deal on the repairs.

- You can offer to deliver the car with a full tank of gas
- Have it cleaned and waxed
- New floor mats
- Or something else of perceived value like an extra tire you might have lying around

Drop Your Price in Decreasing Increments

Remember the psychology of pricing. You want to price it high enough to leave room to back off so that the buyer will feel that he or she has "won." Here's how professional car people do this. Let's say your asking $9,000 and the prospect offers $7,800. You've already decided that the lowest you'll go is $8,200. Your counterbid might be a drop of $400. However, before you make your offer, you might want to emulate the professionals. Get out your calculator and do a lot of figuring and adding. Shake your head a lot and show some "pain." You make your counteroffer and then say nothing. Make the buyer respond before you say anything, even if you end up with five minutes of silence. Let's say he responds by upping his bid to $8,000. Go through the same process as before and show some more pain, then offer a reduction of $175. That puts your price at $8,425 and the buyer raises his offer to $8,250.

At this point, you've got your bottom price, but don't leave any money on the table. Back to your calculator and then counter with an even smaller drop of, say, $75. Now you're at $8,375. With every drop, of course, you should convey the impression that the buyer is one heck of a negotiator. At this point he says $8,300 and you agree to split the difference. By carefully countering his or her bid with *descending amounts* accompanied by a measured amount of visible pain, you're telling the buyer that he or she is getting closer to your bottom line. If you were to drop your bids by $200, then $100, and then $300, the buyer might assume that there is a lot more play in your price and keep negotiating. By decreasing your counterbid in ever smaller amounts, you are creating the impression that you have a number below which you will not or cannot go.

Think this part of the negotiation through ahead of time. Rehearse in your mind how you plan to drop your asking price. Remember, go slowly. And don't drop your price until you're absolutely sure that the buyer won't meet your asking price. If you feel that the buyer is in love with your car and is only looking for a face-saving negotiation victory, you might begin your counteroffer by agreeing to toss in one of the extras mentioned above.

Be Prepared to Walk Away

Always be prepared to walk away from the deal. If you're asking $9,000 and you know that the same car is on the used-car lots for $9,800 and that the wholesale value is $6,800 and the buyer is offering no more than the wholesale price and refuses to budge, there is nothing that says you can't just thank the buyer and end the negotiation. The key is to have a bottom line when you start your negotiation. If several potential buyers suggest that your price is too high and refuse to negotiate their bids up, you may want to go back and reexamine your evaluation of the car's value and the validity of your asking price.

The Offer

The buyer gives you a price. Let's say for the sake of discussion that your asking price is $9,000 and that your bottom line is $8,000. No matter what the buyer offers, unless it's $9,000, pretend to go into deep thought and say nothing. Generally, most people will offer something below that which they are really prepared to pay as a means of testing your price. As we explained on the previous page, your goal is to get them to up their bid before you make a counteroffer. To do that—and this won't always work, but it does most of the time—say nothing. Appear to be deep in thought. Create a large silence. If the buyer is like most people, he or she will try to fill that silence with apologies or excuses for the bid.

"Well, I'm sure that's less than you want."

"I could probably do a little better than that."

If you get a statement that suggests the person is prepared to go higher, ask how much more they can go. And again, say nothing. Force the buyer by your silence to up the offer.

Let's Say the Negotiation Goes as Follows:

Buyer: Offers $7,500
You: Say nothing
Buyer: Indicates he/she could go higher
You: How much higher?
Buyer: Maybe $8,000

At this point what you've done is narrowed the negotiation gap from $1,500 to $1,000. Keep in mind that the buyer is fully aware of your asking price and that he or she is probably not expecting you to part with the car for $7,000. But if they don't ask, they'll never know. And it could be that they might hope you're one of those people who get discouraged quickly and will be happy to get any price above the wholesale value and be done with the whole thing.

However, if you're looking to maximize your profit, you'll negotiate. Again, remember the clock story: If the buyer feels that he has had to work for the price, he'll leave feeling he has won, whatever the price.

Will This Strategy Always Work?

Nothing will *always* work. Professional automotive sales trainers tell salespeople to think of themselves as improvisational actors. These are actors who are given a scenario by someone in the audience, and the actors are then required to make up their lines as they go along. In this case the potential buyer is creating the scenario, and you, as seller, are going to have to adjust your responses to the buyer's scenario.

Closing the Deal

You and the buyer have agreed on the price. You're ready to close. Here are some tips to keep in mind:

As any car dealer will tell you, the best deals are those that close on the spot. If you agree to a price and the buyer says he or she will be back the next day with the money, there is always the chance that the buyer will decide to keep looking in hopes of finding yet a better deal or that for some other reason he or she will get cold feet.

To help minimize the risk of the deal falling through, you can ask the buyer for a small deposit. Fifty to one hundred dollars will usually assure that the buyer will come back. You might say something like this:

"Wednesday will be fine to close the deal. Now that we've agreed on the price, I'm assuming that the car is sold and I'll take the car off the market and not show it to anyone else." At that point you might want to produce a form like the one shown on the next page.

INTENT TO PURCHASE AGREEMENT

I agree to sell my ______________________________ with VIN# __________to
(NAME, MAKE, AND MODEL)
____________________________________ for a total price of $ _________.
(NAME OF BUYER)

It is agreed that we will conclude this transaction on __________(date). At that time I will deliver a clear title in exchange for cash or a certified check for the full amount less the deposit.

With this agreement I acknowledge the receipt of $ __________ against the purchase price. This deposit represents the buyer's good-faith intention to buy the car at the stated price and the seller's promise to deliver the car as shown to the buyer on this date.

Received $ _________
From ______________________________
Address ______________________________
Date __________

____
Seller's Signature

Buyer's acknowledgment of agreement
Name ______________________________Date ____________________

This document serves much the same purpose as the buyer's order in a dealership. First, it gives monetary credibility to the buyer's agreement to buy the car. If they won't leave a deposit, you have to assume that the buyer is not sure of his or her decision and wants time to back out.

Furthermore, this document helps create a sense of *"my shopping is done and I don't have to look any further"* attitude on the part of the buyer.

How Long Before the Close?

Unless you feel very confident of the buyer's intentions—remember, even friends back out of deals—you might want to insist that the deal be consummated within no more than three days.

Are You Obliged to Give the Deposit Back?

As with the deposit asked by dealerships, if there is no stipulation in the agreement saying that the deposit will be forfeited should the buyer decide not to buy, most sellers return the deposit. But since the buyer will have to return to pick up the deposit, you will have another opportunity to try to close the deal. If you decide to make the deposit nonrefundable, that's your choice. While you may want to check with a lawyer, generally any agreement that both parties sign is binding.

Form of Payment

Unless you know the person to whom you are selling and have trust in that person, you should never accept any form of payment other than cash, a certified bank check, or a bank draft. No personal checks. (Even friends have been known to bounce checks.)

Clear Title

Obviously, you can't sell the car without the title, and if you still owe money on the car you will have to pay it off before the lender (the holder of the note) will release the title. If you owe money you can:

1. Pay off the note before you sell the car.
2. If the note is too large to pay it off before selling the car, arrange for the close to take place at the bank or wherever the note is being held. That way you can pay off the note, take possession of the title, sign it over, and release it to the new buyer in one transaction. We suggest that you discuss with the lender how they would like to handle the close.

Sales Tax, Plates, Registration Fees, Insurance

These are all the responsibility of the buyer. Remember, however, to cancel your own insurance on the car immediately after the sale.

Closing Checklist

To conclude your transaction, you should be prepared with the following at the close:

1. Go to your local stationery or business supply store and buy a bill of sale form. Fill it out and keep a copy for your records.

   Bill of sale should include the following items:
   - Date of sale
   - Year, make, and model description
   - Tag number and state of registration
   - Vehicle identification number
   - Odometer reading
   - Amount paid for car and type of payment
   - Conditions of the sale, if any
   - Seller's and buyer's names, addresses, and phone numbers
2. Be sure that all the blanks are filled in on anything you and the buyer sign.

3. Be sure that the wording on any agreement that you might have made with the buyer, e.g., to provide mats or to pay for part of the repairs, is clear and exact in its meaning. If the car is to be sold "as is," note this fact on the bill of sale.
4. A clear title to the car
5. Check to see whether you need to fill out any relevant state or local forms for completion of the sale.

PRE-CLOSING CHECKLIST

Be sure to give the buyer:

- Title with VIN corresponding to car ❑
- Odometer statement ❑
- Owner's manual ❑
- Maintenance books and records ❑

VII

The Checklists

NEW-VEHICLE EVALUATION CHECKLIST

1 Poor, 2 Fair, 3 Okay, 4 Good, 5 Excellent

	1	2	3	4	5
General Quality Impression					
Exterior (fit, finish, paint)	❑	❑	❑	❑	❑
Interior (workmanship)	❑	❑	❑	❑	❑
Comfort					
Ease of entry front and back	❑	❑	❑	❑	❑
Headroom front	❑	❑	❑	❑	❑
Headroom back	❑	❑	❑	❑	❑
Legroom front	❑	❑	❑	❑	❑
Legroom back	❑	❑	❑	❑	❑
Seat support/comfort	❑	❑	❑	❑	❑
Ease of access to controls	❑	❑	❑	❑	❑
Visibility	❑	❑	❑	❑	❑
Trunk space	❑	❑	❑	❑	❑
Riding and Handling					
Acceleration	❑	❑	❑	❑	❑
Passing acceleration	❑	❑	❑	❑	❑
Hill climb power	❑	❑	❑	❑	❑
Cornering	❑	❑	❑	❑	❑
Steering response	❑	❑	❑	❑	❑
Road feel—bumps	❑	❑	❑	❑	❑
Braking	❑	❑	❑	❑	❑
General Impression					
Interior noise	❑	❑	❑	❑	❑
Rattles/Squeaks	❑	❑	❑	❑	❑
Sound system	❑	❑	❑	❑	❑
Convenience features	❑	❑	❑	❑	❑
Safety Equipment	**Yes**	**No**			
Air bags—driver	❑	❑			
passenger	❑	❑			
side	❑	❑			
ABS brakes	❑	❑			
Traction control	❑	❑			

PRICE INFORMATION WORK SHEET

Make ______________________ Model ______________________ Year __________

VIN Number* ______________________ City Mileage ______________________ Highway __________

1	2 MSRP— List Price	3 Dealer Cost	4 Difference/ Profit
Price of Vehicle	________	________	________
Options			
______________	________	________	________
______________	________	________	________
______________	________	________	________
______________	________	________	________
______________	________	________	________
Totals	________	________	________
Supplemental Charges— "Dealer Packs"			
______________	________		________
______________	________		________
______________	________		________

*VIN number is the identifying number of the vehicle, which is usually found by looking through the left front of the windshield at the bottom of the support pillar. Or you can find it on the Monroney sticker itself.

FINANCIAL WORK SHEET

1. If you have a trade-in: Enter the wholesale value of your trade-in as determined by having car appraised by three different dealers $ ________
2. The amount, if any, that you owe on trade-in $ ________
3. The amount of equity you have in your trade (line 1 minus line 2) $ ________
4. The amount of cash you plan to use as down payment $ ________

---

5. Total amount of cash and trade-in equity you have to put against new car (add lines 3 and 4) $ ________

---

6. MSRP (window sticker price) $ ________
7. Invoice (cost to dealer of car/options—use your *Edmund's* or similar source) $ ________
8. Dealer hold-back (Use 3% of MSRP as estimate) $ ________
9. Factory-to-dealer incentive (check second-to-last page in recent issue of *Automotive News* in library) $ ________

---

10. Actual dealer cost (lines 8 plus 9 minus line 7) $ ________
11. Total potential dealer profit were car sold for MSRP. Line 6 minus line 10 (this primarily for your reference) $ ________

---

12. Maximum amount of profit you plan to offer over dealer's cost (line 10) $ ________

---

13. Total amount you plan to pay for vehicle (line 10 plus line 12) before taxes, title, registration, and transportation charges $ ________

---

14. All other charges
    - Transportation $ ________

- State sales taxes* $ ________
- Title fees $ ________
- Registration $ ________

Total $ ________

15. Total amount of transaction (line 13 plus line 14) $ ________

16. The amount to be financed (line 15 minus line 5)** $ ________

17. Difference between the equity in your trade (line 3) and amount you plan to pay (line 13)*** $ ________

*Remember, if you have a trade-in, you pay sales tax only on the difference between what you receive for your trade-in and the final negotiated price of the car.

**It would be wise to be sure that this amount is at least 20 percent below the invoice (cost) of the car. If you plan to finance through the dealership, check their rates before you shop for the car.

***The reason for establishing this figure is so that you can compare it to the number the salesperson writes on the order as the *amount owed*. If your "difference" and their "difference" are not the same, make sure you know why and that you agree.

BUYER'S ORDER CHECK SHEET

1. The date of the transaction
2. Make and model of the car you are buying
3. The VIN number of the car you are buying
4. The total amount that you have agreed to pay for the car
5. The amount of money they are giving you for your trade
6. The amount of the payoff on your current car
7. The VIN number of your trade-in
8. The difference in dollars between what you have agreed to accept for your trade (less any payoff due) and the amount you have agreed to pay for the car
9. The amount to be financed if you are financing through the dealership
10. The number of payments if you are financing through the dealership
11. Annual percentage rate (APR) if you are financing
12. A list of all the fees beyond the price you've agreed to pay: e.g., title, taxes, etc.
13. A clear statement of the warranty that will come with the car

BEFORE YOU SIGN—CHECKLIST

- ❑ **Mileage Statement**
  - Has the mileage of your trade-in been entered?
  - Are all the blanks filled out?
- ❑ **New-Vehicle Mileage**
  - Is the mileage statement on the new car the same as on the odometer?
- ❑ **Used-Vehicle Mileage (used vehicle purchase only)**
- ❑ **Power of Attorney**
- ❑ **Finance Contracts**
  - Is the VIN number the same on the buyer's order and finance contract?
  - Is the figure for the amount you intend to finance the same on both?
  - Are the finance charges the same as you agreed?
  - Are there other charges to which you have agreed?
  - Check the other fees normally associated with a new car purchase.
- ❑ **Is the APR (annual percentage rate) as agreed?**
- ❑ **Do the amount and number of payments reflect the total number of months you have agreed to pay?**
- ❑ **Warranty Agreements**
  - Have you read the warranty?
  - Do you understand what is and what is not covered?
  - Are the agreed exceptions in writing?
  - Has the warranty been signed by management?
- ❑ **Have you received the owner's manual and maintenance record books?**
- ❑ **Did you receive two sets of keys?**
- ❑ **Has the dealership arranged for the license and registration?**
  - Do you have all registration records?
  - Have you arranged for your insurance?
  - Is your insurance form in the glove compartment?

WHAT TO ASK WHEN CALLING ABOUT A CLASSIFIED AD

Use the following chart to develop a fact list of the car you're calling on. Review it with the seller to be sure that the ad reflects reality.

Vehicle Description

Make ____________________ Model designation ____________________
Year __________ Number of miles showing on odometer __________________
Color exterior __________ Color interior __________
Seat covering: Fabric ❑ Leather ❑
Engine size (number of cylinders) ________
Gas ❑ Diesel ❑
Doors: Two-door coupe ❑ Four-door ❑ Hatchback ❑ Sun roof ❑
Power equipment: Electric windows ❑ Electric seats ❑
Radio: AM/FM ❑ Cassette ❑ CD player ❑
Full spare ❑ or space saver ❑
Other items ____

After you've confirmed the description and content of the vehicle, we suggest that you ask the following questions.

1. **Tell me about the condition of the car.**

   (Phrasing the question this way should motivate the seller to provide more information. Don't waste your time with a seller who tells you that it "runs good." This usually means that the car has problems and that even he or she can't think of anything good to say about it.)

Notes:

____

____

____

____

2. **What features does it have?**

Notes:

____

____

____

____

3. **How many miles does the car have on it?**
(Write this down and check it against the odometer when you inspect the car.)

Owner's declared mileage: __________

4. **Are you a used-car dealer?**
(Sometimes used-car dealers put ads in the classifieds, and you'll want to know this before going any further. They could be selling a lemon or a car without a title or a car that won't pass inspection or one that they would prefer not to have associated with the car lot. This is called "curbing." Avoid these people.)

❑ YES ❑ NO

5. **Are you the original owner of the car?**
(If the answer is no, ask how long they have owned the car. Obviously, it's best to buy a used car from the original owner if only because you'll have a better chance of determining its maintenance and repair history. Recently we ran into a situation in which a wholesaler sells cars by masquerading as a private owner. What he does is buy cars at auction that legitimate dealers won't touch, cars that have been in a wreck and then fully repaired. The wholesaler buys them for a very low price, brings them home, and sells them out of his front yard for a price equal to those that one could charge for the car had it not been wrecked. Obviously, he never informs the buyer of the car's history, and most buyers never take the time to have the car fully inspected. Here again is another reason to take any used vehicle to a professional for evaluation.)

❑ YES ❑ NO How long owned? __________

6. **Do you have the maintenance and repair records?**
(Any owner that has kept the maintenance and repair records probably has taken good care of the car.)

❑ YES ❑ NO

7. **What would you estimate it's going to cost to put the car in A-1 condition?**
(This question forces the seller into making an on-the-spot evaluation. Most will try to give you a reasonable estimate, even though it will probably be a conservative one. If the seller tells you that it's in mint condition and you arrive to find a bucket of bolts, you'd be advised to say good-bye.)

Owner's estimated amount of repairs: $ __________

Notes:

______

______

______

______

8. Why are you selling the car?

(This question may help you learn how anxious he or she is to sell the car, and it may supply some information you can use in your negotiation.)

______

______

______

______

9. What is your asking price?

(By using the term "asking price" you are letting the seller know that you're assuming that the "asking price" is higher than what you will actually accept. Here's another question designed to test the seller's pricing resolve. This question should be asked once you feel that you've established a good rapport with the seller. Asked in a conversational, matter-of-fact manner, it can reveal much about the seller's eagerness to make a deal. *What do you expect to get for your car?*

Asking price: $ ______

PRICE ESTIMATE WORK SHEET

Make ________________ Model designation ________________

Year ________ Number of miles showing on odometer ________________

Color exterior ________ Color interior ________ Seat covering: Fabric ❑ Leather ❑

Engine size (number of cylinders) ________ Gas ❑ Diesel ❑

Doors: Two-door coupe ❑ Four-door ❑ Hatchback ❑ Sun roof ❑

Equipment: Power windows ❑ Power seats ❑ Power rearview mirrors ❑

Cruise control ❑ AM/FM ❑ Cassette ❑ CD player ❑ Full spare ❑ space saver ❑

Other items ________________________________

Private seller's asking price ________

Dealer price quoted to buy car ________

Used car dealer price quote ________

EXTERIOR CHECK SHEET

(The items with "$" indicate potentially expensive repair costs.)

Exterior Body Condition	**Good**	**Fair**	**Poor**
Body condition(i.e., signs of rust)	❑	❑	❑
Finish and paint condition	❑	❑	❑
Door fit/open & close	❑	❑	❑

Tires	**Yes**	**No**	
Good condition	❑	❑	$
Pass "penny" test	❑	❑	
Even wear	❑	❑	
Matched set of tires	❑	❑	

Shock Absorbers	**Yes**	**No**	
Good condition	❑	❑	$

Exhaust System	**Yes**	**No**	
System appears well secured to car	❑	❑	$
Pressure test is good	❑	❑	$

Engine	**Pass**	**Fail**	
Smoke from tailpipe	❑	❑	$
Engine idle	❑	❑	
Knocking sounds	❑	❑	$
Engine runs hot at idle	❑	❑	$
Signs of oil on engine	❑	❑	$
Coolant low	❑	❑	
Oil is low	❑	❑	
Transmission fluid is orange	❑	❑	$
Transmission fluid smells burnt	❑	❑	$
Signs of leaking fluids under car	❑	❑	

INTERIOR CHECKLIST

(The items with "$" indicate potentially expensive repair costs.)

Books and Records	Yes	No
Owner's manual	❑	❑
Maintenance records	❑	❑

General Appearance	Excel.	Good	Fair	Poor
Upholstery wear/stains	❑	❑	❑	❑
Rug wear/stains	❑	❑	❑	❑
Overall impression of interior	❑	❑	❑	❑
Front seats—check how they move/adjust	❑	❑	❑	❑
Window cranks (manual)	❑	❑	❑	❑
Smell (mildew, oil, gas, etc.)	❑	❑	❑	❑

Mechanical	OK	Problem
Glove box door	❑	❑
Ashtrays	❑	❑
Center armrests	❑	❑
Exterior rearview mirrors	❑	❑
Inside rearview mirror	❑	❑
Inside door handles	❑	❑
Seat adjustments	❑	❑

Electrical	OK	Problem	
Headlights—high/low beam	❑	❑	
Parking lights	❑	❑	
Taillights	❑	❑	
Brake lights	❑	❑	
Turn signals	❑	❑	
Emergency flashers	❑	❑	
Wipers (washers)	❑	❑	
Heater/Blowers	❑	❑	$
Windshield defroster	❑	❑	
Air conditioner	❑	❑	$
Radio/Stereo	❑	❑	$
Lighter	❑	❑	
Glove box light	❑	❑	
Interior dome light	❑	❑	
Rearview mirror adjustment	❑	❑	

Rear defrost	❑	❑
Horn	❑	❑
Power windows	❑	❑
Power seats	❑	❑

Instrument Panel Indicator Lights/Gauges	**OK**	**Problem**	
Oil pressure	❑	❑	$
Temperature gauge/light	❑	❑	
High beam/Low beam indicator	❑	❑	
Turn signal indicators	❑	❑	
Battery charging system (Light/gauge)	❑	❑	
Speedometer	❑	❑	
Tachometer (RPM indicator)	❑	❑	

Trunk	**Yes**	**No**
Spare tire (full spare or space saver)	❑	❑
Jack	❑	❑
Lug wrench	❑	❑
Other tools	❑	❑

Important Note: Don't let the seller hurry you in this inspection or suggest that it isn't necessary. Remember whose money you're spending.

TEST-DRIVE EVALUATION CHECKLIST

(The items with "$" indicate potentially expensive repair costs.)

Brakes	**Pass**	**Fail**	
Straight-line stopping	❑	❑	
Brake pedal firm	❑	❑	$
Parking brake holds	❑	❑	
Acceleration			
Hill test	❑	❑	
Acceleration	❑	❑	
Highway speed test (sounds/overheating)	❑	❑	$
Car at idle (overheating test)	❑	❑	
Alignment and Suspension			
Rough road at 25 MPH test—holds straight line	❑	❑	$
Rattles or squeaks	❑	❑	
Steering—veer/drift test	❑	❑	$
Transmission			
No unusual sounds	❑	❑	$
Shift quality	❑	❑	$
Back and forth test—no clanks or thuds	❑	❑	$
Standard Transmission			
Shifting test—smooth, no grab, slip, or chatter	❑	❑	$
Hill test—clutch does not slip	❑	❑	$
Driving Evaluation			
Highway speed performance test	❑	❑	
Shimmy and vibration test	❑	❑	$
Steering			
Steering input—no sloppiness	❑	❑	
Wheel turn test—car stopped	❑	❑	
Turn wheel hard left/right and check for squeal	❑	❑	
Retest the Accessories			
Accessory retest—turn everything on	❑	❑	
Charging system	❑	❑	
Cruise Control			
Holds speed	❑	❑	
Disengages at touch of brake	❑	❑	

Engine Restart test			
Engine restarts without hesitation	❑	❑	$
Recheck the Fluids			
Oil level	❑	❑	
Coolant level	❑	❑	
Transmission fluid level	❑	❑	
Evidence of drips or leaks underneath	❑	❑	$

Important Note: Anytime you need to start the car, either during the walk-around or for the test drive, you should be the one to do it. However, the owner should tell you if there are any tricks to starting such as having the seat belts on, the transmission in park, a foot on the brake, etc.

PROFESSIONAL MECHANIC'S INSPECTION

Test Items	**OK**	**Needs Repair**	**Est. Cost**
Brake check	❑	❑	$ ________
Engine test	❑	❑	$ ________
Charging system	❑	❑	$ ________
Cooling system test	❑	❑	$ ________
Spark plugs	❑	❑	$ ________
Emission-level test	❑	❑	$ ________
Drive axle	❑	❑	$ ________
Suspension	❑	❑	$ ________
Alignment	❑	❑	$ ________
Tires	❑	❑	$ ________
Shocks	❑	❑	$ ________
Exhaust system	❑	❑	$ ________
Brake lines/Fuel lines	❑	❑	$ ________
Underbody rust	❑	❑	$ ________
Accident damage	❑	❑	$ ________
Total Repair Cost Estimate			$ ________

Odometer accuracy ❑ Appears accurate ❑ Questionable

Explain:

BEFORE YOU SIGN

1. Read everything . . . twice!
2. Be sure that anything you sign has all the blanks filled in.
3. Be sure that the wording on any agreement, bill of sale, and/or warranty is specific, clear, and exact in its meaning.
4. An Odometer Mileage Statement must be provided stating that, to the best of the seller's knowledge, the odometer has not been tampered with. The odometer statement can be made part of the bill of sale. (In some states this is part of the title.)
5. Be sure you fully understand and agree with the warranty—if it has one. (See explanation of warranties in Part II, Chapter 2.)
6. Bill of sale should include the following items:
   - Date of sale
   - Year, make, and model description
   - Tag number and state of registration
   - Vehicle identification number
   - Odometer reading
   - Amount paid for car and type of payment
   - Conditions of the sale, if any
   - Seller's and buyer's names, addresses, and phone numbers
7. Be sure that the title has the correct VIN on it.
8. Examine the title to be sure that the seller has clear ownership of the vehicle. Determine if there is a bank lien against the car. Is there a co-owner? Is the name of the seller the same as on the title?

PRE-CLOSING CHECKLIST

Be sure the seller gives you:

- Title with VIN corresponding to car ❑
- Odometer statement ❑
- Warranty agreement or service contract ❑
- Owner's manual ❑
- Maintenance books and records ❑

Be sure to:

- Register vehicle ❑
- Pay sales tax ❑
- Get state inspection if required ❑

LEASE ANALYSIS CHECK SHEET

Competitive Lease Information

Make and model of car ____________________

Money factor: __________ as a percentage (24 × money factor) __________

Term of lease: __________ Monthly advertised payment: $ __________

Clarification Questions

- Has the offer been confirmed during a visit to the dealership? Yes❑ No❑
- Is this number fixed or is it conditional on dealer participation? Yes❑ No❑
- Will the factory warranty last as long as the lease? Yes❑ No❑
- How much of the maintenance is lessee's responsibility? __________

Financial Questions

1. How much down payment is required? $ __________
2. What is the total of the advertised monthly payments (payment × number of months)? $ __________
3. How much is the acquisition or bank fee? $ __________
4. How much is the security deposit?* $ __________
5. How much is the lease termination or "disposal" fee? $ __________
6. Does the lease offer 15,000 free miles? Yes❑ No❑
   a. If not, what is the cost of the additional miles? $ ________
   b. Excess miles likely to be added each year. mi ______
   c. Excess per mile cost × estimated excess miles $ __________
7. What is the cost of any additional equipment/services? $ __________
8. Does the lease include gap insurance? Yes❑ No❑
   If not, how much does it cost over the term? $ __________
9. What is the cost of your insurance? $ __________
   (Certain cars have very high rates.)
10. Are the luxury taxes factored into the lease? Yes❑ No❑
    If not, how much are they? $ __________
11. Gas-guzzler taxes if applicable $ __________
12. Cost of registration, license, and sales tax $ __________

---

13. TOTAL (add up all the costs) **$** __________

Divide by the number of months in lease, and $ __________

compare to advertised monthly payment. $ ________**

*Even though the deposit is conditionally refundable, it's still money out-of-pocket that does not earn interest.

**This is the approximate projected out-of-pocket cost that you will be paying over the life of the lease less applicable sales taxes, license, registration, and fees.

LEASE VS. FINANCING WORK SHEET

Sticker price: ___________
Negotiated price: ___________
Residual value: ___________% of sticker price. Residual $ ___________
Purchase finance rate ___________% Finance monthly payments ___________
Lease monthly payments ___________*
Lease money factor ___________

______ MONTH LEASE

		Finance	Lease
Down payment	(1)	______	______
Total monthly payments	(2)	______	______
(TOTAL)	(3)		
Your equity at end of period (Based on estimated residual)	(4)	$______	0
Line 3 minus line 4 **Your cost of driving**		______	______

Plus taxes and other after sales costs to which you might agree.

*For formula to determine monthly lease, review chapter 3.

LEASED-CAR EVALUATION CHECKLIST

1 Poor, 2 Fair, 3 Okay, 4 Good, 5 Excellent

General Quality Impression	**1**	**2**	**3**	**4**	**5**
Exterior (fit, finish, paint)	❑	❑	❑	❑	❑
Interior (workmanship, fit)	❑	❑	❑	❑	❑
Comfort					
Ease of entry front and back	❑	❑	❑	❑	❑
Headroom front	❑	❑	❑	❑	❑
Headroom back	❑	❑	❑	❑	❑
Legroom front	❑	❑	❑	❑	❑
Legroom back	❑	❑	❑	❑	❑
Seat support/comfort	❑	❑	❑	❑	❑
Ease of access to controls, dash buttons	❑	❑	❑	❑	❑
Visibility	❑	❑	❑	❑	❑
Trunk space	❑	❑	❑	❑	❑
Ride and Handling					
Acceleration	❑	❑	❑	❑	❑
Passing acceleration	❑	❑	❑	❑	❑
Hill climb power	❑	❑	❑	❑	❑
Cornering	❑	❑	❑	❑	❑
Steering response	❑	❑	❑	❑	❑
Road feel—bumps	❑	❑	❑	❑	❑
Braking	❑	❑	❑	❑	❑
General Impression					
Interior noise	❑	❑	❑	❑	❑
Rattles/Squeaks	❑	❑	❑	❑	❑
Sound system	❑	❑	❑	❑	❑
Convenience features	❑	❑	❑	❑	❑
Safety Equipment					
Air bags—driver	❑	❑	❑	❑	❑
side passenger	❑	❑	❑	❑	❑
ABS brakes	❑	❑	❑	❑	❑
Traction control	❑	❑	❑	❑	❑
Total Rating—Each Column	—	—	—	—	—

Sum Total of All Five Columns
(130 is highest possible score) ________

THE RETAIL NUMBERS

Even though you plan to lease, you still want to know the true invoice cost of the car and the true cost of the options the manufacturer charges the dealer. This becomes important when you begin to negotiate your lease agreement. For that reason, before you leave the dealership, copy down the information shown on the manufacturer's price sticker. Put down the price of the car and the price of all the options, plus all of the extras the dealer may be tacking on to the car.

Make ______________ Model ______________ VIN# ______________

	MSRP—List Price	Invoice/Dealer cost
Car	$______________	$______________
Destination charge	$______________	$______________
Options		
______________	$______________	$______________
______________	$______________	$______________
______________	$______________	$______________
______________	$______________	$______________
Dealer charges		
______________		$______________
______________		$______________
______________		$______________
TOTALS	$______________	$______________

LEASE WORK SHEET

As a reminder, here are some of the figures you'll need for your calculations.

MSRP	$ ________
Dealer invoice	$ ________
Your target capitalized cost— i.e., the price on which your lease is based	$ ________
Money factor	$ ________
Term of lease	$ ________
Depreciation amount (what you're paying for)	$ ________
Residual value	$ ________

INTERIOR CHECKLIST

(The items with "$" indicate potentially expensive repair costs.)

Books and Records	Yes	No
Owner's manual	❑	❑
Maintenance records	❑	❑

General Appearance	Excel.	Good	Fair	Poor
Upholstery wear/stains	❑	❑	❑	❑
Rug wear/stains	❑	❑	❑	❑
General impression of interior	❑	❑	❑	❑
Front seats—check how they move/adjust	❑	❑	❑	❑
Window cranks (manual)	❑	❑	❑	❑
Smell (mildew, oil, gas, etc.)	❑	❑	❑	❑

Mechanical	OK	Problem
Glove box door	❑	❑
Ashtrays	❑	❑
Center armrests	❑	❑
Exterior rearview mirrors	❑	❑
Inside rearview mirror	❑	❑
Inside door handles	❑	❑
Seat adjustments	❑	❑

Electrical	OK	Problem	
Headlights—high/low beam	❑	❑	
Parking lights	❑	❑	
Taillights	❑	❑	
Brake lights	❑	❑	
Turn signals	❑	❑	
Emergency flashers	❑	❑	
Wipers (washers)	❑	❑	
Heater/Blowers	❑	❑	$
Defrost	❑	❑	
Air conditioner	❑	❑	$
Radio/Stereo	❑	❑	$
Lighter	❑	❑	
Glove box light	❑	❑	
Interior dome light	❑	❑	
Rearview mirror adjustment	❑	❑	
Rear defrost	❑	❑	
Horn	❑	❑	
Power windows	❑	❑	
Power seats	❑	❑	

Instrument Panel Indicator Lights/Gauges	**OK**	**Problem**	
Oil pressure	❑	❑	$
Temperature gauge/light	❑	❑	
High beam/Low beam indicator	❑	❑	
Turn signal indicators	❑	❑	
Battery charging system (light/gauge)	❑	❑	
Speedometer	❑	❑	
Tachometer (RPM indicator)	❑	❑	

Trunk	**Yes**	**No**
Spare tire (Full spare or space saver)	❑	❑
Jack	❑	❑
Lug wrench	❑	❑
Other tools	❑	❑

EXTERIOR CHECK SHEET

(The items with "$" indicate potentially expensive repair costs.)

Exterior Body Condition	**Good**	**Fair**	**Poor**
Body condition (i.e., signs of rust)	❑	❑	❑
Finish and paint condition	❑	❑	❑
Door fit/open & close	❑	❑	❑

Tires	**Yes**	**No**	
Good condition	❑	❑	$
Pass "penny" test	❑	❑	
Even wear	❑	❑	
Matched set of tires	❑	❑	

Shock Absorbers	**Yes**	**No**	
Good condition	❑	❑	$
Exhaust System	**Yes**	**No**	
System appears well secured to car	❑	❑	$
Pressure test is good	❑	❑	$

Engine	**Pass**	**Fail**	
Smoke from tailpipe	❑	❑	$
Engine idle	❑	❑	
Knocking sounds	❑	❑	$
Engine runs hot at idle	❑	❑	$
Signs of oil on engine	❑	❑	$
Coolant low	❑	❑	
Oil is low	❑	❑	
Transmission fluid is orange	❑	❑	$
Transmission fluid smells burnt	❑	❑	$
Signs of leaking fluids under car	❑	❑	

TEST-DRIVE EVALUATION

(The items with "$" indicate potentially expensive repair costs.)

Brakes	**Pass**	**Fail**	
Straight-line stopping	❑	❑	
Brake pedal firm	❑	❑	$
Parking brake holds	❑	❑	
Acceleration			
Hill test	❑	❑	
Acceleration	❑	❑	
Highway speed test (sounds/overheating)	❑	❑	$
Car at idle (overheating test)	❑	❑	
Alignment and Suspension			
Rough road at 25 MPH test—holds straight line	❑	❑	$
Rattles or squeaks	❑	❑	
Steering—veer/drift test	❑	❑	$
Transmission			
No unusual sounds	❑	❑	$
Shift quality	❑	❑	$
Back and forth test—no clanks or thuds	❑	❑	$
Standard Transmission			
Shifting test—smooth, no grab, slip, or chatter	❑	❑	$
Hill test—clutch does not slip	❑	❑	$
Driving Evaluation			
Highway speed performance test	❑	❑	
Shimmy and vibration test	❑	❑	$
Steering			
Steering input—no sloppiness	❑	❑	
Wheel turn test—car stopped	❑	❑	
Turn wheel hard left/right and check for squeal	❑	❑	
Retest the Accessories			
Accessory retest—turn everything on	❑	❑	
Charging system	❑	❑	
Cruise Control			
Holds speed	❑	❑	
Disengages at touch of brake	❑	❑	

Engine Restart Test

Engine restarts without hesitation	❑	❑	$

Recheck the Fluids

Oil level	❑	❑	
Coolant level	❑	❑	
Transmission fluid level	❑	❑	
Evidence of drips or leaks underneath	❑	❑	$

Notes:

PROFESSIONAL MECHANIC'S INSPECTION

Test Items	OK	Needs Repair	Est. Cost
Brake check	❑	❑	$ ________
Engine test	❑	❑	$ ________
Charging system	❑	❑	$ ________
Cooling system test	❑	❑	$ ________
Spark plugs	❑	❑	$ ________
Emission level test	❑	❑	$ ________
Drive axle	❑	❑	$ ________
Suspension	❑	❑	$ ________
Alignment	❑	❑	$ ________
Tires	❑	❑	$ ________
Shocks	❑	❑	$ ________
Exhaust system	❑	❑	$ ________
Brake lines/Fuel lines	❑	❑	$ ________
Underbody rust	❑	❑	$ ________
Accident damage	❑	❑	$ ________
Total Repair Costs			**$** ________

Odometer accuracy ❑ Appears accurate

________________________ ________________________

Professional Mechanic Date Inspected

PERSONAL INVENTORY EVALUATION

In your opinion, does each of the following represent a liability or an asset in terms of a potential buyer's interest in your car? Remember, even a bucket of bolts might be an asset to someone looking for parts. The purpose of this evaluation is to help you identify those features which can help sell the car or potentially kill the deal or force you to take less for your car. Recognizing your car's assets will also be useful in writing your classified ad. As you'll note, we've tried to suggest some guidelines for assets and liabilities. The guidelines are just that and subject to your personal evaluation.

Item	Liability	No Impact	Asset
Exterior Appearance			
Body condition	❑	❑	❑
Glass—no stars, cracks	❑	❑	❑
Bumpers	❑	❑	❑
Interior Appearance			
Mats and rugs	❑	❑	❑
Gas and brake rubber pedal covers	❑	❑	❑
Upholstery	❑	❑	❑
Door trim pieces	❑	❑	❑
Dashboard surface	❑	❑	❑
Headliner (cloth/plastic cover inside roof)	❑	❑	❑
Maintenance Costs			
What do your records show?	❑	❑	❑
How does *Consumer Reports* rate your car?	❑	❑	❑
Performance			
Pickup	❑	❑	❑
Mileage (odometer reading)			
10,000 per year or less is asset	❑	❑	❑
15,000 and up is liability	❑	❑	❑
Gas Mileage	❑	❑	❑
Safety Features			
Seat belts front/rear—asset	❑	❑	❑
Air bag(s)—asset	❑	❑	❑
Other—full-size car, crumple zones	❑	❑	❑

Accessories—assets			
Air conditioning	❑	❑	❑
Radio AM/FM	❑	❑	❑
Stereo	❑	❑	❑
Cassette player	❑	❑	❑
CD player	❑	❑	❑
Phone	❑	❑	❑
Power seats	❑	❑	❑
Power windows	❑	❑	❑
Other ___________	❑	❑	❑
Trunk Size	❑	❑	❑
Tires			
Under 10,000 miles—asset	❑	❑	❑
Over 30,000—liability	❑	❑	❑
Spare Tire			
Full size—asset	❑	❑	❑
Space saver—no impact	❑	❑	❑
Jack & tools	❑	❑	❑
Records & Ownership History			
Maintenance records—asset	❑	❑	❑
All warranties and car-related records	❑	❑	❑
One owner—asset	❑	❑	❑
Previous owner—liability	❑	❑	❑
Mechanic's Assessment			
Under $300 repairs—asset	❑	❑	❑
Over $300—liability	❑	❑	❑

INTENT TO PURCHASE AGREEMENT

I agree to sell my ______________________________ with VIN# __________ to

(NAME, MAKE, AND MODEL)

____________________________________ for a total price of $ __________.

(NAME OF BUYER)

It is agreed that we will conclude this transaction on __________(date). At that time I will deliver a clear title in exchange for cash or a certified check for the full amount less the deposit.

With this agreement I acknowledge the receipt of $ __________ against the purchase price. This deposit represents the buyer's good-faith intention to buy the car at the stated price and the seller's promise to deliver the car as shown to the buyer on this date.

Received $ __________

From ______________________________

Address ______________________________

Date __________

____

Seller's Signature

Buyer's acknowledgment of agreement

Name ______________________________Date ____________________

Index